Linda Calvey has served 18 years behind bars, making her Britain's longest-serving female prisoner. She moved to 14 different prisons, doing time with Rose West and Myra Hindley. Since her release, Linda has become a full-time author. She has previously written 3 books, across both fiction and non-fiction, the first of them being her memoir *The Black Widow*.

LIFE INSIDE

The Hard Reality of Prison and What It Takes to Survive

Linda Calvey

WELBECK

First published in 2024 by Headline Welbeck Narrative Non-Fiction
An imprint of Headline Publishing Group Limited

This paperback edition published in 2024

2

Photos © Linda Calvey
Rise of a Broken Man, poem on pages vii-viii courtesy of Jason Moore.

Cataloguing in Publication Data is available from the British Library

Paperback ISBN 978 1 8027 9595 0

Offset in 8.55/14.70pt Georgia by Jouve (UK), Milton Keynes

Printed and bound in Great Britain by Clays Ltd, Elcograf S.p.A.

Headline's policy is to use papers that are natural, renewable and
recyclable products and made from wood grown in sustainable
forests. The logging and manufacturing processes are expected to
conform to the environmental regulations of the country of origin.

HEADLINE PUBLISHING GROUP
An Hachette UK Company
Carmelite House
50 Victoria Embankment
London EC4Y 0DZ

The authorised representative in the EEA is Hachette Ireland, 8 Castlecourt
Centre, Dublin 15, D15 XTP3, Ireland (email: info@hbgi.ie)

www.headline.co.uk
www.hachette.co.uk

Dedicated to my solicitor and very dear friend
Julian Hardy (we both kept our promise)
and also to my wonderful agent Kerr MacRae.
From day one of meeting them, they have
both always been in my corner. x

In memory of all the inmates that never survived
the prison system, far too many, including
Joey and little Scottie (razors).

RISE OF A BROKEN MAN
BY JASON MOORE

You have taken my life; it wasn't yours to take.

You have broken my heart; it wasn't yours to break.

You stole my spirit; it wasn't yours to steal.

Now I am a tortured soul that may never heal.

In prison now, a broken man left to die,

I stare at the ceiling, as days pass me by.

Life in tatters, dreams destroyed,

I stare at the heavens, very annoyed.

I'm in darkness now, going through hell,

Life passing me by as I rot in this cell,

In this living hell, where I didn't do anything wrong.

I must find a way to be strong.

I stare at the sky and shout, "Why me?

I was once happy and, above all, free."

But something within the depths of me has awoken,

It's pleading with me, "Don't stay broken."

It's pleading with me, "Stay alive any way you can,

It pleads with me; stand a man."

So I will now wipe away the tears of anger,

The tears of despair,

The tears that say life isn't fair.

As a once broken man in prison, surrounded by sin,
My new attitude is, never give in.
I will mend my heart and find my soul.
I will get my spirit back and become whole.
Now my spirit says, "Hold on."
Now my heart, it beats strong.
I've found my soul, and to my surprise,
A once broken man has begun to rise.

Once starved of inspiration, and looking at defeat,
This new broken man, doesn't know when he is beat.
I will stare down the demons, I will find the light,
When I come across evil, I will put up a fight.
And when I am finally free of this prison,
The world will know; a broken man has risen.

CONTENTS

PROLOGUE

The cell door shuts with a loud clang.

Inside the tiny bleak space is a metal army bed, a stained mattress, a pile of bedlinen consisting of a starched sheet, pillow and a scratchy woollen blanket. There is a small Formica table, a single chair and a toilet behind a waist-height screen in the cell, which cannot measure more than 11ft by 6ft. Outside, the wing corridor is alive with screams and wailing sounds from other inmates. Some sound demented. Some shout insults or laugh uproariously. Some bang on the doors, trying to shout through their closed hatches. Everywhere there is the pervasive smell of disinfectant and sweat.

"Alright, Calvey. We'll check on ya during the night. Try to get some sleep."

I look back at the prison officer, catching her eye briefly through the hatch before she shuts it. I am alone, very scared, and wondering how on earth I managed to end up here in Holloway, the infamous women's prison. I shuffle forward, the regulation jelly shoes they gave me earlier replacing my high heels. I'm still wearing the silk suit from Harrods which I wore in the dock today for the end of my trial, but it is now creased and dirty.

Shockwaves course through me, as does disbelief. How stupid I've been. How reckless. How could I have done what I did and expect to get away with it?

The awful truth is that tonight, my children are starting their new lives in different homes to mine. For seven years, I will miss them grow, miss their schooling, miss their tears and triumphs. I will miss everything. Shaking, feeling nauseous and overwhelmed with guilt, I lie down on the thin mattress, the bed creaking underneath me, knowing I won't sleep.

Somewhere, a woman yells out, whether in pain or anger, I can't tell. Somewhere, my teenage children, Melanie and Neil, will learn their mother has gone to prison, leaving them to grow up without me by their side. I turn over and try to cover my ears but the shrieking continues. Somewhere, a door is being kicked from the inside. My first night as a prisoner, banged up for armed robbery, has begun. I know before I shut my eyes that this will be the longest, loneliest night of my life.

CHAPTER 1

GUILTY

FIVE HOURS EARLIER

"On the charge of armed robbery, how do you find the defendant?" the judge says, turning to face the juror who is standing at the end of the jury box.

There is a brief moment's pause.

The courtroom at Southwark Crown Court falls silent. My family – my mum, sisters Shelley and Maxine, and my brother Terry – lean forward in the public gallery to hear better. Even the reporters covering the case stop their scribbling and look up.

My co-defendants, Brian Thorogood and Carl Gibney, pleaded guilty to a string of armed robberies using sawn-off shotguns, and are waiting to be sentenced. My brother, Anthony Welford, has been found guilty of handling stolen cash, though he was nothing to do with the robberies, while his wife Sandra was found not guilty (rightly so).

Now, it's my turn.

I blink, thinking, *Why on earth is he takin' so long to answer? Surely he just says 'not guilty' and I can go home?* I just want this whole thing to finish so I can get back to my cosy flat, make a cup of tea, and give my children, Melanie and Neil, a big cuddle.

Instead, I am standing in the dock, a female prison guard beside me, the first time this has happened since the trial began.

Then, the word I hadn't expected to hear, the one I hadn't prepared for, is spoken.

"Guilty," the foreman of the jury says.

There is a cry from the gallery. I recognise my mother's voice but I am too stunned to react.

The juror coughs as if embarrassed, and fidgets with a pen or something he's holding. He is an average-height man, with brown hair and a smart suit. He sits down, the verdict reached. For a moment, I think I will faint.

Shockwaves smash into me, overwhelming me completely. I know it sounds corny, but it really is like time has stopped and there is only this moment, everyone frozen like a statue while the impact slams into me. I look over to the jury. None of them look back to meet my gaze. They are all staring somewhere else in the room as if I do not exist, as if none of this is really happening. I feel my heart pounding, my legs shaking, and it takes every bit of strength I possess not to cry out in disbelief.

All I can do is try not to break down in front of everyone in the chamber, where all eyes have turned to me. There is the sound of sobbing. I look around and see it is my mother who has burst into tears, followed by my sisters, who are both comforting her. My brother Terry is shaking his head. My children aren't there, thank God. I insisted they shouldn't come for this, the last day of our weeks-long trial. They're in Cornwall being looked after by my sister Hazel, as far away from all this as I could get them.

Brian and Carl are sentenced but I can barely hear the words. All I can think is, *I'm not prepared for this.* No one, not even the police and my lawyers, thought I was going down. I hadn't even been held on remand, which, I was told by my legal team, was really unusual for an offence as serious as the one I was accused of. I had gone regularly to visit Brian and Carl, who had been placed on remand awaiting the trial. Both of them had told me not to worry, they'd done deals with the police. They'd told them about other robberies, on condition I would go free. I had believed them. Why wouldn't I? They were my gang of robbers. They did everything I told them to do, and more. Between us, we'd robbed more post offices and shops than I could recall, and stolen hundreds of thousands of pounds. A lot of money in those days. If Brian and Carl told me I was safe, I wouldn't take the rap, I believed them. I look down then at my suit: a silk designer outfit Brian had bought me from Harrods, matched with a pair of ruinously expensive crocodile skin high heels. Hardly an outfit fit for prison.

Then, I hear my name again.

Still dazed. Still reeling from the hammer blow of the jury's verdict, I see Judge Derek Clarkson turn to me as he speaks. From the minute I stepped onto the stands, I'd known he disliked me. I could see it in his face. I could see his eyes narrowed and his eyebrows raised at what I was saying. I couldn't blame him, there was a lot I had twisted to suit our story that I was an unwilling participant in a series of raids on post offices in Essex.

His words shock me almost as much as the verdict did.

He clears his throat. His white wig is slightly askew and, bizarrely, I want to giggle. It must be the shock. He leans forward and stares into my eyes, making sure I know he is talking about me, Linda Calvey, the armed robber.

"Far from being a small cog in this operation, you were, in fact, the whole machine."

There is another moment of silence.

How does he know?

My lawyers and the guys had all painted a picture of me as a victim of Brian and Carl's crimes. They testified they had forced me into committing the robberies, and that I was only a getaway driver, a look-out, no one who could be blamed for taking part. They said I was scared of Brian, a gangster who thought nothing of raiding post offices and showering his friends and family in stolen cash. We created a whole story – and yet the judge saw right through us all.

He's right, of course.

Far from being the blameless victim, I was, in fact, the ringleader, the queen robber, the mastermind of the raids we did. It was me who had cased out the targets, walking miles around each area to check for exit routes and other ways the guys could escape if it went wrong. I had checked the timings, noting down when the security vans arrived, when the busiest and slowest times of the day were, how many post masters or mistresses were in charge. I had known it all – and it was me the men had trusted to pick the right victims of our craze for money and the thrill of robbing.

When they had asked me if I wanted to brandish a sawn-off shotgun, I said yes. I didn't need to. They said I could stay out of it, in the car, away from the actual robbery, but I had been determined to be with them, holding a gun, just like my dead husband Mickey had taught me to do. I had learned from the best. My husband Mickey Calvey had been a respected armed robber in the underworld, a "blagger", as robbers are called. For years, before he was shot and killed by the Flying Squad on a raid, I had listened and learned as his gang formulated their robberies around my kitchen table. This time, it had been me leading the men. They sat at the kitchen table in my flat in Bethnal Green with a plate of ham sandwiches and a pot of tea and listened to what I had to say. I had known exactly what I was doing – but, apparently, so did the judge.

I may have had a husband who was in and out of jail, but I had never been inside one before, except to visit.

All that is about to change.

"This is an amazingly horrifying case. It must be one of the worst ever heard in front of a British court," the judge says.

I don't know where to look. I don't know what to think. I keep listening as the words beat against my brain.

"These robberies were carefully planned and organised. They were skilfully, effectively and ruthlessly carried out. There is no reason I cannot sentence you today, and so, Linda Calvey, I am sentencing you to seven years in prison."

"Fuckin' hell..." whistles the prison officer standing next to me, under her breath.

What does that mean? I think. *Why did she say that?*

This time the shockwaves are felt throughout the court. A sentence this long is unheard of for a woman, except for life sentences for murder. It is a time when women are given much shorter jail terms than men – except for mine, it seems.

I glance over at Mum, who is being comforted by Shelley. Someone in the gallery cries out; it's an angry shout and I wonder if it is a relative of a post-office employee. Suddenly, the fun and the thrill are gone. The confidence – the *arrogance* – I had in thinking I would go home tonight scot-free is completely blown apart. How could I have been so naïve, so stupid? What will my kids do tonight? They were coming back and we haven't made plans, so sure was I that I would be coming home. Bewildered, I look down at my legal counsel. My barrister shakes his head. There's nothing anyone can do. Panic rises in me now. I stumble a little as I am led down the steps into the bowels of the building.

"Wait here until the sweat box arrives," the prison officer beside me says.

"The what?" I say, completely confused. Terror coming in waves now.

"The sweat box, the meat wagon, or prison van if you'd rather say that," the officer says and raises her eyebrows at another officer, a large lady, who is knitting something, sitting on the only chair.

"What did she get?" the knitter says as if I am not there.

"Seven years. Can you fuckin' believe it?"

The knitter whistles just as the other officer did when the sentence was read out.

"Fuckin' hell..." she says, just like the other.

I must look as confused as I feel because they take pity on me.

"You'll have the longest prison time in Holloway except for the lifers, the ones who've murdered people," the officer who is casting another line, explains.

"Oh my God, will I?" I say. I look around. The corridor is harshly lit with no other furniture. There is nothing to do except wait for the van that will take me to my new home – a jail cell at notorious Holloway Prison.

How will I survive? I think to myself. *How will I ever get through this, and what'll happen to my children?*

I realise, as the door to the outside parking area opens, that I'm about to find out.

CHAPTER 2

SWEAT BOX

Nothing could've prepared me for the horror of being sent down.

When the guilty verdict was read out, my life collapsed completely. Suddenly, I wasn't a human being any longer, I was a prisoner, a convicted armed robber. How could I have ever thought that anything was worth that risk?

"Hold out your wrists," the officer, who has now stopped knitting, says.

I hold them out and realise what's about to happen.

She snaps the handcuffs onto my wrists. They feel cold and clunky. I look up at the officer who is already turning away. I'm starting to feel invisible.

It's so degrading. Is this what I've come to? Standing here, with my hands cuffed together, wondering what on earth comes next. I've never met a single other woman who has been to prison. I have no idea what I'm facing.

"The van's 'ere. Calvey, this way."

I step outside, two prison guards by my side, and stare into the filthy insides of the large vehicle with blacked-out windows. I feel numb. One of the prison officers steps in front of me and into the back of the van. Handcuffed, I get in awkwardly, while the other officer gets in behind me. There are no other prisoners in here as it's the afternoon and I appear to be the last person sentenced today. Looking down, I see the seat is ripped and dirty, the floor littered with cigarette butts, and it stinks of diesel, stale nicotine – and sweat. These are the days when you can smoke anywhere, and of course, the windows can't be opened.

God, if this is what the vans are like, what the hell is the prison goin' to be like? I think, feeling it can only get worse.

As I step into the appropriately named "sweat box", I'm in deep shock. By then I'm also thinking *fuckin' hell* too. Largely, though, I feel numb. The windows are blackened glass, but within seconds of pulling away we're surrounded by press photographers and people who are jeering. There's a flash as a photographer's camera goes off, catching me inside the van for tomorrow's newspapers. I'm starting to realise that being a female armed robber is quite an unusual thing. The press seems hooked by the story, but I don't care about any of that.

All I can think about are Melanie, who is 16 years old, and 12-year-old Neil. How they're going to feel when someone in my family sits them down tonight and tells them I've gone to prison. *Oh God, where are they goin' to end up? What's goin' to happen to them? My poor kids!* The thoughts race through my mind. I feel nauseous. Already I feel trapped and I've got seven years to get through. I don't know if I can do this, but what other choice is there?

My imagination is running riot as we drive from the court through central London, towards the north of the city. With every mile we cover, I feel less human, as if I'm losing my humanity. I'm desperately scared. I'm full of regret for my actions, and I'm already homesick for the life I've now been forced to leave behind. I'm utterly helpless. As we move ever forward towards HMP Holloway, I see people going about their normal business, walking a dog, or crossing the road with a sheaf of papers under their arm, a woman sipping from a coffee cup, a gaggle of teenagers wearing headphones and smoking ciggies. All of them free.

I feel like I'm disappearing from the world, I'm separated from everything. How am I going to cope?

Half an hour later, and we reach the gates of the prison. I grew up in the East End, a place with plenty of crime, of course, but no prisons at all. I have a large, law-abiding family, and it wasn't until I met Mickey, the love of my life, at the age of 19 that I came into contact with anything illegal. I quickly learned he was a bank robber, a blagger, and even though I hated the thought of committing crimes, he was such a lovely man. I fell head over heels in love with him, and it confused my view of the world. How could a man who treated me, his family and his friends so well, be a criminal at the same time? How could a good person be going out and committing serious crimes? Could enjoy it, even? My Mickey was banged up during our relationship and subsequent marriage. He would laugh off his sentence, regaling me with funny stories when I visited him. He met our daughter Mel for the first time while he was locked away in Wandsworth. He never gave me any impression that prison was difficult or horrible, and so all this is coming as a shock. I am 38 years old but nothing Mickey ever said has prepared me for this. This time it's different. This time it's me being locked up. In a place that looks foreboding as hell.

The Victorian Holloway Prison that housed suffragette Emmeline Pankhurst and the last woman to be hanged, Ruth Ellis, was torn down and rebuilt in the 1970s. It has bright red brick walls and a huge gate that is now sliding open to let us through. My heart is pounding, my palms are sweating. My wrists feel sore where the cuffs are rubbing, and I feel physically sick at the stench inside the van. All I can think is, *I want to go home.* As the gate slides shut, a jolt of panic hits me.

"We call this no man's land," says one of the officers. This doesn't bode well.

The van goes through another gate, where we stop and the side door is opened. With difficulty I get out, my skirt crumpled, my fear building to fever pitch.

Inside, the reception area has a desk and a couple of plastic chairs, underneath harsh strip lighting. Two female officers are sitting at the desk. One of my guards says to them (again, as if I'm not there): "She's just got seven years!"

Both officers look up at me.

Both whistle. "Bloody hell!"

One of them, a dumpy woman with nondescript hair, says: "How come you wasn't on remand?"

"Because I got bail," I reply and shrug. How do I know why that decision was made? But I am starting to understand the ramifications – I am starting my sentence from nothing.

"So, you've got to start seven years without a day behind you in prison," the officer says and nudges her co-worker.

"Yes, obviously, that's right," I reply, wishing I could be anywhere on earth but here.

"How will you do it?" my guard says.

I turn to her. She has a surprisingly kind face for someone who works here.

"Because I 'ave to. I'm guilty of the crime so I 'ave to do the time."

Well, I see instantly they don't hear that very often!

They all laugh, stunned.

"Blimey that's refreshin'!" one of the seated Holloway officers says. "We get some who come in here for a week and insist they didn't do it. Not many admit they're guilty."

"Listen, just so you're aware, there's a lot of bullying in Holloway..."

I nod. I'd expected it. That's one thing Mickey mentioned, though as he was a blagger he was top of the prison hierarchy, but he used to tell me stories of young guys robbed and beaten regularly.

"Well then, I'll just have to stand my ground," I say.

I'm told to sit at the desk while I give them my name, date of birth, the sentence I received and what I've been convicted of. My head is reeling and I jump at every sound. They ask what religion I am and I say I am Church of England. All of this is written in a book and onto a card. The officer hands me the card. I look down at it and see: N56981, Calvey.

"What's this?" I say.

"That's your prison number. From now on you're N56981, Calvey."

For a moment, I'm too shocked to speak. *Oh God, how horrible is that? I'm already just a number, not a person.*

"And that card goes outside your cell door so everyone knows what you're in for."

Then, it gets worse.

"You can't have earrings, you can't have your watch neither 'cos they've got diamonds on. The only ring you can keep is your wedding ring, the others 'ave got to come off."

Well, that really hits home. I love wearing nice things; diamonds and designer dresses. I've been spoiled by my boyfriend Ron Cook, who's a big-time gangster. My husband Mickey always used to buy me a necklace or bracelet when he pulled off a big heist, and so I'm used to wearing them. I slide off the two solitaire rings I'm wearing, and my fingers look naked.

As I take out my earrings, a set of simple diamonds bought as another gift by Ron, and as I release the clasp of my watch, I feel like I am losing my personality. All the bits that made me *me*, are being gradually erased, being taken off me. I feel suddenly exposed without them.

"Sorry, this is how prison works," the plain-faced guard says, spotting my discomfort. "Oh, and you can't 'ave your handbag neither."

I look down at my Gucci bag. There isn't much inside it; a lipstick, some tissues, my keys. I realise with a pang of homesickness, that I won't be using my door or car keys again for a very long time. I can't comprehend this even though it's now my reality. Everything feels surreal. I've lost my freedom. Every second that goes past, a new part of me is stripped away. I hand over my bag, and I'm left sitting in my suit, wondering if there is anything else they can possibly take off me. Then, she spots my shoes. Now, these shoes are my favourite pair. I bought them especially for court, thinking I'd get a not-guilty verdict and could wear them for posh functions like weddings or parties afterwards. Again, how naïve I've been. They were the least practical, most expensive, most stylish shoes I could find, made from crocodile skin with high heels that clack satisfyingly as I walk. They make me feel a million dollars, and now I have to hand them over to someone I've never met before.

"What size are ya?" the guard says, ignoring my look of devastation.

"I'm a size six," I manage to say as I slip each one off and find my nylon-clad feet resting on the cold linoleum floor. The floor is at least relatively clean, unlike the van.

"Here you go, they'll do for now," says the guard, returning from whichever cupboard holds the correct prison shoes. I look down and in her hand is a pair of blue plastic jelly shoes. I feel like crying, as if this is the straw that breaks my back, but I remind myself that shoes don't matter. If I'm going to cry for anyone, it'll be for my kids having to go through their teenage years without their mother.

"OK," I say, swallowing hard. "What do I do now?"

"You need to go over there to the cubicle," the guard replies, but this time she does not catch my eye.

"What for?" I ask, feeling suddenly filled with dread.

"You 'ave to be strip-searched."

Shoes are one thing. Being divested of your clothes and made to take them off in front of two strangers is quite another.

Stepping inside the cubicle I can smell sweat again, though thankfully it's not my own. The floor of the cubicle looks like it needs a clean. Two officers who I don't recognise come in. Above my head is the same intense white of fluorescent lights.

"You strip 'alf and 'alf. What that means is, you can do your bottom 'alf first and then your top, or vice versa. It's up to you."

My body starts to shake. This is beyond humiliation. Reluctantly I opt to have my top half inspected first. I take off my silk jacket and blouse, then my bra. They both look at me intently, then they go through every stitch of my clothing, checking the seams, checking the wiring of my bra. I don't have a clue what they're doing, but it occurs to me that this is how they look for drugs being smuggled in. Once I put everything back on, they do the same to my bottom half. I take off my skirt, tights and knickers. They check pockets and seams again, while I look at a small black spot on the wall and try not to think about what's happening. I've never felt as low in my life as at this moment, and it takes all my strength not to cry.

When they finish, and I'm dressed again, they tell me to have a bath. At this point they realise I have nothing with me, no toiletries, absolutely nothing, I'm given a basic pack. It contains a flannel stamped with HMP on it, a toothbrush, a roll-on deodorant and a small packet with a green powder inside. I barely glance at the things. It's so far from what I'm used to. I think of my bathroom at home with nice soft towels, posh bubble bath and scented candles.

"I don't want a bath," I say, looking around the small, basic bathroom, which again could do with a good scrub. There's a rim of grime around the enamel tub and a mess of hair in the plughole. I shudder.

The prison guard raises her eyebrows.

"Listen, Calvey. You might not get another for a week, so I suggest you 'ave one."

I look down at the bath tub again and try not to think of all the other women who'd got inside it today.

"Alright, I'll 'ave a bath," I say with a shrug. No point fighting her.

"Good, though you can only have six inches of water."

If my face looks aghast, the guard doesn't appear to notice. She shuts the door without locking it. I undress for the second time.

I run the regulation six inches of water, wondering if they come in and check. I open the packet and sniff it. It smells minty, but I assume it's Radox as no one has told me any different, so I sprinkle the green powder into the water.

A few minutes later, after dousing myself feebly with lukewarm water, I decide I've had enough.

"Calvey, when you're out, you'll need a bed pack," comes the officer's voice from the other side of the door. I realise I could've run a proper bath as no one actually seems bothered about checking how many inches I'd dared to run, but I do as I'm told. I'm starting to see this is the only way I'll get through this.

Once out I'm handed a bed pack. It consists of two starched white sheets, a starched pillowcase, an itchy blanket stamped with HMP and a green towel – again, stamped with HMP.

I look down at the pile, realising there's something missing.

"Sorry, but I don't have any toothpaste."

"What are you on about? We gave ya some. The tooth powder's in the packet."

"Tooth powder?" I say. "Ohhh, I thought it was Radox, so I put it in my bath!" I start to giggle, like all this is a joke that'll end soon so I can go home. It isn't, of course. But for a moment, I feel like me again.

The officer laughs.

"Alright, well you can 'ave this. It's brand new. I confiscated it off someone earlier today."

She hands me a tube of Boots own-brand toothpaste, like it's a lump of solid gold.

"Thank you," I say, wondering if I've ever had a stranger day in my life.

CHAPTER 3

THE FIRST NIGHT

Still waiting to be taken to my cell, I'm shown into a holding room. It must've been packed with people earlier because the floor is littered with cigarette butts, used tissues and bits of Rizla papers.

There are two other women in the room, the last of the day to be sent to a wing, apart from me.

"Face the wall and pray to Jesus!" one of the woman, a mixed-race lady in her forties, is saying repeatedly. Seemingly in a state of agitation, she's facing the wall, her back to me, repeating her strange mantra. "Turn yer head and pray to Jesus! Face the wall and pray to Jesus!"

I sit as far away from her as I can. The only other woman in there is pacing up and down, muttering something to herself. She's a young girl, and her eyes look like they're on stalks. Whatever drug she's taken earlier in the day is beginning to wear off. She's gaunt, her skin is grey and she looks dishevelled. Her eyes seem to stare elsewhere, and for a moment I feel afraid of her too.

My God, how am I goin' to cope if I'm spendin' the next seven years with women in these states? If everyone's like this, I'll go insane... I think to myself, fear rising inside me again.

Both women obviously need some kind of psychiatric help, but that help is clearly not forthcoming. They pace and mutter, pray and chant, and all the while, I'm trying not to think too much about my situation. About 15 minutes later, a guard looks in.

"Calvey, bring your stuff. We're taking you to a cell for a couple of nights. You're going to be put on C1 for obs."

"Obs?" I say, not having a clue what C1 means either.

"It's just for a couple of days. We'll observe you in your cell. You're an unknown quantity to us. You weren't on remand, so we don't know you. In a couple of days, you'll be moved to another wing, I'm sure. It'll be fine."

How wrong she was, though I did not know it yet.

C1 – the psychiatric wing – is going to be anything but fine, but I feel a little reassured as she takes me down. Instantly, I realise that everything is restricted. The prison officer has a big set of keys that jangle on her hip. She pulls out one and unlocks a large door. We stop. I wait. We walk through.

"Stop there, Calvey. I'll lock up." She turns and secures the door, as I wait again. I can't even walk through a door by myself now. Then we walk along a long corridor that is gleamingly clean, a far cry from the mess of the holding area. There's the harsh strip lighting, the same linoleum that has been fitted to run up the walls, a little above the floor, that same institutional bleakness. Though Holloway is a modern prison, it's built more like a hospital, it seems, with long corridors and the same kind of white-green lighting.

We stop again as we reach another door.

The officer does the same – unlocks it, ushers me through, tells me to stop, locks it again – then we carry on walking. This happens a couple more times. I don't know where I'm being taken, or why. They've told me I'm going to C1, but I could be going to the moon for all I know about it. I know these are my last moments before I'm put into a cell. Every footstep feels onerous. I'm tired, the events of the day are catching up with me, but I'm also wired and scared, more scared than I've ever been in my life. I've never seen inside a cell. In my mind are pictures of Victorian prisons, overrun with rats.

As it turns out, this isn't far from the truth.

My jelly shoes squeak on the floor as we reach C1. This door has a huge lock.

When the door is opened, the first thing I notice is the noise. It sounds like a load of stray cats are wailing and shrieking. Women are banging against cell doors, rattling the closed hatches, screaming and shouting through the ones that are open. It's like walking into a zoo filled with desperate, angry, caged animals.

The main door clangs shut behind us.

The second thing I notice is the smell of disinfectant. It's so strong that for a moment I think I'll retch.

"Don't worry, you'll only be on C1 for a couple of days."

"What's C1?' I ask, not at all sure I want to know the answer. "And why's there a nurse sitting on the wing with a prison officer?"

The officer doesn't look me in the eyes. "It's the hospital wing," she says.

"Why on earth am I 'ere? I'm not ill! I don't need to be observed! I just want to get on and get my sentence done," I say.

The officer shrugs. "You're an armed robber, you've got a big sentence, we don't know if you're dangerous. We don't know anything about you, so you'll be monitored until they decide where you'll be allocated."

"Oh God," is all I manage to say. "What if they leave me 'ere?"

She doesn't reply.

The nurse comes over. "Linda Calvey?"

I nod, mute with shock.

"Right then, you'll be here for assessment."

"Why am I 'ere? I haven't got anythin' wrong with me," I say to her this time.

The nurse, who is a tall woman in a white uniform, shakes her head at the officer, who turns to leave.

"Good luck, Calvey," the officer says as she walks back down the wing. The noises are getting worse, or perhaps it's me, panicking now, which makes everything feel more intense, as if I have had an outer layer of skin removed.

"You're here because of the length of your sentence. This is your cell. You'll be locked in the whole time."

For a moment, I hesitate. Every cell in my body is screaming not to go in there. The floor looks filthy. There is food splattered up one of the walls and a whole load of scratchy graffiti carved into the wall by the bed.

"Just see how it goes," the nurse says as if I have a choice in the matter.

The cell door shuts and I'm left alone.

I look around and I discover that all I have now is a metal army bed and a stained mattress. I'm clutching a small pile of bedlinen consisting of a starched sheet, a pillowcase for the also-stained saggy pillow and a scratchy woollen blanket. There is a small Formica table, a single chair and a toilet behind a waist-height screen in the cell. My whole living space cannot measure more than 11ft by 6ft. Outside, the wing corridor is alive with the screams and wailing sounds of other inmates. There is a cacophony of noise, from shrieking to wailing and laughing. Some bang on the doors, while others are trying to shout through their closed hatches.

"Alright, Calvey. We'll check on ya during the night. Try to get some sleep."

I look back at the prison officer, catching her eye briefly through the hatch before she shuts it.

I sit down heavily on the bed. It creaks beneath me, and I instantly burst into tears. I can't open my door. The window is open but only by a couple of inches. The screams don't seem to be stopping, and I think again of the two women in the holding area, and assume every inmate in prison must be like this. I feel frightened, and very alone.

There's nothing for me to do in here. No radio. No telly, just me and my thoughts. My heart is racing and I feel claustrophobic.

I'm torn between terror at being banged up like this, and utter grief at the thought of my children Melanie and Neil, who tonight are with my sister. Cornwall isn't their home, and when they come back, where will they go? I know they'll be with my family, so they'll be safe and loved, but other than that, I have no idea who's looking after them. At least they won't have to go into care. That, at least, I'm grateful for.

Family is the most important thing to me. Perhaps it's why I lost the plot when my Mickey was killed by the Flying Squad during a botched raid on a supermarket. He was an experienced robber. He knew what he was doing, but it only takes one raid to go wrong and you lose everything. This was the raid that ended his life – and, in some ways, mine too. He was shot and died at the scene, and that night I lost the love of my life and the man who'd provided everything for me and our kids. When my brother-in-law Terry told me Mickey was dead, I remember hearing a woman scream and scream. In my head I was thinking, *Someone shut that woman up!* That woman was me though, and something happened to me that day, something changed inside of me. I was no longer the gangster's moll on the sidelines; I was a woman hell bent on finishing what Mickey had started.

Something crystallised inside me. It was a hard mixture of grief and fury. The love of my life had been taken from me. I'd also been left with no way of supporting myself and the kids.

I managed for 18 months. When a crook dies, the underworld puts on benefits for the grieving family, raising money to see them through. Two benefits were done for me – and at this point I met Ron who also insisted on giving me money though I was too busy grieving to notice his interest in me. I worked on Mum's stall and for a while I got by, but my brain had literally changed and I feel I became another person. I became anti-police, and anti-authority; looking back, I believe it was a type of post-traumatic stress. I decided, wrongly it turns out, that I was entitled to go and do what I did. I thought I wasn't hurting anybody, and nobody except the post office were losing money, so I formed my own gang. It wasn't hard to do. I had many contacts in the underworld and something burned deep inside me: a need for revenge on anyone who I felt had wronged me.

I'd never have stolen from a person, whether a granny with a pound in her purse or someone getting out of a Bentley dropping a wad of money. I wouldn't go into a sweet shop and pinch a bar of chocolate, but I'd go into a post office holding a gun and demand they hand over the cash. The first time I held a gun I forgot to breathe. I felt a connection to my dead husband. I felt I was carrying on his work. I did that first raid on auto-pilot. The guys said I didn't have to hold a gun, but I said I wanted to, for Mickey. I was determined this was what I was going to do. My thought process, however twisted, felt quite rational. They'd taken Mickey from me and destroyed my life and family, so I felt justified. When he was in his coffin, with lavender posies in each hand from the children, I stood with him, holding his toes, and I said: "I promise you Mick, I'll make sure they (the kids) 'ave everythin' you died tryin' to get them."

Mickey always gave his children the best of everything – designer clothes, expensive toys, holidays abroad – and we'd got used to living a certain way. All of it had been funded by crime – and I saw no other way of living. It was what I was used to. I must've gone temporarily mad. It was a crazy mix of grief, survival and adrenalin. It was like a perfect storm – with all the reasons and justifications rolling into one long pillaging spree.

A pillaging spree that has brought me here to this cell, in this stinking, crazy wing. I can see that I'm going to have plenty of time to reflect on my crimes, and unpick all the strands of my life that have led me here. From Mickey and from the thrill-seeking part of me, to the single mother who wanted to give her kids the best. None of it justifies what I did, and all of it brought me here – to this creaking bed, this scratchy woollen blanket, the screeching and wailing around me.

I wasn't a stupid woman. I knew that robbers ended up going to jail or being killed. I had all the proof in the world of that. Mickey and I even married when he was behind bars. I'd seen his friends get long jail sentences, and I'd visited some of them in prison on Mickey's behalf. I knew the score – but somehow, I hadn't imagined it would happen to me.

It did, of course. It ended almost as quickly as it began. Within a few months of starting the raids, armed police arrested me at my flat in Bethnal Green, knocking me to the ground when I opened my front door. That day, more than a year ago now, was the first time I had a gun held to my face. Literally looking down the barrel of a gun, I was snapped instantly out of the trance I'd been in. It was like I became myself again and not that grieving, vengeful, maddened, frightened widow. In that moment, I knew what I'd done to people – and all I felt was remorse.

So, here I am.

Alone under the harsh light of the cell, waiting for goodness-knows-what to happen, wondering for the millionth time why I did what I did. The fact I enjoyed the thrill of those robberies is some-thing I know I'll find hard to reconcile with the disaster that has now befallen my family. I think family is everything to me, yet I've broken mine by my actions, and this thought leaves me desolate. None of it makes any sense. All I know is, I did what I did, and now I have to atone for it.

Thinking about Mickey I'm reminded of the funny stories he told me about prison. It wasn't anything like this. When I used to visit him, it was in pleasant visitors' rooms with tea and coffee, and books on shelves, and even pot plants. Had Mickey been lying to me? Is this what all of my prison life will be like? I have no answers for any of my questions.

It's got to get better... I think. *This is a nightmare, but it just has to get better.*

Just then, a woman shrieks that she wants to kill herself. Another shouts that she'll do it, too. An alarm sounds and I can hear someone running across the wing. Another inmate moans and starts shouting swear words. I don't think I can get through this, not if this is my life now. I have no night clothes, so I slip off the jelly shoes and lie down, pulling the scratchy blanket over me. The bed creaks underneath me and the metal frame hurt my hips. Every second feels like an hour.

Through the night, the screams continue. There are also voices calling from further away, from other wings perhaps. Women are shouting to each other like they're chatting, but it's done over an expanse of the prison. Now and then, an argument breaks out. And someone, somewhere is laughing manically.

God, this is a madhouse, an absolute madhouse, I think as I close my eyes and try to sleep. I'm hungry by now. I've had no water or coffee for hours. It occurs to me that I can't even get up and make a cup of coffee or a slice of toast now. Those simple privileges are now denied me, and the loss of even such tiny freedoms feels devastating.

Each time I feel myself drifting off, the light is switched back on and a pair of eyes looks through the hatch. This is the observation, and it goes the same way every hour or so.

"You OK, Linda?"

"Yes, thank you," I reply.

Then again, an hour later.

"You OK, Linda?"

"Yes, I'm OK, thank you."

Then again, and again, all through the night.

I don't sleep at all. I try not to wonder why there's food up the walls or why there are people's names scribbled on the cell. I try not to think about the dirty bed and the exposed toilet. I try to think of Melanie and Neil, hoping they are OK, hoping that one day, they will forgive me.

CHAPTER 4

NORMAL OR VEGGIE?

BANG! BANG!

"It's 7 a.m.! N56981 Calvey, rise and shine!"

For a moment, I'm confused. I'm disorientated with exhaustion. Then I remember. This is my prison number, and I wonder if I will ever get used to it. I need a wash and a new set of clothes. I'm starving now but the smell coming from the wing is the disinfectant mixed with an oily meat odour.

All night I've been dreading this moment, when the wing wakes up and the day begins, because I don't know what's coming next. Prison is worse – much worse – than I'd ever dreamed of. It's as close to hell as I ever want to get.

The hatch in my door is opened, increasing the volume of the commotion in the wing. It sounds like the nurse is doing the rounds as I can hear her saying: "Take your medication," and "Just swallow it down. Here's a cup of water." As well as this, women are shouting: "How long 'till breakfast? Where's my toast?" and "Bloody screws, never do what I ask, do ya?"

One of the screws – which I am learning is prison slang for prison officer – looks through the hatch.

"Are ya normal or veggie?" the voice says, brusquely.

"Am I a normal or veggie what?" I say, bemused.

"Breakfast. Do ya want a normal breakfast or a veggie one?"

The eyes in the hatch are not unkind.

"Well, I suppose I'm normal then," I say, and through the hole comes a blue plastic plate, laid out on which is a single strip of streaky bacon, two stiff slices of cheap white bread and a small scraping of margarine.

I take it and the screw hands me a set of white plastic cutlery, which I have to keep for my other meals.

I look down at the plate in my hand. If that's how much you get given, I'll die of starvation before my sentence is through.

"Cup of tea?"

"I only drink coffee," I reply, expecting her to hand me a cup of Nescafé at the very least.

"There ain't no coffee. You'll 'ave to drink water then."

A matching plastic blue mug is passed through my hatch, containing tepid water.

If I was despondent before breakfast, then it's getting worse by the minute.

"You'll 'ave to keep the plate and mug, and wash them in the sink where you wash yourself. I'll pour a drop of washing-up liquid in a cup for ya."

I can't help it, I'm horrified.

"I 'ave to clean my plate in my sink where I 'ave a wash?"

There's no reply. The officer has moved on. I can hear her saying the same to another new inmate.

"You veggie or normal?"

Once I've eaten the prison offering, I realise there's absolutely nothing to do. The night before I was too shocked to really think beyond trying to shut my eyes for a while. Though I'm just as terrified, possibly more so now I'm here on this hellish wing, I suddenly realise there is nothing: no television, no radio, no books. Absolutely nothing.

I realise that time drags slowly here – and the thought makes me feel even lower, if that is possible.

Just as I'm sinking into a pit of despair, a screw I haven't seen before comes to my hatch. She unlocks my door and takes me out to the wing office nearby. The wing seems quieter while people eat their food, but later I realise it's also because they've taken their medication.

"Calvey, you get one reception letter which the prison pays for. If you want to send more letters you'll 'ave to pay for them."

I don't have any money, but I nod anyway, wondering how on earth I get money sent to me. I take the offered letter: two pieces of paper and a second-class stamp.

"Do you want a VO as well?"

This term I know. My Mickey used to send visiting orders so I could go and see him in Wandsworth Prison.

"Yes, thank you, I'd like one," I say

"Do you know who you want it sent to?" the screw asks. She is a large woman with long brown hair tied in a severe bun. She seems quite nice though. None of the screws have been horrible so far, so at least that's something positive. I'm already finding I need to snatch at each good thing like it's a diamond inside a rock.

"Yes, please send it to my mum and two of my sisters."

"You can do an app for clothes as well. You're allowed three sets of clothes and a small amount of underwear. They'll have to bring it in for you when they visit."

"What's an app?" I say. I don't know this one. I realise there was loads that Mickey didn't tell me about the way prison works, probably because he was protecting me from the hard reality. It was so like him to make a joke and make light of things. I wish I'd asked more questions at the time now. I had no idea what he'd really been through.

"It's an application, but in 'ere it's called an 'app'. Don't worry, Linda, we'll sort it for you. Don't forget not to seal the envelope, it has to be read by staff before it can be posted out."

It is the first time since I came onto the wing that someone's called me by my first name. How strange that in less than 24 hours, this could feel so foreign.

By now, I'm very aware that I'm still wearing the same set of clothes that I wore to court only yesterday – the same suit, the same knickers and bra, the same blouse. I feel quite disgusting. The screw tells me what I'm allowed to have brought in, and it's a far cry from my wardrobe stuffed with fur coats, designer suits and heels.

As I hadn't been on remand, I'd lived a normal life up until I went to court. I had never thought I should take some clothes with me, it had never entered my mind! I went into my trial totally blind, with nothing that might be useful if I was sent down. I had no plan in place for my kids, no clothes, nothing.

"The wing guv'nor'll see you soon," the screw says, taking me back to my cell where she shuts the door again but leaves the hatch open.

"Oh right, thank you," I reply, not sure I want to meet the governor. He won't let me go home, so what's the point?

I look down at the paper and take hold of the pen. For a moment, I'm not sure what to write, there's too much to say. I know I won't tell them anything about the reality in here, just as Mickey did for me. They don't need to know about being stuck inside a tiny cell all day and all night, without anything to distract from the hellish conditions.

I begin writing my letter, trying not to cry as I do so.

Mum,

I hope everybody's OK. Give the children my love. Please tell me who they are with and what is happening with them. Everything is all very different here but I'm getting used to it. I wish Mickey had told me what prison is really like, though. It might've helped, but then again, I don't suppose any of it makes any sense until you actually get banged up.

I'm so sorry for what I did. Please say this to Melanie and Neil. I thought I was giving them the best, being able to buy whatever they wanted with the money I stole, but I got it all so wrong. I can't live with myself knowing they don't have a mother for the next few years.

The screws are sending you, Shelley and Maxine a visiting order. When you come, please bring me some clothes as I'm still wearing the suit from my trial.

Here is the list of the things I can have:

Three outfits – the screw suggested you bring me track-suits (don't laugh, you know I've never worn one in my life!) because they're more durable than dresses, so please bring me two tracksuits, and a smart skirt and blouse, which I can wear for visits. Also, a pair of flat pumps, a pair of trainers and a pair of slippers plus two nightdresses, please. I'm also allowed a dressing gown, three bras, a few pairs of knickers and I think that's it. Could you please bring it all with you?

I'm counting the days until I see you. I've sent the VO just to you and my sisters. I don't want my children to see me as I am right now in here. When I'm more settled then, assuming they want to see me, I can send another VO.

Give everyone my love,

Linda xxx

I know my family would never, ever reject me, even as a convicted armed robber.

I grew up in the East End of London, a place notorious for crime and poverty, but I have been one of the lucky ones. My family has always been one of my greatest strengths. They are law-abiding and close-knit, a rarity in those days.

My dad Charlie was a soldier in World War Two, who then became a blacksmith afterwards, working near Limehouse Docks and Smithfield

Market. My mum Eileen ran a stall selling wigs at Roman Road Market, and brought up nine children. It seems unbelievable now. I was born in Ilford, and we moved to Stepney when I was five, right into the heart of the East End, streets away from where the Kray twins grew up. We've always rallied round each other, it's just what we do. As I sign my letter, I know without a doubt that my family will come through for me.

I have days to wait until the visit, and I'm starting to realise that I'll have to make do with the clothes I'm standing up in until then.

When I finish my letter, I hand it back through the hatch, without sealing it so that strangers can read the words I've written. I'm fast learning there is no such thing as privacy. There's one thing I remember Mickey telling me during a visit I paid him. He had just been banged up and he mentioned that inmates are allowed to seal letters to their solicitors, but you have to write the solicitor's address on the envelope alongside "Rule 39", which means for the lawyer's eyes only. I hadn't paid much attention at the time as I was so happy to see him, but it comes back to me now, with a strange, sinking feeling. I had no idea back then of the course my life – our lives – would take. We were young, in love, and in trouble with the law. I could never have guessed that one day, years later, I would be sitting in his place, a widow and a jailbird.

Lunchtime in Holloway is 11.30 a.m. I'm actually quite glad when I hear the lunch trolley go round as I'm still hungry from breakfast.

Again, a pair of eyes peers through my hatch.

"Veggie or normal?" the staff member says.

"What are the choices?" I ask.

"Shepherd's pie if you're normal, or rice with mushrooms and peppers if you're veggie."

"Oh God. I don't eat mince, and I don't eat rice neither," I say. This is no time to be a fussy eater.

"Take a shepherd's pie and just eat the top," the screw says.

I shrug and pass her through my blue plastic plate.

A large portion of the food is passed back through.

"I've given you a bit more. Just eat the potato, love," the voice says.

"Thank you," I say, looking down at the plate. Everything is swimming in grease. There is a sheen of cheap margarine on the potatoes, but I'm grateful for the staff's kindness. Without salt or pepper, it's difficult to eat, but I manage a few mouthfuls, more for the sake of the screw who was so generous.

I finish what I can, then wash my plate in my sink.

Just then, another set of eyes appears at my hatch. A key turns in the lock and my cell door is opened.

"The wing guv'nor'll see you now," the screw I met earlier, the one who took me to the wing office, says. She's quite young, probably in her thirties, and has brown hair pulled back off her face. I'm getting used to the sight of the uniforms now. She's wearing a dark blue skirt and a white shirt, with a navy jacket and flat, black shoes.

I'm taken along the corridor. Someone's screaming and banging something against her door. It takes a moment before I realise it's probably her head. The thud, thud, thud continues.

"Can't you help her, poor soul?" I say to the screw.

"It's in hand. She does it all the time," she replies, but I'm not convinced. I look down the corridor then back at the screw. I can't see anyone coming to help her. And she seems to be only one of many who are clearly disturbed. I can see where food has been chucked through the hatches, there are plates and splattered mince on the floor now, which a cleaner is already trying to mop up half-heartedly.

In another cell a woman is shrieking almost continually. Her voice echoes down the long corridor as we walk. I feel sick, though whether it's from the lunch or shock, I don't know.

By the time I get to the wing governor's office I'm more shaken up than I was inside my cell.

A woman in her fifties, with a plain face and dark brown hair and wearing an expensive-looking suit is sitting at a large desk.

"Why didn't we have you in here already?" she says, without any other greeting.

I blink, unsure what she means.

"You got seven years and you weren't held on remand before your trial. That's very unusual. Linda, please sit."

There must've been a look on my face because she adds: "This is going to be a culture shock for you."

I look at her and manage a smile. "It is already."

"Listen, the reason you're locked in, and will be again tomorrow, is because of the length of your sentence. I know this has already been explained to you. The charge you were found guilty of is extremely serious and we don't know yet if you're a danger to yourself or others.

"We need to observe you to see your reactions, but actually you seem very pleasant. The staff have all said so."

I have to laugh at that.

"Well actually, I am really pleasant!" I reply. "Will I be stayin' 'ere?"

"No, you won't, Linda. You were an unknown quantity to us, but we're satisfied with how things have gone so far, and so tomorrow you're going up to D3."

"Oh," I say, wondering if this is good news. "What's D3?"

"That's the working wing, it's a lot more pleasant than down here," the governor says, getting up out of her seat, and indicating that the interview is over.

I take this as a glimmer of hope.

Thank God, I think to myself as we walk back, past the shouting and distressed women, *at least it sounds better. I don't think it could get any worse...*

Back inside my cell the screw asks if I want her newspaper. A small gesture it might be, but actually, inside jail, it's another piece of kindness amid all the horror.

"It's only the *Daily Mirror*, but it'll give you something to read."

When I thank her I wonder if such a little thing has ever made me feel as grateful as I do now. It cheers me up enough to think more positive thoughts.

I'll just get tonight over with and then I'll be up in D3. It'll all work out for the best...

I've always been a glass-half-full person. I always try to see the positive, even when things are bleak, and they don't get much bleaker than being inside Holloway's psychiatric wing.

That night I refuse the dinner of pasta, as that is something else I don't like to eat. Luckily, they serve pudding and so I polish off a jam and coconut sponge with custard. Time passes much like it did before. All night there are the sounds of women screaming. I have nothing but my thoughts to accompany me, and this makes me feel lonely. I wonder what Mel and Neil are doing. I wonder what Mum and my sisters are up to. It seems unbelievable I can't pick up the phone and call them as I would if I ever felt this way at home. I can't call them. I have to lie on my scratchy blanket, staring out of the tiny rectangle of window at the night sky.

Eventually, I manage to drift off but again, I'm woken by my light being clicked on, and the periodic sounds of ambulances wailing.

"What's happenin'?" I say sleepily to one of the pairs of eyes who looks through my hatch to observe me. I've got no idea what time it is, but it's late because much of the screeching from the wing seems to have settled down.

"One of the girls has slashed herself with a broken lightbulb. I wouldn't normally tell you, but as you're off the wing tomorrow, it doesn't matter." The night staff's voice is totally normal, not shocked at all, as if she's talking about when breakfast will be or what the weather will be like tomorrow. In some ways, I find this more shocking than what she's telling me. It feels like people don't care, though I know enough to understand this must be a frequent event. This thought makes me shudder.

"Oh my God, is she OK?" I say.

"The medics are 'ere. There's not a lot more we can do. Get some rest, Calvey."

I lie back, wondering how on earth this prison is allowed to exist. Surely, there must be better ways of dealing with mentally ill inmates other than locking them in isolation 24 hours a day? It's no wonder that some of the girls go mad, kicking doors, throwing food and hurting themselves so brutally. Of course, there are no answers to my questions. I lie awake, listening to the chaos. More ambulance sirens wail in the darkness. There are sounds of footsteps running up the wing, presumably to the woman's cell. I lie, willing away the time until I can leave this part of my sentence behind. Whatever's coming next must be better. And if it isn't? I'll cross that bridge tomorrow. For tonight, I send up a prayer for that poor woman who may already be dead.

CHAPTER 5

D3

"N56981, Calvey, get ready to be moved!" a screw says, poking her head through my hatch.

I've already eaten my meagre breakfast of a single rasher of bacon again with two slices of white bread, and drunk a cup of water. Yawning, I pack my few belongings, as well as my bedding, placing my toiletry bits into my pillowcase as I don't even have a plastic bag to carry them in.

A few moments later, another officer appears.

"Linda Calvey? I'm moving you up to our wing."

I follow the woman who is a big lady, quite tall and imposing. I don't know what to think as we go through each set of large wooden doors. I'm exhausted from the past two nights of broken sleep and the sheer horror of finding myself banged up. The guard's keys jangle again as we walk. At every door, we have to stop, wait for it to be unlocked, go through, stop again while it's locked, then carry on. Here and there doors slam, while every single light is fluorescent with this extremely bright light. The corridors all gleam though. There isn't a scrap of dust or dirt anywhere, which I find strangely comforting. I'm taken up the stairs and into D3. A woman in a white coat is sweeping the floor. She looks up at me.

"Alright," she says.

"Alright," I reply, wondering if this is another hospital area.

There's no one else on the landing because everyone is working. We get to the wing office. Inside is another screw, who looks up at me as we enter.

"Linda Calvey, come up from C1?" she says.

"Yes, I'm Linda," I say.

"I bet you're glad you've come up from there!" she adds, looking down at my card.

"It was horrible," I agree, "but I don't know what it's like up 'ere yet."

The screw leans back in her chair. Her desk has piles of papers on it and a large computer, which takes up most of the space.

"You've had the worst; as long as you do a job, you get to stay on this wing."

"Right." I nod. "Well, I'd much rather work than be locked in, that's good."

The screw gets up, brushes off a few biscuit crumbs from her shirt and gestures for me to follow her. The guard from C1 leaves, saying goodbye. I hope fervently that I never see her, or that wing, ever again.

The cell is a single cell, like the one down on the ground floor psychiatric wing but clean. The bed is still an army-style metal one. The mattress is still tatty and thin but not as bad. There are still no curtains at the window, and there is a table and chair, a sink and toilet, just like before. The screw tells me to get my stuff sorted. As she walks away, I realise she's left my door open. Already, this feels odd after being locked in solidly. My heart lifts a little. It's like freedom in a small way.

As I'm making my bed, the woman in the white coat walks up.

"We was all wonderin' when you'd get up 'ere. We read about you in the paper. My name's Diane. Would ya like a cuppa?"

Her manner is almost deferential, and she hovers in the doorway, not coming into my cell.

"Sorry, Diane, I don't drink tea, and I know what you're goin' to say, there's no coffee and I'll 'ave to 'ave a cup of water!" I smile, realising she is another inmate working on the wing and not a nurse.

"No, I won't say that 'cos I've got coffee. I'll make you a cup."

"How comes you got coffee? I was told I couldn't 'ave it," I say.

"We can buy it from the canteen with our wages, or if ya family can send in money. A lot of girls in 'ere don't 'ave that, but them's the usual ways." Diane beckons for me to follow her, and I do so, looking around to see if I might get caught, feeling already like I'll get into trouble as I don't yet know the rules.

"Don't worry, Linda. We can move about 'cos it's work time. We don't get locked in till later."

I follow her to the kitchen. A couple more women are sweeping floors and dusting. Diane says hello, and so do I, but they just stare back at me.

Diane hands me a steaming hot cup of coffee. It's my first in three days. I don't think I've ever been as grateful for a cup of instant coffee as I am right now.

"Thank you," I say, sipping the dark liquid. "Can I ask a question?"

"Course you can," my new friend says.

"How come those others just stared at me? Is it because I'm new, or the fact I look like I do in the same clothes?"

Diane is a young girl, probably in her late twenties. She looks older than her years and has a pale complexion with black hair scraped off her face.

"Don't worry about them," she says, mysteriously. "Listen, I've got to get back. Nice to meet ya."

"You too," I say. "And thanks for the coffee, you're a lifesaver."

After the drink I walk back to the office, wanting to know when I'll have my first visit – and receive my clothes. They can't seriously expect me to stay in these until my family can get here to see me.

"In the morning when we unlock, someone'll shout if anybody wants any apps. You can put in an app to get your regulation clothes brought in, and then you do a second one to give out your existing clothes the following week."

"OK," I say, not really sure I understand. "I've been wearin' this outfit for three days, since my trial ended, and it's gettin' rough now. I've already written a letter to my family askin' for clothes. Can't they just drop them in?"

The screw looks back at me as if I'm an idiot.

"No, Linda, they can't just drop them in... You 'ave to do an app, and do the proper process. I'm sorry about your clothes, but unfortunately you'll 'ave to wear them until your family can bring you in new ones."

"Right," I reply, still confused. "But can't I borrow somethin' off one of the other girls on the wing?" I say. It seems an obvious solution to me, as it's pretty barbaric expecting people to fester in their dirty clothes.

"We can't let you do that," the screw says, turning back to her paperwork. "If you wear someone else's clothes, you both get put on report."

"What does that mean?" I say.

"That means you 'ave to go downstairs and see the prison guv'nor, and be adjudicated. You'll be told your charge beforehand, then it's like a mini court, where you're charged with borrowing clothes, or fighting, or whatever it is you've done. You could get a fine or lose a privilege, or, in some cases, your sentence could be increased. And it wouldn't just be you that's charged if ya did borrow clothes, it'd be the person who lent you them as well."

"But why?' I say. This sounds really harsh.

"I know it's strange, but we don't know if you've bullied that person into givin' you somethin' to wear. In the past we've had women bully girls into givin' up nice clothes, so this measure was introduced."

"So, what you're tellin' me is, I 'ave to stay like this," I say, feeling quite annoyed.

"I'm afraid so, Calvey. It isn't all bad, you get a single cell because of your long sentence. Most of the girls 'ave to share dorm rooms, four to a sink and toilet."

"Oh right, well that's somethin'," I reply. That, at least, I can be thankful for. Even so, I can't help glancing down at my crumpled blouse and wrinkled skirt.

. . .

That night, I venture out of my cell for the evening meal, feeling quite nervous and unsure what to expect. There is a large room used as the canteen, with guards standing around the walls or milling about. Women queue up at a hatch where the meal is served. There still doesn't appear to be any more choice than the usual normal or veggie options. When I finally get to the hatch, women eyeing me up as a newcomer while I shuffle forward, the inmate in the kitchen says: "Normal or veggie?"

I sigh.

"Neither, thank you," I say. From what I can see, there are pork chops or a rice dish. This looks more promising. I ask for the chop and jam roly-poly and custard for pudding. Hardly a balanced meal, but at least it's something.

While I'm waiting for my pudding to be dished up, I look around me. Every sense in my body is on alert. I've seen films and telly documentaries about prison, and they usually involve a scene of violence erupting in the food hall as inmates throw food and punches. Nothing like that happens, though I see a few eyebrows raised as I walk to the table Diane is sitting at. Heads turn as I sit down, but I ignore them.

"They've read the papers," she says.

I shrug. There's not much I can do about that.

"It'll go good for ya," she says. "Everyone thinks you're a big gangster. You won't 'ave any trouble from the girls."

I look around. A few faces look back at me but most turn away as if I've caught them doing something wrong.

"I can see that," I say.

Just as I start to eat, a rough-looking woman with a partly shaved head, probably in her late twenties, pushes past a young girl, then strides up to the table next to us.

There's a girl sitting there. She looks pretty bedraggled with long greasy hair tied back in a ponytail and skin covered in some kind of rash.

"She's a druggie," Diane says. "They're looked down on in 'ere. They're the bottom of the heap. I think she's a prostitute as well."

"Poor soul," I murmur, wondering what's going on.

I don't have to wait long to find out.

"I'm 'avin' that," the rough older woman says, and reaches down, taking the meat off her plate, She grins then walks off, leaving the younger woman with just a bit of mash and a few vegetables. I can't believe what I'm seeing.

"God, the bullyin's blatant 'ere! She can't do that, surely? What's that girl goin' to eat?" I start to ask but Diane shakes her head.

"There's a peckin' order. She's at the bottom and there's nothin' you can do about it."

This, at least, I had heard of from Mickey and his friends, who all served time over the years. I'd been told by them that blaggers were at the top of this pecking order, and it seems this is the same in women's prison.

"Don't worry, they won't bully you, they're in awe of ya," Diane says.

Thank bloody God, I think. *At least my charge has done some good for me*, though I can't say the same about the young girl who's lost her dinner.

"So, what are you in for?" I say, turning to my new friend. "And why weren't you afraid to approach me?"

"Credit card fraud. I nicked cards then put my name on them and spent a fuckin' fortune. It's nearer the top of the peckin' order than the others and I thought you looked like a nice person," Diane replies, grinning.

"Fair enough," I say.

Already, I'm changing to fit this environment.

In the outside world I wouldn't be able to stop myself butting in if I saw something as blatant as that. I'd feel really uncomfortable watching someone vulnerable getting treated like dirt. I know I'd say something. In here, I'm learning very quickly not to say a word. I've only just arrived. I don't know the lie of the land, so even though I'd dearly like to tell that rough bitch what I think of her, I don't.

Diane seems to read my mind.

"As long as they're not botherin' you, keep out of it."

Afterwards I head to the association room as the girls are allowed to watch telly for an hour before lock-up.

I walk in, and see immediately there are no seats. Some girls are standing, leaning against the wall. A couple of nasty-looking women clock me as soon as I arrive. One of them looks over at a young woman who has a chair, and says: "Oi you, get up, she's 'avin' your seat."

The girl, who seems quite timid, doesn't question this or argue back. She stands up and scurries to the back of the room.

I know, without having to ask anyone, that if I turn around and tell the younger girl to keep her seat, this new status of mine, earned because of my charge of armed robbery, will be gone instantly, and I could end up being bullied the same way. This is survival. This is a dog-eat-dog world, and I'm fortunate to be at the top of this hierarchy. I know they expect me to be treated better, they expect me to go and take that girl's seat, and so what do I do? I walk over and sit down. I don't acknowledge the bully who made it happen. I certainly don't acknowledge the girl who gave up her place. I watch TV as if all this is normal.

Even though they don't know me, they know who I am. My name and face have been plastered over most national newspapers. My reputation as the queen robber comes before me, and I'm given respect. My crime, serious as it is, is standing me in good stead inside prison.

It's like playing a role, and one I'm grateful for. Already I can see a little of what life must be like for the girls who come here without status – the crack heads and junkies, the prostitutes and shoplifters – and I don't envy them. If life for them is hard, prison is harder – and I also know I can't change it so I have to take it as it comes.

Just as the episode of *EastEnders* is finishing, a girl comes in. She has dirty blonde hair and is fidgeting restlessly by the bully women who'd given me my seat. I look round and catch her eye.

"Oh, you're Linda," she says. Her eyes are gleaming and I wonder if she's high.

"Yes, I'm Linda," I reply and begin to turn away.

"I'm in for armed robbery, like you," she goes on.

"Are you now," I say. It isn't a question. I don't feel like inviting this conversation.

A voice comes from the side of the room. It is the other of the bully women who hasn't said anything yet. She has a tattoo up her arm that looks like a blade.

"Fuck off, you ain't like her!" she says. "Goin' into an off-licence with a knife was muggy, how can you compare yourself to her, she's the real McCoy..."

"I'm just sayin', I got the same charge..." the jumpy girl replies. She keeps looking over at me but I say nothing. It feels like this might kick off.

"No, you ain't like her. Move away from her." The bully stands up and actually blocks the girl from speaking to me. She has a rock-solid frame and hair bleached at the ends of her dark roots.

I don't even know who these two women are that seem to be my protectors, but I don't ask. I say nothing still, hoping this will pass.

The room is open to the corridor, with material chairs that are like a cross between an armchair and a dining chair, all pushed together in rows. There are about 20 women lounging about, chatting or bickering now as the programme ends and lock-up approaches.

At 7.55 p.m. exactly a screw appears and turns off the TV, making some of the women groan.

"It's time to lock in," the guard says, as they start to troop back to their cells. Inwardly, I give a sigh of relief as the two bullies walk off and the twitchy girl disappears to her cell.

"Oh and Calvey, you'll be starting work as a wing cleaner tomorrow," the screw says.

"Oh right," I say, not sure if that's a good thing or not.

"It's a good job, they must like you," Diane says, appearing from the other side of the room. We walk back to the cells together, as I start my third night locked up in Holloway.

· · ·

All night I can hear women calling out to each other across the prison. Convicted girls from the wings shout over to those on remand, who are held in cells on the opposite side of the prison. Somewhere, a woman is screaming a series of swear words and won't stop. Elsewhere, it's more like the kind of chat heard over the garden fence.

"Rosie! How d'ya get on today?" one voice yells.

"Oh, they were right shits! I got six months and they told me I'd only get three!" another voice replies, loudly.

"Oh well, I'll see ya tomorra!"

It's like being in one of the soaps they watch each evening.

Despite the racket, I'm starting to get used to the thin mattress, the scratchy bedding and the continual cat-calls. I look back at how appalled I was when I arrived, and wonder at how quickly the human spirit adapts to adversity. That night I sleep well, and when a screw bangs on my door, key turning in the lock to let me out, I realise I feel almost normal for the first time since I arrived in prison.

Diane greets me once I have had a shower and got dressed.

"We're up a bit earlier than the girls to get the breakfast ready," she says.

As we begin to sort out the kitchen, putting out boxes of cereal and milk, one of the women from the kitchens appears with a huge industrial trolley.

"Alright Di," she says. "Who's this?"

"I'm Linda," I say. "I only came up to the wing yesterday so I'm the new girl."

They both smile at that.

"You'll soon get used to it," the woman, who has shaggy permed hair, says with a grin.

"I hope so," I answer, "'cos I've got a long time before I get out."

The woman looks like a lightbulb has been switched on somewhere in her brain.

"Oh, you're Linda Calvey! I know who you are now. All the girls are talkin' about you. A proper gangster! You won't get any trouble 'ere then," she says, nudging Diane with her elbow before she ambles off.

"Everyone keeps tellin' me that," I say as I help Diane push the bloody great big trolley into the kitchen. On it are rows and rows of fried eggs and strips of that horrible greasy bacon. Saying that, by now I'm starving, and would eat greasy bacon and more right now. We eat all our meals early, so everyone has to go from dinner at 5 p.m. through to being unlocked at 7.30 a.m. for breakfast.

"Right, let's count the number of eggs. OK, there's enough left over for us to 'ave an extra one each. Put them aside so we can eat later. How many strips of bacon are there?" I'm amazed at what Diane is saying. It looks like we'll get a bit more than the others, though I'm not sure yet how I feel about that. Seems unfair, but then again I'm learning that this place operates on being unjust.

"Fifty-five," I say.

"The kitchen girls are good," Diane says, smiling. "They always send a few more so us wing cleaners can have extra rations. OK, put a few rashers aside and we can 'ave those too."

I'm starting to realise why being a cleaner might be a good job. I definitely didn't expect this. I was dreading scrubbing floors and cleaning toilets.

Diane shows me how to turn on the tea urn and the hot plate. I carry out loaves of cheap white bread for the girls to toast themselves when they come in, while Diane unloads a huge vat of porridge from the trolley.

The women slope in from 7.30 a.m. and queue at the hatch.

"Why 'ave some of them got Marmite and jam when others don't?" I say, as they shuffle past. Some say hello, most eye me with curiosity. I realise I'm a bit of a novelty in here. Most women seem to be in for petty crimes or soliciting, but there are definitely no other female armed robbers as far as I'm aware. The lifers are kept on the same wing, so I'm realising that other than them, I have the longest sentence of anyone on this floor.

"They've just bought themselves some bits. You can spend your earnings, buy some nicer shampoo, a jar of face cream, or some jam for your bread," Diane says, humming as she works.

"We get paid?" I say in disbelief. Things are looking up!

"We do, in a manner of speakin'," Diane says. "It isn't much, so don't get too excited..."

"Well go on, how much do we get?" I say, eager to hear, wondering what I might be able to buy. I've spent my life being bought wonderful things by men. I don't know why they do this, but men have always liked to look after me, bought me expensive perfume, Dior lipsticks and make-up, Clinique or Estée Lauder face cream. The thought of being able to spend my own money on something nice makes me feel quite giddy.

"Seventy-five pence. A week."

There is a moment's silence.

"Bloody hell, at that rate it'll take me a month to get a jar of coffee," I reply.

Diane looks at me, and I can see she's struggling not to laugh.

"Didn't you know?" Diane says, eventually.

How could I have known that? Mickey never mentioned money when he was banged up. This is all new to me. I look back at Diane, and we both burst into laughter. Suddenly this whole situation feels less of a tragedy and more a farce. It's a welcome moment of hilarity, like the sun's rays suddenly poking through the clouds.

"No, I didn't know. I shoulda carried on robbin' post offices," I say.

Once everyone is served and we finish dishing out food, Diane shuts the hatch and we sit down to eat.

"OK, so there's two rashers each and two eggs. Not bad, eh!"

I smile at Diane.

"It's a lot better than C1, though I don't know why they've picked me for this job. There must be girls who deserve this more than me?" I say.

Diane shrugs.

"Perhaps they expected ya to be a nasty piece of work, but you ain't. Or maybe they're scared of ya." She snorts. I look over at Diane, but she drops her gaze and grabs a scrubbing brush, getting ready to clean the floors.

CHAPTER 6

FIRST VISIT

"I have to do what?" I say in disbelief.

Diane points to the scrubbing brush and the bar of chemical yellow soap that are sitting on the landing floor.

"It's your choice, Lin. You can scrub the floor with a brush and soap or a scouring pad with a tin of Chemco."

I look at my new friend as if she's gone mad.

"Are you tellin' me that I've got to clean the wing floor on my hands and knees. Where are the mops and buckets?"

Diane shrugs.

"It's just the way they do things 'ere. Sorry, can't do nothin' about it."

I am four days into my seven-year sentence. I'm still wearing the clothes I was sent down in, and now I have to get down on my hands and knees and scrub prison floors. Every time I hit a low point, I think it can't get worse, and then something else comes along.

"Alright. I'll use the scrubbing brush and carbolic," I say.

All morning I kneel down in my silk skirt that is now only good enough for the rubbish bins and wonder, not for the first time, how on earth I'm going to get through this.

During the day the wing is quiet as everyone is out doing their jobs and only the wing cleaners stay. By 11 a.m. the floor is gleaming and I stand up. Diane gestures for me to go with her back to the canteen as the lunch trolley is due. Bang on 11.30 in comes the woman from the kitchens who greets us cheerily again.

"Linda, it was you, wasn't it, who doesn't eat mince or pasta?" she says.

"It was, thank you for rememberin'," I reply. "Why, what's for lunch?" I feel the familiar dread at the thought of having nothing I want to eat. I'm starving after the past few hours of scrubbing floors, and really quite fed up with it all.

What can I make do with today? I think, with dread, expecting to find nothing I want to eat yet again.

"Don't look so worried! I've made ya an omelette. Will that do ya?"

"It will! Thank you, that's kind of you."

Sure enough, a delicious looking cheese omelette is sitting on a plate with some salad. I look at the other dishes and it looks like everyone else is having either spaghetti bolognese or rice and vegetables again, neither of which I would've eaten. I'm thrilled by the sight of the omelette in a way that would've been laughable before being banged up!

"The guv'nor sent us kitchen girls a box of peaches, so I've put a few there for you two as well. Enjoy, ladies..."

Certainly, in the real world a few peaches or an omelette would be nice but not a huge deal. Inside prison, it feels like unimaginable riches. I can't stop thinking about those peaches while we serve up lunch. Women file past. I'm starting to recognise faces now. I say hello and some nod back at me. When everyone has finished it's the same drill. We tidy up, wipe down the tables, and stack the plates in the kitchen, ready to be put into the huge industrial dishwashers. Sitting down to eat I can barely contain my excitement. A real peach. I cut out the stone and take a bite. It's sweet and juicy, and I relish every mouthful as if it's the first time I've tasted it. Kindness is not something I expected to find in Holloway.

. . .

That evening, I'm told I am to take the tea trolley around to each cell and give the women a last cuppa and whatever the kitchen has set up for supper. Tonight it's an orange each. As I go, I shout, "Ice creams! Choc ices!" just like they used to do at the cinema, and I make a few girls laugh.

"Oi, Linda, would ya go to my mate's cell and ask her if I can borrow two cigs? Tell her I'll replace them on Friday." A mixed-race girl I've seen on the wing peers through her hatch. She has the most beautiful almond-shaped eyes.

Round at the friend's I get the cigarettes for her and take them back.

"I'm Maria. Thanks, Linda."

"You're welcome, Maria. Nice to meet you," I say, as if we're guests at some sort of strange party.

"Would ya do the same for me, Linda? Tell Jane I'll lend a cig and pay her back on Friday."

So, I go over, and Jane pokes her face up to the hatch.

"I ain't got none. Sorry, Linda, tell her I'm all out."

After that, I end up pushing that trolley up and down the corridor, running backwards and forwards handing out ciggies and chatting to each of the inmates. I fill up their flasks with hot water for overnight drinks and give them an orange each for supper.

"Don't worry, you 'ave my orange, Lin, for getting me the ciggies," one girl says.

Another offers me a scoop of her coffee, knowing I don't drink tea.

"Thank you, darlin'," I say, touched by the spirit of cooperation I'm seeing, though I'm aware I'm probably receiving this treatment because of who I am rather than what I'm doing. I never expected prison to be like this. I expected fights, bullying, even rioting, but I never thought people might try to help each other.

. . .

Finally, the day of my first visit arrives, a week after I was sent down.

I've been counting the hours until today, and yet, strangely, I start to feel nervous as I sit in my cell, waiting for a screw to take me down. My mum and sisters, Shelley and Maxine, are coming. I asked them not to bring my children. I think seeing them might break me, and I want to know how they are before I ask them to come. Deep down, I realise they may not want to see me, and I have no intention of forcing them. I've done enough damage. I want it to be their choice, though, of course, I desperately hope they'll come soon.

"Visit for Calvey. Time to go," one of the screws says. *She's new*, I think as we begin the start-stop journey through locked doors to get to the visiting room.

My nerves must've been apparent, because when I arrive in the holding room, with other inmates waiting to see people, Maria comes up and plonks herself down next to me.

"Who you got comin'?" she says. She has a long scratch on the side of her face, which I'm trying not to notice. It looks like she's been in a fight.

"My mum and my sisters," I reply. "Who 'ave you got comin'?"

"Oh, a mate," Maria says, looking away.

"Don't you 'ave any family?" I say with surprise, thinking it's normal to have mums and siblings who love you and want to see you.

She looks at me like I've said something outrageous.

"Nah, not many of the girls do. My mum's a junkie and on the game, and my dad fucked off, so I was in care. Lots of us in 'ere were."

I look back at Maria. Her hair is pulled off her face. She's wearing large hooped earrings and a pink Nike sweatshirt and joggers. She is a prostitute as well. I'm told that's what she's inside for, that and drugs. Apparently, she's one of the ones who bounces in and out, where Holloway is like a second home, and one that might actually be better than what lies outside these walls. I'm starting to realise that many girls don't have homes to go to. They have pimps and dealers, their kids are in care and nobody is looking out for them. Women like Maria are the real victims of an uncaring system. Living through chaotic child-hoods, broken homes, drugs, violence and poverty. How on earth are they meant to know how to live?

It seems to me that life was unfair for Maria from day one. She didn't have a chance. A prostitute mother addicted to drugs, and a neglectful father. Is it a surprise she's in here, a place that provides regular meals, though the food is basic, a safe enough bed to sleep in and a routine of sorts? I don't think so.

"I'm so sorry to hear that," I say. It strikes me yet again, how lucky I am to have a family that cares about me.

Maria shrugs, tucking a cigarette behind her ear.

"I'm used to it," she says. "Listen, Lin. When ya go out there, remem-ber to play it down."

"What d'you mean?" I say.

"Smile. Pretend things are OK, even if they're blatantly not. Don't make them worry any more than they are already. D'ya know what I'm gettin' at?" Maria says.

Just then, a voice tells me I can go in to the visiting room. Sitting at a table are Mum, Maxine and Shelley. They all stand up when they see me and it takes every bit of self-discipline I have not to run over and hug them. I also feel disgusting in my dishevelled suit. Glancing at the clock, I see that we're 15 minutes late starting, so we'll only have three-quarters of the allotted hour.

"The queues, Linda. It took ages gettin' in 'ere," says Maxine. Both her and Mum are crying.

"Oh God, have you had to wear that all week!" Shelley exclaims. "That's awful!"

I smile but can feel myself welling up. Maria's words have not left me though. I realise in a flash of memory, that's what Mickey was doing when he was laughing and joking with me when I visited him. I always came away from those visits thinking prison couldn't be too bad. Mickey was happy, so I didn't go away suffering any more than I already was. I see that's what I need to do for my family now, too.

"Don't worry about me. I'm fine in this suit. They don't let you borrow another girl's clothing 'cos they think you might've bullied her into it. But, it's fine, I'm fine. Honestly." My face is already hurting from grinning so widely, and I'm unsure how convincing I am. If there is one kindness I can do for my family, it's this. Give them nothing more to worry about. They don't need to know about my sleepless nights worrying about my children, or the feeling of being trapped in a tiny cell. They don't need to know about the bullying and fights, the drugs and the despair. No, they deserve more than my misery, and I'm determined to make this as easy as I can for them. It's the least I can do.

Looking around, the room is quite pleasant. There's a tea bar with coffee and snacks, bits of cake and crisps.

"How are you, love?" Mum says. Is it my imagination or does she have more worry lines than she did even a week ago?

"Honestly, it's not as bad as you think. I'm fine. I just want you all to be OK," I reply.

"They only let us hand in two outfits 'cos what you're wearin' counts as your third. Next time we come, pack up your suit, and we can bring the third fresh set of clothes," Shelley says. She smiles back at me, and behind her eyes I can see she knows what I'm doing. I'm grateful to her for playing along.

"How are Melanie and Neil? I hope they understand why I said for you to come first?

"They're fine too, course they understand. Don't worry about them. Mel's with Mum, and our older brother Terry has Neil. They're with family so they're safe and loved."

"Will they want to come and see me, d'you think?" I ask, not sure if I want to hear the answer. My greatest fear is losing them because of this, because of my actions.

"Of course, they want to see you," Mum says. She is sniffing and searching in her pocket for a tissue. I can see she's about to burst into tears again and I hope and pray this won't set me off as well.

"Tell them I love them, and I miss them so much..." My voice trails off.

"Of course, we will. They miss you, too," Maxine says. She is crying still, so Shelley gets us all a hot drink and a bar of chocolate. Tasting the chocolate and sipping the scalding hot coffee, I say: "Who would've thought a KitKat and a Nescafé could feel like luxury."

Shelley smiles and I see pity in her gaze.

Just then, there is a sudden movement. We all look round to see a screw place their hands around Maria's throat. She is standing up after seemingly just having kissed the guy who came in to visit her.

"Don't swallow!" the screw shouts. "Spit it out!"

"Oh my God, what's happenin'?" I say, alarmed.

Maria turns away and retches loudly. She spits something out into her hand. I can't see what it is, but the screw grabs it and marches her off. I catch Maria's eye as she goes, and look back at the man who is now being held by another officer.

"Drugs," an inmate mouths from across the room, turning back to her visit as if nothing happened.

"Poor girl, I hope she's OK," Mum says, oblivious to the reason for the interruption.

Shelley and I share a look, but there's nothing we can do. The room buzzes with the shock of the sudden movement then returns back to how it was.

Poor Maria, I think, *she'll be put on report for that.* I know enough by now to know she'll be in real trouble for trying to smuggle drugs into Holloway.

"Listen, Linda. Your solicitor told us he's booked a legal visit with ya. Your sentence is so big, everyone's goin' to appeal and they're sure you'll all get time off," Shelley begins. "That judge was excessively harsh in your case, and they all agree. All isn't lost, there's an appeal underway, and hopefully you'll get time off and be back at home a lot quicker."

"I hope so," I say, "for Melanie and Neil's sake. And look, I know they're not OK. I know they must be missin' me, so thank you for everythin' you're doin' for them."

"They were devastated," Mum admits. "Bear in mind they lost their dad when they were young."

"I know, Mum. I lost Mickey, too," I say quietly. "Tell them whatever happens, I will never do anythin' to risk bein' taken away from them ever again."

My children had already lost their father, and now they're having to deal with a mother in prison, a long separation and new lives in different, albeit kind and loving, households. My heart is breaking anew, and I'm almost glad when we're called back to the cells. I give Mum and my sisters a cheery wave and a smile as I walk away, but as soon as my back is turned, the tears slide down my face, and I wonder if they'll ever stop.

CHAPTER 7

KICKING OFF

Stepping out into the exercise yard, I'm grateful for the only piece of advice Brian and Carl gave me when I visited them in prison before our trial.

Though they both said they'd done deals with the Old Bill to keep me out of jail, they still offered me this wisdom in case it all went wrong, which, of course, it did: *Don't rush to be friends with anyone. The prison is like a miniature world – the yardies stick with the yardies, the junkies stick with the junkies, the travellers do the same. Wait until you find your group, 'cos you'll be with them a long time.*

Turns out, it was good advice. Women eye me warily as I walk out into the summer heat, though I've been banged up for more than a week now. I've only really spoken to Diane and the kitchen girls, apart from when I slop food onto plastic plates at mealtimes or pass them their flasks filled with hot water at lock-up.

"It's because you're the "Black Widow", you're the big armed robber," Diane says, trying to fan herself ineffectually with her hand when I ask why they're still all staring. Perhaps it's different when I'm behind a hatch, or serving tea through the hole in their doors in the evening. Now I'm here and walking around with everyone, it feels different, like people are deliberately keeping their distance.

"They're too scared to speak to ya," Diane laughs. "You're the top of the prison pecking order in 'ere. God, ain't it hot!"

"Go on! I'm a nice person, how can they still be too scared to approach me? They see me on my hands and knees scrubbin' floors all day!"

Diane giggles. Just then, Maria appears. She walks straight up to me. I haven't seen her for a couple of days after what happened in the visitor's room. She looks pale in the sunshine, and seems on edge.

"See, Maria isn't too scared to say hello," I counter. The warmth of the sunshine feels good on my face after days spent inside. At home, I don't have much of a garden, just a small patch of lawn and some pots where I grow my flowers, but one of the things I love doing is sitting outside, watching the world go by. Being stuck indoors, in a small cell or the hot kitchens, has been its own punishment.

We're standing on a large square of tarmac where women are jogging, while others sit on the grass surround. A few women with babies from the mother and baby wing sit on a bench, their buggies parked haphazardly beside them. I'm amazed to see them because prison yards are volatile places, not exactly where you'd want to bring a baby or small child. Mickey used to tell me that fights always broke out in the yards because everyone was thrown in together: lifers, shoplifters, druggies and thugs. There are three girls who're heavily pregnant, and that also feels odd. Surprisingly, there's no fence, but we are surrounded by screws.

"Alright, girls," Maria seems distracted. She's looking round, her shoulders hunched.

"You OK?" I say, alluding to the screw grabbing her throat.

She laughs.

"I'm alright. They stuck me in solitary for two days but I'm fuckin' out now and cluckin'."

I've got no idea what this means but I nod anyway.

"Got any salmon, Lin?"

"Any what?' I say. Maria is fidgeting and restless. I've been watching her march up and down the exercise yard, getting progressively more frantic for the past 20 minutes.

"Can we get salmon in 'ere? Well, the food's posher than I thought!" I say.

"You what?" Maria says. Then she bursts out laughing again. "No, not the fish! I mean cigarettes! 'Ave you got any ciggies? I'm desperate..."

I look at her. My face must be a picture. "Sorry, Maria, I don't smoke. Why on earth d'you call cigarettes salmon?" I ask, realising I've heard girls say this before but assumed they were talking about what they'd like for dinner.

She shrugs, but one of the women who has followed her over says: "Salmon trout – snout – cigarette."

"Oh," I reply, not sure I really understand. The prison slang is taking some getting used to. Maria has walked off already. There is a jumpy, twitchy energy about her. It doesn't take me long to find out why.

A few minutes later, Maria reappears, with a cigarette pushed behind her ear. She is with a few of the women, all of whom look shifty.

"Lin, did ya want to score?" Maria says, her voice lowered.

That, I do understand. My Mickey never did heavy drugs like heroin, though he always puffed, meaning he smoked cannabis. None of the guys I knew in the East End touched the filthy stuff, but the terminology was widespread.

"I don't do drugs neither," I say. For a moment I think this young woman will reply, but she just walks on, off to her cell, no doubt, where they'll take whatever it is they've smuggled in.

"Is it easy to get drugs in 'ere?" I say to Diane, squinting in the sunshine.

"Yeah, it's pretty easy, they all do it. If they've got money, they bribe a guard. If they haven't, then they get it brought in. People have it in their mouths so when they kiss they pass them over that way. Well, sometimes it goes wrong, you saw what happened the other day."

I know I've got a lot to learn, but this fact really saddens me. I can already see how the drugs are ravaging women like Maria. Her face is stunning, but there are signs already there: her teeth aren't great, her skin is starting to look spotty. Why do they do it?

I don't have time to ponder this.

"You've been tryin' to pull my bird!" A large butch woman with tattoos up her arms and neck marches up to another inmate. All heads swivel round to see what is happening.

"Fuck you, I don't want that slag!" the other woman replies. She is now glaring at the other, her head shaved, a cigarette in her mouth.

"Well, I think you did pull her." The larger of the two puts her face right up to the other. They look like two stags locking horns.

Everyone seems to stop what they're doing. Conversations drift as people realise things are about to kick off.

Tensions run high in the heat. All day there's been an unsettled feel, even more than usual. I hardly slept the night before as the noise the women made was even worse than a normal night. This was punctured by yet another visit from the fire brigade; sirens screaming, people running, shouting and noises because someone in C1 had set light to their cell again. It seems like this is a common occurrence. A woman had been badly injured when she'd set light to toilet paper wrapped around herself. She'd tried to end her life – and we didn't know yet whether she'd succeeded. There is so much self-harm on that wing, so many troubled people who shouldn't be in prison. This morning, the whole prison had been abuzz with the news, and it seemed to tip some women over the edge, that and the July heat.

Every time the firemen are called, I think they must hate it. As soon as they step out of the engines and make their way onto the wings, there's a chorus of women shouting from their cells: "Show us your cock!" "Get your kit off!", cat-calling and jeering at them.

Back at the fight, things are escalating. "Go fuck yourself, wouldn't touch her with a shitty stick!" The cigarette gets thrown to the ground. The women step around each other, face to face.

"The shit's hittin' the fan," Diane says.

"What if one of the babies gets hurt..." I begin to say. Then the two women launch at each other. A crowd forms almost instantaneously around the women screaming and lashing out. Some of the inmates start shouting encouragement to either one of the girls.

"Oh my God, what's happenin'? Why are they fightin' like that?" I ask.

"A lot of the butch girls are tough, so the straight girls 'ave relationships with them 'cos it gives them protection. There're always fights over girlfriends in Holloway."

As Diane finishes, there is a sudden commotion. Several screws seem to run over at once.

The crowd scatters.

"Get the babies in! Get the babies in!"

One of the screws launches at the inmates, while another starts to usher out the girls and their prams. A baby is screaming. Another is wailing as her mum tries to pick up a nappy and bottle from a bench.

"Oh my God, this is bedlam! Those poor girls!"

Both inmates are still trying to lash out and kick each other as the two burly prison officers try to contain the fight. Now the children are out of the way, the officers drag the women inside, both screaming insults at each other, and making it very clear what they'd like to do to each other.

It's almost funny.

"It's like a bloody zoo in 'ere," I say to Diane. "Where will they take them?" I ask, as we all follow behind. Even though we we're nothing to do with the altercation, we've all been ordered back to our cells to be locked in as punishment. Bang goes my sunbathing.

"They march them down to the punishment block. They'll be locked in all day and all night, and all their privileges gone. They'll probably be charged with assault or fightin', somethin' like that."

"That doesn't sound good," I say as we watch them struggle out.

"Then there are the ones who've been in before. They fall out, get released, end up back in 'ere and they start their battles again. Lots of 'em are enemies on the outside."

"Wait till I get hold of her!" is the last we hear of them as we line up to be escorted back inside.

. . .

That night, despite the drama of the day, I smile as I hear women calling out to each other. I'm starting to understand what they're saying.

"Anyone got a salmon? I'm on floor one..."

"I'm above ya. I can drop you one down..." comes a voice nearby. The cell windows measure roughly three feet by four feet, and they're divided into strips six inches wide. At either end is a window that opens out, measuring roughly three inches. You can't get your head through but you can pass objects, or drop stuff down to other inmates, which is exactly what happens next. Prisoners are allowed to smoke inside their cells, and so the trade in cigarettes is rife. They seem to be more like currency than anything else.

"Thanks..."

Two dressing-gown belts tied together edge downwards past my window. A few seconds later, there's a jolt and they come back up again, this time with a cigarette tied to the end.

"Can ya swing it across to me? I ain't got a lighter," comes another voice. This goes on for a while as we settle down for the night. Some of the girls share dorm rooms, cells with four beds in. Despite having a single cell because of my long sentence, I don't feel so lucky when the door is slammed shut and I'm locked in alone. Tonight, we've got hours added to lock-up because of the fight, and it's now that the enormity of my sentence and my crimes really hits home. There's a reason a lot of the girls go mad. It's uncomfortable as hell being shut up with just your thoughts. I could easily hate myself for what I've done. It isn't such a big step from that to thoughts of self-harm or even suicide. There's no one to listen, no one to comfort me, no one at all except for me, and the constant noise from across the wings.

CHAPTER 8

APPEAL

"N56981, Calvey. Legal visit for Calvey!"

I get up from my kneeling position as one of the screws appears. I put down my scrubbing brush and follow her to the office.

"Your solicitor is here to see you, Linda. Sharon'll take you down," a guard says.

The screw named Sharon nods. She is one of the regulars who works on this floor, but we have only spoken a few times, despite the fact I've been here nearly three weeks now. She is quite tall with a stern face but she's friendly enough. I follow her down to the rooms used for appointments with our legal teams. They are tiny, pretty barren, with a bare table, a couple of chairs and a red panic button.

My solicitor, Peter Hughman, is waiting for me. He has a polystyrene cup of tea, which leaves a brown ring on the surface of the Formica table. He is a tall, slim man who always wears a smart navy suit and carries a briefcase stuffed full with papers and documents.

"Is there any hope of an appeal?" I say straight away. There's no point either of us wasting our time.

"Hello Linda, it's good to see you too." He smiles. "Sit down, let's see what we can do... there's always hope."

"But the judge hated me on sight! He gave me the biggest sentence in the prison apart from the lifers," I say. The air is stale in this room,

.and I have the sudden urge to run out. My breathing feels laboured and I realise I feel scared. So much is expected from legal visits. I've seen how the other women on the wing wait, expecting miracles to happen, only to be disappointed. I don't want to give myself false hope, but hope is really all I have right now.

"I know, and so there's room for your sentence to be reduced. I think we should go for it. At least they can't increase your sentence. The judge's remarks were stern, granted, but we should be able to do something."

I look at him and he shrugs.

"How much can they reduce it?" I say, starting to feel hopeful again, thinking perhaps I might go home in a year if I'm lucky.

"It's hard to say," Peter says, frowning. "But they might put it down to five years, hopefully."

"Five years!" I burst into tears. "It's such a long time to be away from my family," I say, dabbing a tissue at my eyes. There's a box of them on the table; obviously I'm not the first to need them.

"I don't know if I can handle five years in 'ere..."

"Sorry, Linda. I think that's the best we can hope for. If they reduce your sentence, you won't spend five years in Holloway. You'll be moved to other prisons, less secure ones, to begin the process of going home, but that won't be for a while yet. Hold tight, Linda. We'll do everything we can."

We chat for a while, running over what my solicitor is going to say and when the hearing might be.

"Alright, thank you. Let me know as soon as you hear anythin' won't ya," I say, getting up. The chair scrapes on the lino floor as I leave, a screw by my side, stopping at each door, waiting at every lock for it to be opened then shut again. My thoughts are far away from here. I'm thinking of Mel and Neil, wondering what they're doing at school today, who their friends are, whether they're coping as well as my family say they are. I think of the risks I took, the heists I planned, even the shot guns I carried, the danger and the thrill of stealing all that money. I think of how my gang and I took spray guns filled with ammonia and threatened people with them during the robberies. We did it for effect, but I didn't give a thought to what that effect might be beyond getting the cash handed over to us faster.

It makes me feel sick to think of the terror we inflicted on people. I always used to think of robbery as a victimless crime. The post offices were insured. The people who worked there didn't lose anything personally. What I had been too arrogant or naïve to realise was that it cost them hugely. It cost them their piece of mind. It cost them the impact of each robbery on their families. With every step I take back up to my wing, I know I'm paying the price for this as much as anything else, and I know I deserve it.

It's too late to change things, though I wish fervently I could. I have to pay the price, do my time as graciously as I'm able, then go home as soon as I can.

When I see people arguing with the screws or fighting each other, I wonder why they do it. How can adding time to your sentence be a good thing? I'm learning the only way to do this is to keep my head down and to carry on. Hope is a luxury I'm not sure I can afford.

Back on the wing, I'm given a white coat, like the one a doctor wears, and told I can wear this to do my cleaning in so I don't get my two new outfits dirty. I get changed into it with just my underwear on underneath and join the other cleaners on the wing.

I'm sweeping the landing when a woman wearing a bobble hat walks past.

"Alright, Di," she says, then throws me a quick glance. She is walking with another woman, who whispers loudly: "That's the armed robber..."

The bobble-hat-wearing inmate stops and turns around.

"Oh shut up. She don't look nothin' like an armed robber!"

"Yeah," the other woman, who is wearing a grey sweatshirt and jogging bottoms, replies, "that's the lady from the newspapers."

They both stand staring, like I'm an exhibit in a zoo.

Neither of them has actually addressed me personally. They continue to ignore me, turning to Diane instead.

"Ohhh, what's she like?" says the hat-wearer.

"She's nice," Di says.

"I am nice!" I say, laughing at this absurd conversation.

"Want a cup of tea?"

"I don't drink tea, thanks," I reply, thinking that's going to be the end of this bizarre exchange.

"I've got coffee. Come and meet the other girls. My name's Bobble."

"Bobble?" I say. Could this get more surreal?

"Yeah, after my hat. It's what everyone calls me."

I don't know what to say to that.

"OK, I'll 'ave a coffee, darlin'," I say and follow Bobble to the dorm she shares with two others. It is a bigger cell than mine with four metal beds, each one with a wooden cupboard, but it is just as dingy. Paint is flaking off the walls, there are no curtains, so no privacy at all, and dirt is ingrained in the floor and window ledges.

"This is Linda, you'll 'ave read about her," Bobble says by way of an introduction. Two women look back at me. One, who I discover is called Bibble, which has to be a joke, is a young woman who is in for shoplifting, which is called "heisting" in prison.

"Pleased to meet ya," I say as Bobble passes me a mug of coffee.

"This is another Linda," she says and points to the woman sitting with her head leaning against the wall.

"Alright," the woman says. Her voice is almost as low as a man's and she is scratching her back as she speaks. There are badly drawn tattoos running up both her arms, and her face looks hardened by life. She barely looks over at us, just sits there, scratching.

"Right," I say, unsure what else to add. "Pleased to meet you too," though I'm not sure I am.

"Bibble here is in for heistin'. I'm in for counterfeit fraud, car tax discs mostly. We know what you're in for..." Bobble says, grinning.

I sip my coffee.

"I was caught heistin' in Sainsbury's, ta-ras. Got caught 29 times and they put me in 'ere," Bibble says in a small voice. She looks half-terrified, and I notice the slang she uses, something I've not heard before.

"Why didn't you try a different shop?" I say, and everyone – except poor Bibble – laughs. I later discover that Bibble is rightly nervous of everyone. Originating from Mauritius, she has a sister who's in prison for a very nasty crime, and she is constantly terrified that other inmates may recognise her real name and mete out a punishment on her that they can't get to her sister to inflict. Bibble often hides in the cell's only cupboard and is a frightened young thing, probably no more than 20 years old.

Just as we finish giggling, Bobble nudges me. I look at her, wondering what she means, and I see why. There is a giant cockroach walking across the wall, its long antennae wiggling. I gasp but Bobble shakes her head and I can see she's suppressing a smile. We stare, fascinated, as if transfixed, as the creature heads for the other Linda's hair. The woman, who is still leaning her head against the wall, appears not to notice and is now scratching her arse and offering to make toast, which we all decline politely.

"Nearly there," whispers Bobble.

The cockroach disappears into Linda's hair.

A second later she screams.

She jumps up off the bed, shakes her head and the cockroach comes flying out.

"You fuckin' bitches!" she yells, hopping about, scratching her hair, at which point Bobble starts to belly laugh. Her amusement is contagious. I find myself bent over almost crying with laughter. It feels so good to laugh properly again. I feel like I haven't since I arrived. Even Bibble is smiling.

"You bitches! You just watched it crawl up!"

"Oh we did, Linda, and it was worth it to see your face!" Bobble says. She is crying with mirth now.

Linda storms out, and heads back to work as a wing cleaner on C1. Not the nicest job in the prison as she has to deal with mopping up blood and food spilt by the self-harmers and mentally unwell inmates. I know enough already to know that a cleaning job in the psychiatric wing is not for the faint-hearted. Having to work amid the wails and screeching, the violent fits and attempts at suicide, putting down bleach and disinfectant everywhere, must be pretty awful. In contrast, my cleaning job is much lighter. There's no one around on the wing for a start, so it's quieter, and it involves a degree of freedom in the kitchens and taking the trolley around each night. I wouldn't swap my job for the other Linda's for ten times the wages.

There are also cleaning parties that go around the yard, picking up litter and no doubt sweeping up the legions of dead cockroaches that seem to be everywhere in Holloway. That, and rats of course, not to mention the piles of rubbish that are thrown out of the cells each night. Every morning the yard is strewn with cigarette packets, cigarette butts, food wrapping, tabloid newspapers and a whole host of rubbish. Every day the cleaning party goes around, collecting it up, but every day it is always the same mess again.

"Sorry, I don't mean to be nasty, but I couldn't resist that," Bobble says, wiping her eyes. "Look, we need another cell mate in 'ere. Why don't you come and join us?" she adds.

"What d'you mean?" I say. This is the first time I've genuinely enjoyed the company of other inmates since being banged up, and suddenly I don't feel so lonely any more.

"Well, it's nice to 'ave a single cell, but it's not the same as bein' with others."

Bobble has a point. The nights are very long. I'm in my cell alone for 11 hours between lock-up and wake-up. Perhaps some company, even in the form of the other Linda, might be better.

"Alright," I say. "I'll give it a go. How do I go about it?"

"Oh, just let the office know that you want to move into our dorm cell, and they'll be happy. They like to keep the single cells free anyway in case of new people comin' up," Bobble says. "Let's toast our newest recruit!"

Bobble, Bibble and I knock cups, and even though my coffee has gone cold, I feel a new warmth spread through me. Things are looking up at Holloway.

* * *

Later, I'm called to the office.

"Calvey, you've been sent a couple of photos in the post." The screw is holding what looks like them in her hands.

"Oh right," I say, wondering what I'm expected to come out with.

The screw looks at me like I should know.

"You've already got ten photos pinned on your board." This is true. I have pictures sent in from family, mostly of my children, and they're on display in my cell, like all the other inmates.

"You need to decide which photos you're taking down, if you want to put these up," the screw says, a little impatiently.

"I do? Oh, right." I look down at the images. They show Melanie and Neil grinning at the camera, the sun in their faces. I think of the pictures I have in my cell. A picture of Mickey holding Neil as a newborn. A black-and-white photo of me with baby Melanie in her pram. Pictures of me with all my siblings. How can I choose which to keep and which to hand back to the screw?

"But why only ten? Is it so terrible to 'ave 12 photos in my cell?" I ask. It doesn't make any sense to me.

"That's the rule. Ten photos, Calvey. Did you want these?"

"Of course I do. OK, I'll bring two back, give me a minute."

As I walk back to my cell, I don't know whether to laugh or cry.

CHAPTER 9

REGRET

A month after arriving in prison, my children come to visit me.

I'd told them to wait until I was settled as I didn't want them seeing me in a state. My mum brought them over, but they're taking ages to come through security. I don't think I've ever been so nervous in my life, except for that moment before my guilty verdict was read out.

Eventually I see my daughter's blonde hair, closely followed by Neil's tall frame. My mum follows behind them. My heart is pounding and I well up inside as they look over and see me.

The children both look terrified and so I'm relieved when their faces break into smiles as they walk over to me. All morning I've been worrying about whether they'll come, or how it'll be with them when they get here. I can see immediately that they're intimidated by this place (Who wouldn't be? The visiting room is clean and bright but badly in need of a refurbishment, with basic chairs in groups of four which are fixed to the floor around a small table, and bare walls), but my heart soars as they sit opposite me.

"Hello darlin'," I say to them both. "I wish I could give you both a big kiss. How are you? How's school? Are you OK?" The questions fall out of my lips before I can think straight. All I really want to tell them is I love them and I'm desperately sorry.

"Calm down, Mum. We're OK," Neil says. He's a typical teenage boy with trendy clothes and trainers and a slouch when he walks. Even in the time I've been here now, he seems to have changed, to have grown up a little perhaps.

"Let me get you a drink or a cake, look there's Coke or Pepsi... How was your journey?"

They both shake their heads.

"We're alright, Mum, honestly," says Neil. "Except it took ages to get through. They searched us, made us wait for ages, then we had to go through security again before they let us through."

"No wonder you were all late through then," I say, looking over at my daughter now.

Melanie is the same. She looks like she has matured. Both look older than their years. She is wearing a leather jacket and a new pair of trainers. Her blonde hair is worn long and she is wearing make-up. She looks so grown up, but I wonder if she's had to grow up quickly even in the short time I've been banged up.

It can't be easy on them, all their friends at school knowing their mum's in prison, especially as Mel had her seventeenth birthday two weeks after I was sentenced. That must've been so hard for her, but my mum wrote to say they'd organised her presents and a party and for me not to worry. How could I not? I was so sad to miss it, and felt so guilty too. Before I can ask how they are, Melanie speaks.

"Mum, we miss you..." she says.

"I miss you, too," I say.

There is a moment's silence.

"Why did you do it, Mum? We only wanted you, not all that stuff. We didn't want anythin' but you..."

"Don't upset your mother tellin' her that," my mum says, defending me even though she'd already asked me the same question.

"I'm glad they've said that," I reply. "They've told me the truth, and that's all I want. I got it all so wrong."

I look over at them both and sigh. How do I explain what I can barely understand myself? I look down at my hands and my wedding band glints gold on my left ring finger.

"I really don't know," I reply. "Looking back, I wasn't myself after your dad was killed. I lost the plot, I guess you could say. I wanted to give you the best of everythin' like your dad did, and there was no other way of doin' it... It was really the only way I knew how to survive... but I also thought I was gettin' one over on the police. I'd be lyin' if I said it was all about survival and paying bills and buying nice things. It wasn't. I wanted revenge for your dad's death..."

There is a moment's silence as we all digest this.

"I regret it now," I continue. "I regret all of it. If I could change what I did, I would, you 'ave to believe me."

They both listen, still taking in my words. I know my explanation is inadequate, and they'll probably be feeling deeply angry at me for being so reckless with our lives. My heart is still pounding and I'm starting to feel tearful.

Eventually, Mel shakes her head.

"But Mum, all we wanted was you. We didn't care about toys or clothes, or any of that, not after Dad died anyway."

I feel like a knife has been put through my heart.

"Mum, why did you do it when it was so risky and people could've been hurt?" Neil says now.

I look over at him and I wish I could turn back time and start again, from the day Mickey died, and be the mother they needed, not the one I thought I should be. I've made so many mistakes, and I don't know if I can ever put them right. Perhaps I can't. This thought brings me real despair.

"I'm so sorry. I thought I was doin' the best for you both, I really did..." Even as I say it, I know that is not the whole truth, and they know this too now. Of course, my kids were at the forefront of my mind, but there was also the thrill, the risk itself, which, I'll admit, I found intoxicating.

"But you weren't, Mum. You weren't doin' the best for us. If you were, then you wouldn't be 'ere," Neil says, and again, I feel like I have been sliced through, the pain of their words cutting me deeply.

"You left us like Dad did..."

"I'm so sorry..." I don't know what else to say. "But I'm still 'ere, and I will go free one day. My solicitor says I might get my sentence reduced."

"Yes, Peter's been in touch. Let's hope he can do your appeal and get you out as quickly as possible." I see Mum suppress a shudder as she looks around. I see the room through her eyes. It is filled with women, some dishevelled, some tough, some desperate, some just getting through, all of them convicted of different crimes. It's no place to spend an afternoon, especially with kids.

We chat for a while about where they're living, how they're doing at school. Neither feels very settled, though they know they're safe and loved.

"It isn't the same without you," Mel adds. "We know we're lucky to have our family, but it just isn't the same."

"Of course it isn't, it must be so hard for you both," I reply as the end of visiting time is announced.

"It's gone too fast!" I say. "We need more time!"

"Sorry, Calvey, that's your lot," says the screw on duty.

"Alright," I reply, "but can I give them a little hug? They're my children. I don't know when I'll see them next."

I know this isn't really allowed. Some screws let people have a hug but others stick to the rules. I don't recognise this screw, she must be new, and so I wait for her answer, praying she's one of the kinder ones.

"Go on then, Calvey. I'll turn a blind eye."

"Thank you," I reply, feeling like I could hug the screw as well.

I turn to my children, and one by one, I give them a hug. I know they're probably experiencing fear, abandonment, anger and perhaps even shame at their mum being a prisoner. I know it has taken a lot of courage on their part to come here.

"I love you both. I'm sorry for everythin'," I say as they begin to walk away. I wave and smile, but as soon as I'm out of that room the devastation I feel seems to hit me. I somehow manage to get back upstairs to the cell before I break down in tears. It occurs to me that this is my real punishment, this separation from my children, this knowledge that I've done this to them. That night is truly the hardest since I arrived. The full knowledge of the consequences of my actions leaves me heartbroken. I ache for my children. I pick up a pen and try to write the words in my weekly letter to them but nothing comes; instead all I can do is pray that my appeal is successful and I can get home to them as soon as humanly possible.

* * *

The next day, Maria plonks herself down next to me in the association room.

"Were them your kids, yesterday?"

I still feel a bit shaky, so while I'm pleasant enough, I'm not really in the mood to talk about my children. The pain of seeing them is still too much.

"Yes," I say. "That was Melanie and Neil."

"You're lucky," Maria says, which I don't expect to hear.

"Why d'you say that?" I reply, turning to look at her. She looks rough today. She is shaking and her skin looks sallow. Yesterday, I saw her head off to another woman's cell, where I hear they all share a "set of works". In prison slang, this means a syringe and needle. They take heroin, or whatever it is they inject, and the needle just goes around to each woman. These are the days of AIDS, when it's an incurable terror – a certain death sentence to anyone unlucky enough to contract it. I see what Maria and her mates are doing and I shudder. I wonder how long it'll be before they do real harm to themselves.

"I don't know when I'll see my kids again," Maria says, looking down at her fingers, which are stained yellow with nicotine.

"What d'you mean?"

"At least you get to see yours... All my kids are in care."

"Oh my God, I'm so sorry," I say, taking hold of her hand. Maria flinches as if she's not used to being touched gently. "But, what about their dad? Can't he look after them?"

She shakes her head vehemently, a bitter smile on her face.

"They've all got different dads. None of them give a shit. They're using as well. I s'ppose my kids are better off where they are. Out there, I'm on the game, I take drugs. I want to stop but I can't. I don't even know who's lookin' after them 'cos my girl's been fostered out and I think the boys will be too."

I'm learning that prison is a melting pot of people, just like the real world. It's a place where every human tragedy and loss is played out, just like out there, but in a concentrated form. I'm also starting to realise how lucky I am to have a good family, something I've always taken for granted until now. It feels like I'm in the minority, having people who love me, who look after my children, who'll welcome me home with open arms one day.

The ones with no visitors, no extra money to spend, no food sent in, are the ones I feel sorry for. I always share out whatever I have to those who might spend months inside and never see another soul except for the others in here. It is tragic – and extremely common. The one thing that has shocked me about being banged up is the amount of women who have nobody. I've always presumed that everyone has a good family, or at least, some kind of family; a caring mum or dad, a strong network, but they don't.

"What are their names?" I say, softly.

"My boys are Riley and Mason, my girl's called Tara. She had her birthday last week."

"Her birthday? How old is she?"

"She's five. They want to adopt her out but I'll keep fightin' it if I can."

I feel desperately sad for Maria. It's so clear to me that she had everything weighted against her in life. I feel almost ashamed of myself for getting upset at seeing Melanie and Neil, because at least they're cared for, they're safe, and as soon as I get out I'll have them back with me. Mine have not had to go into care because they have a loving family. Maria has none of that. I can't imagine how that feels.

"Don't look so sad, Lin! I'm used to it," Maria adds.

"You always say that but how can you be? I don't think I'd ever get used to my kids bein' taken from me! Can't you get off the drugs? Please try. You never know what might happen if you do."

Maria smiles at me. Her smile is sad, and she shakes her head as if I don't understand at all. She's right. I don't understand what it is to be addicted to drugs, to have boyfriends who are pimps and who abuse me, though my boyfriend Ron has always been very controlling. I didn't really have a choice about whether to go out with him or not. He decided he wanted me (despite the fact he has a wife and kids) while Mickey was alive, and after I became a widow that was that. You can't argue with Ron. People end up injured or dead. He's a gangster, a big-time robber, a powerful man. The only good thing about being locked up is that I don't have to put on a mask as Ron's lover and be at his beck and call.

But there must be hope for Maria and her children? It's clear my friend thinks otherwise. She looks around and catches another inmate's eye. From that glance, I know she's going somewhere to get her next fix. I know a lot of people might judge women like Maria, and all the others who grew up in poverty or broken homes with abuse or violence. They turn to drugs to cope with the pain of all that, and the fact that society is not a level playing field. Stopping taking drugs is not that easy either, especially as the only people you might have outside when released are your boyfriend who got you on drugs in the first place, and the other working girls who stick together because they have no one else. How do you escape that? I can see that for Maria, and countless others like her, it's an impossible task.

CHAPTER 10

CONTRABAND

Things are already changing. In the beginning, during those first few nights and weeks, I felt extremely claustrophobic and trapped. I felt shame and remorse, as well as terror. None of those feelings have gone away, but I've started to adapt to the environment.

Daily life has a rhythm if nothing else, a routine which helps the time pass, at least during weekdays. Every morning I'm up before 7 a.m. to dress and go to the kitchens, where I serve breakfast. Then, after eating, the day unfolds with the same mundane tasks: sweeping floors, scrubbing them, dusting and cleaning everywhere except for the individual cells. Then it's lunch and I help serve that before eating again, then the afternoon disappears quite quickly because dinner is served so early, at 2.30 p.m.! By 3 p.m. everyone has eaten, then it's back to the cells before coming out for association at 7 p.m. I write each evening to my family to maintain contact as best I can. I'd put in an app to be moved into Bobble's cell and it was approved. Now I have company each evening with Bobble and the others, so it isn't all bad, but nothing can distract from the fact we're stuck inside a prison that isn't fit for purpose. Maria has been released and is back out doing what she does, and I worry about her, as well as all the other young girls navigating life on the streets.

We all dread weekends. Staff shortages seem to be announced at the end of every week, and so we know we'll be locked in pretty much the whole time except for mealtimes. It's dispiriting and incredibly boring. I still have no radio, and there's little to occupy us. I have to remind myself that at least I don't have to sit and stare at the walls on my own any more.

I'm even finding ways of getting one up on the establishment.

One of the best scams we have going on is with the remand girls. Their cells look over the exercise yard, and so we ask all those who have visitors to get extra supplies brought in. The allowance is generous. You can have half a bottle of wine, cigarettes, chocolate, cans of lager, six pieces of fruit or even a hot meal brought in for you. People on remand can get a visitor every day, unlike those of us who are convicted and have our allotted three visits a month only. Of course, 75 per cent of the remand girls don't have visitors at all, and some of those that do have them can't afford to bring extra food. But there are always a few who do get visitors, and it's these girls we speak to, asking if they'll do the convicted girls a favour and get in extra supplies. It works like this. The remand girls take our orders for boxes of ciggies or bars of chocolate, and they ask their families or friends to bring them in. When they've got them, they get word to us on the prison grapevine, and my friend Bobble goes out with a large bin bag to collect it all. The girls throw the extras out of their cell windows in the evening.

Bobble goes round calling out: "Anythin' for the convicted?" as she walks under the cell windows of the remand girls, which always makes me laugh, and fills the bag with goodies. She works in one of the painting parties, so she is allowed more freedom around the prison. She can easily do this at the end of each day, saying to the screws she's going outside to collect rubbish. Somehow, they always let her.

Bobble then bursts back into our cell carrying the contraband, grinning like she's won the lottery.

"What a haul! Ain't a bad group of girls on remand at the moment," Bobble says, coming in this evening just after lock-up. Bibble is lying on her side on her bed, watching us both without saying a word, while the other Linda is digging something out of one of her teeth.

"Oh well done, you did well, Bobble!" I exclaim as she tips the haul onto her bed.

Galaxy bars, Mars bars, packets of Marlboro and Camel cigarettes jumble together.

The idea is we split the food with the women who don't have visitors, then we share out what's left between ourselves.

"They actually asked me to go and pick up rubbish on the way back tonight," Bobble says, grinning. "One of the screws told me it's lookin' disgustin' out there. I was happy to oblige!"

This arrangement serves us very well. Without attracting suspicion, Bobble is able to grab a few bin bags and head out to the yard to collect the contraband.

"The screws don't take any notice, do they?" I say to Bobble.

Bobble shrugs.

"They don't care. They just want to do their shift and go home," she adds.

"Pick out what you want then hide the rest in our cupboard so we can hand it out tomorrow."

"Wahooooo," Bibble says, picking up a gigantic bar of Cadbury's.

"That's for sharin'," I say, smiling at her reaction.

"The girls did well," the other Linda says, looking through the spoils. There are about five packets of cigarettes, countless chocolate bars and packets of sweets and biscuits. It doesn't sound like much, but for us it's heaven. It's amazing how much you can miss the normal things in life, like popping to the corner shop for chocolate when you fancy it, or pouring a glass of wine in the evening. It's the simple stuff that makes life what it is.

We're like children let loose in a sweet shop. Bobble and I pick out what we'll keep and what'll be shared among the women on our wing.

That night we feast on illegal chocolate and custard creams. We all agree, food tastes better when it's forbidden.

. . .

The months pass, and though we run these small scams and joke about in our cell, life is undoubtedly dreary. I miss my children and my family. I miss simple things like opening a door for myself, or popping out for a pint of milk, or boiling a kettle to make a cup of decent coffee. Life is endlessly frustrating. Then, of course, there's the bullying and thieving among the girls, which is horrible to witness. It's even worse when it happens to me.

"Which bloody bastard has nicked my bra and knickers?" I shout as I walk into my cell and find all of my new underwear, given to me by my family, has vanished from inside. I'd tied a bit of string from the window to the door frame as a tiny washing line. Everyone does it. It's the only way to dry our smalls as there's a bizarre rule that knickers can't be washed in the washing machines so they have to be done by hand. As people walk past they can see what you've got hanging on there. I'd washed my new white bra and knicker set and hung them on my line.

"Someone's nicked your knickers? Don't worry, Lin, we'll get them back for ya," one of the big butch girls says, looking over my shoulder.

Fifteen minutes later, she appears with my underwear in her hand.

"'Ere ya go. They won't be nicked again, it's all sorted..."

Well, I don't ask what she's done or said to the thief. I'm not opening that can of worms, so I take my things and say: "Lovely. Nice one."

Luckily, I get respect for the seriousness of my charge, otherwise I'd have lost those nice things and never got them back.

Another time, I'm walking across the yard with a new male screw, Mr Jenkins. He's quite a nice guy and we're chatting away, when all of a sudden something whizzes through the air and whacks me on the head.

"What the hell?" I exclaim.

"Jesus, are you OK, Linda?" Mr Jenkins says.

"I think so," I say, rubbing my head. We both look down and see it's a bloody clothes hanger.

"Sorry Lin!" comes a voice from a window above us. "It wasn't meant for you, it was meant for him!"

The screw and I exchange a look of disbelief.

"Who threw that?" he shouts up.

For once, there is silence.

No one says a word.

"Who threw the coat hanger?" he shouts again.

Still, nothing.

Uncharacteristically, you can hear a pin drop.

"If I find out who done that, they're on report," he fumes, picking up speed and almost hurrying me back into the building. Even though I got hurt, I can't help but see the funny side. As soon as I see Bobble, I tell her what happened.

"And no one said a word when he shouted! They were all quiet as mice. They'll never tell him who done it."

Life is always strange at Holloway.

* * *

Christmas is a terrible time to be in prison.

In normal life, people look forward to Christmas as a holiday, or a time of celebration, or a time to be with friends or family. For some it can be lonely, but for prisoners it's a whole new level of isolation. There's a skeleton staff for one thing, so inmates are locked in even more than usual. At Holloway, the staff all want time off, and as time moves on and my first Christmas inside approaches, the same appears to be happening as we're locked in more and more.

I feel incredibly sad knowing I won't be with my children. It's the first time we've ever been parted at this time of year. I'm lucky.

My family always have huge Christmas celebrations. I'm one of nine children and my mum always went to town when we were growing up, with a huge Christmas tree that touched the ceiling, a gigantic turkey, and loads of gifts piled up in the lounge, which meant Christmases have always been joyous occasions. This year there couldn't really be a starker contrast.

Melanie and Neil come for a visit the week before, and we're all very sad as the days count down to the festivities.

"Mum, we can't believe we won't be with you," Mel says, and Neil nods his head. They both look close to tears.

"Look, you'll have lovely Christmases, even though we won't all be together, you're with your family, so it'll be OK." I want desperately to reassure them.

"You're with good people who care for you," I add, trying not to cry.

Christmas is an important time of year for me. I'm dreading it without them.

"It won't be the same," Neil says.

"I know, love. I'm so sorry. It won't be the same for me neither, bein' stuck in 'ere. I wish I could be with ya." I can't even promise them when I'll be home for Christmas because I haven't heard anything about my appeal for a while. I know my solicitor Peter's working on it, and I expect I'll get some news any day, but no one's going to be running the courts at this time of year so I'm resigned to waiting. I feel like I'm always waiting.

I spend the next half an hour of my time with my kids trying to say the right things, to make them realise how much I'll miss them. We reminisce about Christmases we've shared, but I can't change the harsh truth of it. They'll be with other people, in other homes, without their mum by their side. Aside from the first Christmas I spent without Mickey after he was killed, this is the lowest I've ever felt at this time of year.

Christmas Day arrives at last. It's a relief to get this day over and done with. There have been a few more suicide attempts on the wing as women deal with the separation from their kids mostly. It's a horrible atmosphere. Everyone seems sad or angry. There isn't much Christmas spirit on the wing, and I'll be glad when it's over.

We're sent up a full English breakfast with half a grapefruit, which is a real rarity, so that's something. After that, we're locked in until the lunch trolley comes up. The kitchen girls have done a good job of preparing Christmas dinner, with turkey, roast potatoes and vegetables, but it's not like at home. We get Christmas pudding and a mince pie, but as soon as we've finished we're locked in again, with no telly, though we do now have a radio, which my family brought in for me. Apart from that, it's our own thoughts that occupy us, which isn't the best thing at such a poignant time of year. Bobble is her usual chipper self, but Bibble has become quite isolated in herself though we're sharing a cell. The other Linda just grunts and moans as normal, but no one is really up for any banter.

I spend my time thinking about what my family are doing, imagining my children opening the presents given to them on my behalf. Though I'm distraught, I don't lose sight of the fact that many of the girls have no one outside, and no contact with their children in care.

A few days after Christmas, Maria reappears. She looks in an awful state. A couple of her teeth have been knocked out and her skin is riddled with spots and scars. Her eyes look wild and her hair is thinning already. She used to be so beautiful. When I see her, I walk straight over and ask why she's back and what went wrong.

"It's the fuckin' drugs innit, can't get off them," she says, sadly. "Don't know if I'll ever get my kids back. Didn't see them at Christmas, so I went on a bender. Got really messed up. Don't even remember gettin' this," she says, pointing to her teeth.

"Oh, darlin', why can't you get help to come off them? It's the only way you'll 'ave a chance of gettin' your kids back."

I feel so sad for her. Her pimp keeps her hooked on drugs. Her mother's a junkie as well, and I have no idea if she's even still alive. Maria's clothes look tatty and dirty, and she looks like she's "clucking" (which I've learnt is prison slang for detoxing, as she can't get Class As right now because we're mostly locked in and she can't get out of her cell to score). She's all alone in the world and I find I can feel some gratitude for my situation.

Saying that, I must've looked pretty glum, because that night a screw looks through my hatch to ask if I'm OK.

"Yes, thank you," I say. She is not convinced.

"'Ere, pass me your flask," she says.

"I've already got hot water, I'm alright," I answer.

"No, Linda, pass it to me."

I hand it out, puzzled.

A second or two later, she gives it back.

"There's a drop of somethin' in there. You can at least 'ave a drink tonight." She winks and walks off.

I unscrew the lid and taste it. Vodka!

"Thank you," I call out. I don't ask how she manages to smuggle alcohol into a prison. Instead, I sip my drink and settle down, thinking: *One Christmas down, how many more to follow?*

* * *

A few weeks later one of the screws walks up to me while I'm scrubbing the floor.

"Linda, tell the others but you, Bobble, Bibble and Linda need to pack up, because you're all goin' up to B5 in the next few days."

"Oh, why's that?" I reply.

"It's just the way we do things. As girls leave, you move upwards. It's another workin' wing, and actually it's a bit nicer than 'ere."

I look around at the dark blue linoleum floor, the pale yellow walls with peeling paint, the dirt ingrained everywhere, and I feel that this move has to be an improvement.

I've been on D3 for a few months now. Most of the girls have calendars and they tick off each day as they go through their sentence. I refused one, saying my sentence is too long, and the sight of seven years' worth of days to go will only dispirit me. I get through each week by setting my sights on each visit. I focus on the next visit, on a Thursday, then the one after that on a Monday, and that is how I have stayed sane. If I tried to look beyond each visit, I know it would be too daunting. Most women are only doing a few months for soliciting or drugs, then they get released. Marking off the days is much simpler, and they can see the end in sight. The end of my sentence is still a long way off.

"Why's that then?" Bobble says to me when I share the news that evening.

"The screw said that some of the girls have gone home, so there's room up there. It's a bit nicer and it's a workin' wing, so it won't be much different."

There's a moment's silence while we all digest this latest news.

"There's not much we can do about it anyway," I add. It's true. We don't have any say over where we're put. We're quite lucky to be given a reason for the change; most staff don't bother and just bark orders.

The next day, having no bags to carry our small amounts of things, we pack our clothes and toiletries into our pillowcases and fold up the scratchy blankets and sheets. The tall, stern-faced screw called Sharon unlocks our cell door.

"Let's go," she says, and we all troop out in front of her.

Holloway is built like a hospital, not like a prison. Its corridors and walls are all painted blue or yellow, there are the bright strip lights and the same linoleum floor throughout. We stop at the first door leading out of our wing while Sharon unlocks it. We move through, smiling up at the ever-present security cameras, then stop and wait again as the screw locks it. We have only one screw with us because we're a trusted group. They know none of us is going to start a fight or try to attack the officer. We all toe the line and work, so the staff aren't worried about walking through with a group of us. We follow Sharon going up the concrete stairs to B5, which is four storeys up. The wing doors are unlocked, we wait again while they're locked, and eventually we're standing in an identical-looking wing office to the one in D3.

"Hand your cards in. That's it then. Good luck, girls," Sharon says as she walks back to our old wing.

Now, there are prison guards who are just doing their job, who care about the women inside and who do their best every day in difficult circumstances. There are also prison guards who are bullies, those who delight in seeing us suffer and play power games, knowing they'll always win.

As we stand there in our new wing, a screw walks out of a nearby office. She is wearing bright pink lipstick and has a huge mop of black hair. She looks like a Barbie doll, albeit with dark hair and a prison uniform. She is wearing navy-blue heeled shoes and her white shirt is starched to within an inch of its life. Her lipstick is smudged, and it's obvious she's drawn it outside of her lips to make them appear bigger. She walks up and stands directly in front of me. She looks me up and down, slowly. Instantly, I know she hates me on sight. Instantly, I know she's one of those who delights in tormenting those in her care.

It turns out, I'm right.

CHAPTER 11

LIPSTICK

"So, you're the celebrity? You're the armed robber?" she says. Her eyes narrow, her eyebrows arch, and inside, I'm thinking, *'Ere we go, I'm in for it...*

"Well, everyone's the same up here. Don't think you can try and take over anything."

"I'm no celebrity," I reply, staring straight back at her.

I look at her and think to myself: *You really think you're somethin' special.* I'm guessing she thinks the same about me.

"And why would I want to take anythin' over up 'ere?" I add. I don't flinch. I don't look away either. I'm now determined to show this screw I'm not intimidated by her.

The woman, the senior wing officer, who I later discover is nick-named "Lipstick" by the inmates, smiles, and it's one of those unpleasant smiles, more like a grimace. It's clear she doesn't like inmates talking back.

Oh shit, what 'ave I done? I think, wondering whether I should've rolled over when she decided to start putting me down.

"Ladies, one of the officers will show you your cell. You'll be staying with your normal jobs."

There are moments in life when I wish I'd kept my mouth shut. This is one of them.

"One of the girls on D3 told me I'd be cleanin' Mr Brown's office..." My voice trails off as Lipstick stares back at me.

"Who told you that then?" she says, unpleasantly.

"One of the girls who left this wing. She came to find me yesterday, and told me she'd recommended me to the wing governor Mr Brown to clean his office." I feel like I'm digging a hole that's getting deeper and deeper.

Lipstick's eyebrows practically vanish into her hairline.

"Oh, and is this inmate running the prison then?" she sneers.

"No," I say, "but she told me she'd spoken to Mr Brown."

"Do you think you're better than everyone else?" she says. Bobble glances at me. I know it's time to back down.

"No, of course not."

"You'll be a wing cleaner, if that's what I say you'll be."

"Fine," I say. "I'm not bothered."

Just then a man wearing a pale-pink bow tie opens a door, and pokes his head out.

"Where's my cleaner then? Which of you is Linda Calvey?"

Lipstick throws me the dirtiest look.

"Me," I say. "I'm Linda Calvey."

"I'll pick you a cleaner—" Lipstick starts to say, but Mr Brown interrupts her.

"No, thank you. I've chosen my cleaner. Linda, you start tomorrow."

With that, he shuts his door, leaving us all standing there. I give Lipstick my best "up yours" look, and we walk off to find our cell with another screw.

"Good luck." Lipstick's smile is even more unpleasant, and I'm now left wondering what on earth Mr Brown will be like to work for.

"She's got it in for ya," Bobble hisses as we follow the screw.

"I know," I say. "I couldn't help myself. Anyway, she hated the sight of me. Some women just do."

I know it sounds arrogant, and I don't mean it to, but it's true. Some women take one look at me and they just hate my guts. Perhaps it's the same impulse that means men take care of me. I'm not sure why it is exactly, but that's how my life has been. I could see the minute Lipstick set eyes on me that I was in trouble.

"That wasn't the wisest thing to do. She's goin' to make your life difficult..." Bobble says as the door to our cell is shut behind us.

I shrug.

"What's done is done. She was always goin' to hate me. Come on, let's unpack. I'm starving' and lunch'll be soon."

As I make my scratchy bed on yet another thin, stained mattress, I know I've made an enemy.

* * *

The next morning, the routine is the same. I'm woken a bit earlier than the rest, and I go to the canteen room to help with breakfast. The food is brought up on a trolley from the kitchens and there's enough left over to have an extra egg and slice of bacon. Again, it's the small things that get you through.

I know I'm lucky to be given this job, and I'm sure it's because I never argue with the screws, or at least I haven't until I met Lipstick. There are women who take their frustrations and anger at being locked up out on the officers, but the way I see it is it's not their fault we're incarcerated. They're just doing a job, and so we should treat them like the human beings they are, as much as we want them to treat us the same. I don't see the sense in upsetting those in charge – until now, perhaps.

After breakfast I go to Mr Brown's office. I've been warned that he suffers from OCD, obsessive compulsive disorder, or so one of the women on the last wing said. Whether this is true or not, I don't know, but I feel nervous.

"Good morning, Linda, come in," he says. He seems friendly enough.

"Good morning, Mr Brown," I say. "What would you like me to do first?"

I'm surprised at his answer.

"Go and put the percolator on and we'll have a coffee, then you can start with my desk," he replies.

This is luxury.

It's the first time I've been offered a coffee by a member of staff since my trial, and the prospect of drinking a real coffee made from beans rather than having an instant is quite thrilling.

When we've drunk our coffee and my head is buzzing a bit from the caffeine hit, I begin work. I know this is no ordinary cleaning job. It is the wing governor, a man who could make my life as difficult or as easy as he wants. It's essential he likes me. I've been warned that he is very particular about where he places the objects on his desk, and how I must remember where they all sit when I put them back after dusting. He sits watching me as I work. I pick up a paperweight, inside which is a tiny Tower Bridge and plenty of fake snow. I wipe it with my duster. He's still watching me. Then I place it down on his desk, fervently hoping I've put it in the right place. He holds my gaze as he stretches out an arm and nudges it back into the exact position. He does this with every one of the items on his desk. Each pen, each blotter, each coaster is moved slightly, back into the correct place. It's like a strange dance between us. I dust. He watches. I place it back. He moves it. Then, on to the next. By the time I reach his little clock, I've completely forgotten which side of the desk it sat upon before I cleaned it. I stand there, Mr Brown watching me as I dither. Eventually, I put it down on the right side.

Mr Brown shakes his head.

"You messed up, didn't you?" he says.

I nod.

"Yes, sorry, Mr Brown," I say, trying not to laugh at the absurdity of it all.

"Next time, memorise it," he says, not unkindly.

"Yes, I will, Mr Brown," I say, meekly, wondering where on earth I've ended up this time.

"You're a breath of fresh air, Linda. Come back and do the same tomorrow," Mr Brown says later on, when I've finished cleaning his office.

"Thank you, I will, and thank you for givin' me this job. I want you to know I really appreciate it," I reply. Goodness knows why he thinks that, but it has to be a good thing.

Later, when I tell the others how my first day with him went, and how I thanked him to the high heavens for the job, they all say: "Linda, you're such a creep!"

To which, my only reply is: "I know, but I think he likes me!"

•   •   •

Over the following weeks and months on B5, Mr Brown becomes something like a friend, albeit a peculiar one. He often says to me that he's in the wrong job because he hates women and he hates prisons, which makes me giggle. He says it in all seriousness, and I can see he means it.

I realise with a jolt of shock that I've been inside for almost a year now. My birthday comes and goes, as do the seasons, which we are largely unaware of as we're inside for most of the time. I asked everyone not to make a fuss, though my family all visited as usual, and the screws even let me have a slice of the birthday cake at the time.

Life carries on, but this is a place where violence and trauma seem endless. Back in the dorm, the other Linda, the one Bobble calls "Soapy" because she doesn't wash much, is in a state of shock. She's a cleaner on C1 and has come back with some horrific stories in the past, girls cutting off their nipples or even a woman who had broken a china sink in the toilets and tried to saw off her leg. If anything, Linda looks more shocked than she had on those occasions.

"You alright?' I say as I come in. I'm about to get changed out of my white coat as we've finished work for the day.

"Oh my God, Linda, it was worse today. It was awful. I don't want to go back on there!" She is wailing. I've never seen her so distressed.

"What's wrong?" I say. "What happened?"

My heart sinks. This must be bad, even for C1. Lots of the girls are medicated down there, and in very fragile psychological states. They tend to copy each other, so if one throws her food out, the others follow.

"One of the girls on C1 shouted she was goin' to rip her eye out. Then, the rest of them shouted they'd do it, too. The nurse down there said they wouldn't, but the girl started screamin'. I ran to her cell and there was a bloody eyeball lyin' on the floor. She'd torn it out and thrown it through the hatch. I looked through and she'd fainted."

"Oh my God, Linda, that's awful," I say.

"The nurse ran over and picked up the eyeball with a dirty tissue. When I tried to stop her, sayin' not to use it 'cos the eye'd go bad in her head if it was dirty, she looked at me really sadly and said she won't need it any more. Then, I had to run up and down the wing to try and stop the other girls doin' it. They were shoutin' out and everyone was yellin'. It was awful..."

Well, I don't know what to say. Those women on C1 are disturbed and this whole bloody prison should be shut down. Before I can answer, a screw pokes her head through our hatch.

"Calvey?"

"Yes," I say, distractedly.

"Your appeal date's through."

CHAPTER 12

LEAVING HOLLOWAY

I step into the office.

Lipstick is sitting typing something on her massive computer screen. These are the days of huge computers, and lots of complicated wiring. She knows I'm standing there, in front of her desk, but she carries on, seemingly oblivious to my presence.

I wait while she taps on her keyboard. I wait some more. She knows I'm here because I'm standing right in front of her, but she's refusing to acknowledge me. Irritation grows inside me but I know I can't say anything. This really makes me angry. Screws using their power to put us down, to make us feel less than human.

"Ahem," I cough, eventually.

"Oh Calvey, I didn't see you there." She smiles. There's a smudge of pink lipstick on her teeth.

I smile and hope it's as unpleasant as hers.

"I've come to ask about my appeal," I say. "'Ave you heard anythin' yet?"

It's been almost three months since I got the date, and I've waited and waited, hoping for a miracle, just like all the others, though I know I shouldn't expect too much. The appeal against the length of my sentence is held without me having to go to court, so I'm stuck in Holloway while my barristers are arguing my case in front of a new judge today. My solicitor Peter was expecting Brian to get time off, and then it would follow that we would all get time off. We're appealing the length of my sentence, saying the original judge had given excessive prison terms. Peter had said he'd call the wing office as soon as it's over. It's already lunchtime, and I'm sure he told me my case was being heard this morning.

"When I know the result I'll tell you." Lipstick grins, looking back at her screen.

"OK, thank you," I say, and walk out.

"Bloody bitch," I say under my breath.

The day drags on. A couple of times I walk over to Lipstick's office but can't bring myself to walk in. Just before the end of working hours, I go back.

"Any news?' I say. Lipstick ignores me.

When she eventually looks up, she shakes her head.

"No, Calvey. Nothing yet."

When five o'clock comes, I head back to my cell feeling anxious. There's been no word, which is strange. Perhaps my case got postponed? Perhaps they dropped it from the list today? I'm completely in the dark until Lipstick decides to tell me what she knows, assuming she knows anything. The card on our door still says the same: *N56981, Calvey. Seven years for armed robbery.*

Mr Brown is on holiday today otherwise I'd go and ask him. One of the women in a nearby cell calls over to me from her window. I can see her hand holding the cigarette she's smoking out of the window, but not her face as the windows are too thin to poke our heads through.

"Oi Linda! One of the screws was at court today. You must be 'appy with your result?"

"What d'you mean? I haven't heard anythin'," I shout back.

"What? That's odd 'cos the screw said yours was one of the first up this mornin'. Yeah, you got two years taken off!"

"I got what?" I say, not quite able to believe what I'm hearing. "D'you mean I've been waitin' all day and heard nothin', yet mine was done this mornin'?"

"Yeah, so I hear. Congrats anyway..." The inmate withdraws her hand, and disappears inside. I'm left fuming, literally fuming, at the thought that Lipstick has kept me in the dark. I knew Peter would've kept his promise and rung as soon as he knew, so why hadn't Lipstick told me?

When she comes around to lock us all in at 8 p.m., I ask again.

"It's strange there's been no news. My case was definitely heard today and the appeal court will be closed now," I say.

She doesn't blink.

"You'll know when we know."

With that, she walks off, keys jangling in her hands.

"Bloody, bloody bitch."

. . .

The next day, I have a visit booked with my mum, and sisters Maxine and Shelley.

"Thank God, you got two years off, Love," my mum says and bursts into tears.

"Did I?" I say, wishing I could lean over and give her a cuddle to comfort her.

"One of the girls told me I had but nobody official let me know, though I kept askin'..."

This really upsets me. I spend the rest of our visit feeling unsettled and cross. It's a simple thing to let someone know. It shows that if an officer doesn't like an inmate, they have the power to make their life miserable, or even more miserable than it is already given we are all banged up, counting the days until we can go home. The system seems built on personalities and not on processes. This can't be right, but what can I do to challenge it?

"How d'you know?" I say, knowing they wouldn't have been at the court that day as it was just my barristers in attendance.

"We phoned Peter Hughman and he told us," says Shelley.

"D'you mean no one told you? That's terrible," Maxine says.

"No, I wasn't told, and I bet Lipstick knew all along," I say and I can't keep the bitterness out of my voice.

"Peter said he was phonin' the prison, so someone must've known..." Shelley adds. "Try not to get upset. Concentrate on the fact that you'll be home with your family sooner than expected. That's a good thing, Linda."

"I know. Of course it is. We'll celebrate when I get out. I just wish they didn't choose to make life more difficult than it needs to be," I say.

When Mum and my sisters leave, I head straight for the office, Shelley's warnings not to go mad at them ringing in my ears. It's advice I dearly want to ignore.

"I've had a visit, and I'm told I got two years off yesterday, and my solicitor phoned you to inform you."

Lipstick looks up this time, because I don't wait for her permission to speak.

"Oh well then, there you go," is all she says.

I leave before I say something I'll regret, but as I go, she calls out: "And while Mr Brown's away, you'll be scrubbing floors, Calvey."

.   .   .

A few days later I'm on my hands and knees, cleaning the floor with the same scrubbing brush and carbolic.

"Who told you to do that, Linda?" comes Mr Brown's voice. I look up.

"The senior wing officer told me to do the floors," I say, meaning Lipstick, of course.

"Oh no, come with me. We'll see about that."

I follow Mr Brown to Lipstick's office.

Oh Christ, what 'ave I done, tellin' him... I think. *She's goin' to kill me...*

"Linda doesn't clean floors. Linda is my cleaner. I don't mind her doing other light duties, but not the floors. Do you understand?" He is shouting at Lipstick and I'm trying to look anywhere but at her.

Lipstick is livid. Her face blushes scarlet and she throws me yet another filthy look.

At least that put her in her place, I think, knowing she'll hate me even more now.

We head back to my cell, which is where the wing governor sees my card, which still reads seven years.

"Linda, I'm so sorry!"

"What for?" I say.

"Well, you obviously never got your appeal."

"Yes I did. I got two years off," I reply.

"Who told you?"

I can see where this is going.

"My mum on a visit the next day..." I'm cringing, knowing he'll probably get cross at Lipstick again.

Mr Brown frowns.

"Weren't you informed by the prison?"

"No," I say.

Mr Brown, who was locking me in, opens the door again.

"Come with me."

We walk back to Lipstick's office, where Mr Brown, as predicted, begins to berate her.

"Linda Calvey informs me her mother told her she's got two years off, taking her sentence to five years. Is that true?"

"Yes, that's correct," Lipstick says, smiling ingratiatingly.

"Why didn't you tell her?"

She stops smiling.

"I-I thought she'd been informed," she stammers.

"But I asked you at the end of the day, and you said there was no news," I add. In for a penny, in for a pound.

"Right, I want that card taken off her door and I want new sentence dates on it. This affects Linda's dates greatly. I want a fresh date put up on the door and board. I find this very unprofessional."

'Ere we go, I think. *That's goin' to upset her even more now.*

As we walk back, the governor turns to me.

"Right Linda, things have changed dramatically for you now. I'll be referring you to Cookham Wood for the next stage of your sentence."

I'm stunned. I can't believe I'm about to say what I do next.

"But, I'm happy to stay in Holloway, I'm used to it here."

"That may well be, but your sentence is now lower, and so you shouldn't still be in Holloway. This is a big step forward to getting ready to go home."

I digest this for a moment. It's early October 1987, and I've served roughly 15 months inside here. With remission off, I realise I'm now a lot closer to release.

"You'll be going as soon as there's a vacancy."

When I tell my cell mates, Bobble and Bibble are devastated, as am I.

"But I don't want ya to go. It's my birthday next week, I won't let them take ya before then!" Bobble says.

"I know. I asked if I could stay 'ere but Mr Brown says I 'ave to go. I won't be goin' for a few days as they 'ave to wait for a vacancy." I sigh. Whoever would have thought that I'd want to stay in Holloway Prison?

Bobble's birthday arrives. I've gone all out and planned a party for her, and the whole wing, including the screws, are invited. We take over the canteen, and the girls from the kitchens send up a Sara Lee chocolate gateau we all chipped in to buy for Bobble, plus sandwiches, as well as a few bottles of fizzy pop. The screws even hold all her birthday cards back so she gets them on the day, though she'd got upset the night before, having received none.

"Lin," she'd said. "Ain't no one sent me a card and I'm goin' to be 21!"

"Oh dear," I replied, not wanting to ruin the surprise of the party we'd planned for her. "I've got some news though..."

"What's that then?" Bobble asked.

"I was called into the office today. Lipstick told me I'm leavin' the day after your birthday ..."

"The day after my birthday?" Bobble looked like she'd burst into tears.

"Yes, darlin'. I'm so sorry. If I could 'ave it another way, but you know Lipstick. No point arguin' with her as she won't try and change it."

"She's a fuckin' bitch, that woman," Bobble muttered darkly.

"She is, but we won't let her spoil tomorra. Don't worry, you're goin' to 'ave a lovely day," I said, giving Bobble a wink. I didn't want her going to sleep that night thinking no one cared.

*   *   *

Bobble's party is more like a child's birthday party, but my friend is ecstatic. I'm guessing there are women here who've never had a party thrown in their honour, as they all appear really excited, which makes me feel quite sad.

We play some music and have a dance. Everyone has contributed what they can afford to buy Bobble some bits; chocolate and nice shampoo, among the things we are able to get. My friend is emotional, as we all are; this isn't just a birthday do, it's also my last night with the girls before I have to pack up and leave for Cookham Wood Prison. The party is a great success. It's my way of saying goodbye, as well as letting my friend know she's worth it all. I watch Bobble, and even Bibble, as they joke and laugh, and know I'll miss them sorely, even though this is my first step towards my freedom.

CHAPTER 13

MYRA

"Calvey, pack your stuff up, you're goin' down to reception. You're goin' to Cookham today," Lipstick says.

"Yes, I know that, I've already packed my things and I'm ready to go," I reply, staring back at this woman who has made life pretty difficult on B5. We hold our gaze for a few seconds, and I'm delighted when Lipstick looks away first. At least that's one good thing about leaving, saying goodbye to that sour-faced bitch.

I don't want to leave Holloway. I've got friends and I know the routine. I know the prison's ways: how the water's only ever a trickle in the showers, which are basic to say the least, where the fights happen and places to avoid (the yard and the long corridor on the ground floor where girls from every wing walk in lines to education or C1); which cell the druggies score in and when to avoid them too; which tables I sit at, which chair in the association room is always kept empty for me; which inmates are the bullies and which staff are the nicer ones. I'm used to it. Some might say I'm a little institutionalised, and they're probably right. I've had to shut parts of myself down to survive. I've had to toe the line (mostly) and accept behaviour I would never accept outside (like the bullies and some of the staff). I've had to shut my feelings down too and just get my head down and serve my time. What's the point moping about? That won't bring me my kids or my freedom, so I've adapted –

but now it all changes and I have no control over it at all. I feel like I'll be beginning again from scratch, as if I'll be starting my sentence again, just this time in a different place.

Most of what I'm feeling is fear of the unknown, and that continual sense of being powerless, at having no say at all over where I'm put. Of course, I have no choice but to begin my goodbyes. The people going to court get taken down first, while people like me, who are being transferred, are taken down afterwards so I get to hug Bobble and a couple of the others, including Diane, who's also due to leave soon.

"Come and see me when you get out," I say to Bobble, who's only going to be in prison for another few weeks.

"'Course I will, Linda. It's the first thing I'll do when I'm free."

Clutching my small plastic bag of belongings, given to me by a member of staff, I wave to the girls as I go. Both Bobble and I are in tears, while Linda gives me a handshake with a hand I'd seen her wiping her nose with only seconds earlier. Bibble is also due to leave imminently as her sentence has come to an end, though, sadly, I'm sure she'll be back, especially if she insists on robbing that same Sainsbury's again!

Down in reception, I undergo a strip search again; same cubicle, same process, top half first, then bottom half. Once that's done and I'm dressed, my things are rifled through.

"What are ya lookin' for? I haven't got much!" I say with a laugh to the same plain-faced officer who was there when I first stepped out of the sweat box and into Holloway. Her name is Sue and she's a lot friendlier than when I first arrived.

"You know the score, Linda. We 'ave to check everyone in case they're smugglin' weapons or contraband out, though we know you wouldn't do that."

"Course I wouldn't! Anyway, I haven't seen any weapons, only what the girls 'ave told me about. Never needed to carry one," I say, smiling, knowing that my reputation as a gangster goes before me.

It's true. I haven't ever needed to protect myself against the inmates, because lots of the girls have been in awe of me. I'm not saying that's a good thing because it got me into trouble with Lipstick, but after seeing the extent of the bullying between inmates, I know my reputation has saved me from much worse. I became a bit like a mother figure to some of the girls by the end. They used to come to me with their worries, or talk about their children, or their lives on the game outside of the prison, as they'd never before had anyone to actually listen. I know I'm no Mother Teresa, but I cared for some of these girls.

One girl, Gemma, came to me a couple of weeks before Bobble's birthday to say that Maria, the young girl fighting for her kids to be given back to her, had overdosed and died.

"They found her body at King's Cross Station..." Gemma sniffed, tears pouring down her face.

"Oh my God, I'm so sorry to 'ear that!" I said, shocked to my core. I guessed Maria wouldn't get clean. She seemed to be deep into drugs, but I've always thought there's room for hope, even for those as damaged by a shit life as Maria. I felt real sorrow for her – and most especially for her kids. It sounds hard, but every week it seemed we'd hear tell of another young woman who'd died of drug abuse. It was quite common, and you sort of get used to the stories and the hard lives.

"They found her in a toilet cubicle, a needle in her arm. Her pimp had fucked off and left her. She was all alone." Gemma wept and I tried to comfort her but what could I say? How many other girls like Maria were destined to die young, unprotected and alone in this world? How many more kids would be without a mother? I imagined that people outside would see it as society having one fewer working girl and junkie to deal with. Somehow, Maria's humanity – and the horror of her upbringing – was lost in that story of her life.

It upset me that no one would ever really hear the other side of things; her remorse and her regrets too. No one would ever realise the struggles she'd gone through as a child, the lack of anyone to care for her properly. And worse, there are so many like her who are put behind bars each day, part of an uncaring system, a hostile prison environment and a life where having access to your children is a luxury. So sad, and so inevitable.

. . .

As I'm the only one going to Cookham Wood in Rochester, I'm handcuffed to the single guard who'll sit with me in the prison van. It's like a transit van. It's got blackened out windows so I can see out but people can't see in. It's the same fag butts and stench of stale tobacco and sweat in here. The same scruffy seats and dirt. I'm feeling apprehensive. I'd got used to Holloway with all its trials and tribulations, its fights, its cockroaches and hullabaloo. I'm nervous at going to another prison even though the staff assure me it's a forward step. My eyes are glued to the window looking out because I'd been inside all that time. It's refreshing and heartening to see normal life still carrying on. I see the last of the autumn leaves on the trees as we head away from the grime of North London and down into Kent. The prison officer tries to talk to me.

"I'm sorry, I'm not bein' rude. I just want to look outside as I haven't seen life for so long."

"That's OK, Linda, I understand," the screw says, and so I watch, fascinated, as the landscape changes to country lanes and big, grey cloudy skies. This is the next step. Hopefully, it'll be OK.

The first thing that strikes me upon arriving is how different it is to Holloway. Gone are the high walls, replaced by a high metal fence with razor wire on top, which is quite foreboding but not as much as where I've come from.

As we pull in through the gate, I can see a small building, which is only a couple of floors high. It looks more like a bland, 1970s-built red-brick school than a prison, but the sign says *HMP Cookham Wood* so I'm left in no doubt where I've arrived. There are a couple of women attending a pretty little garden, but the overall effect is pretty gloomy.

I'm left in reception, in a small room with a bench, and a window with bars over it. In contrast to Holloway's reception area, it's very clean. There are no cigarette butts, no discarded bits of food littering the floor.

"Hello Linda, you're too late for lunch, would ya like a sandwich?" I assume this woman is an inmate as she's wearing a white coat like the ones we wore in Holloway and a pair of jeans underneath. She must work in the kitchens. It seems strange seeing a prisoner down here, and this is another indication we're in a more relaxed prison. She seems friendly enough.

I say, "Yes, please," and ten minutes later she reappears with a cheese sandwich and an apple.

"You'll be alright 'ere," she says, smiling.

"Thank you. What's it like?" I ask.

She laughs. "It's a lot easier than Holloway!"

"Oh so you've come from there, too?" I ask.

"Most of the girls 'ere 'ave. It's alright, I promise." She winks as she leaves and I feel myself exhale.

A few moments later a screw calls me out to be processed, which means being strip-searched and registered with them. It's the same routine, but I don't think I'll ever get used to the humiliation.

"OK, Linda, let's go to your wing. It's a lot calmer 'ere than Holloway." The screw nods at me to follow her once I'm dressed.

"Everyone's at work now, so it's very quiet. I'll take you up to the north wing, to the office, and from there they'll allocate your cell. There's only two wings 'ere: north and south, so it's much smaller than you're used to. Keep your nose clean and it'll go well for ya."

"Right," I say. "I'll remember that."

I follow the screw. We stop and start as we reach locked doors, and walk down a long corridor, which is very bright and has big barred windows. The exercise yard is visible, and as we walk past there is what looks like a couple of men chatting. They both stop and one of them wolf-whistles as I walk by them.

"Oh, are they workmen?" I say, wondering what the hell men are doing in a women's prison.

"That's not a man, that's a woman!" the screw says.

"Blimey," I say, thinking I should probably shut my mouth next time.

I'm taken to my new cell after a short tour of the wing, showing me where the showers and dining room are. It's not a huge improvement on my cell in Holloway. The walls are painted the same magnolia as Holloway and there's pale-coloured lino on the floor, but apart from that it's the same size, with a single bed, a thin mattress and a Formica desk with a chair. There are still no curtains, which is disappointing, and the only thing that's different is the general cleanliness. Looking around, I can't see the same dirt that seemed to be ingrained everywhere in Holloway. The cell is actually quite bright, and is spotlessly clean. I cast a quick look at the window and under the bed, but I can't see a single cockroach, so things are looking up.

I unpack, knowing I'll be called into the wing office at some point. I feel strangely nervous, though everyone's been kind so far. Holloway is intimidating from the get-go. The reception area is vast and dirty, and generally chaotic with inmates coming in and out, and lots of noise and bustle. The prison itself is endlessly noisy, with arguments, screaming, sirens wailing and people shouting. It seems very quiet here in contrast. As I wait, I try and reassure myself it'll all be fine, but I'm unsettled at the thought of making new acquaintances and dealing with staff I don't know. It feels daunting, and already I'm missing my friends and the routine at the London prison, which is bizarre. I never thought in a million years I'd rather be there than here.

Later, I head down to the dining area for my first meal. There's a long food counter on the ground-floor landing, with tables and chairs to the side. It's a bit livelier and there are a couple of girls having an argument, which is broken up by another screw. People generally don't take as much notice of me, though I see a few nudge each other and look over. I'm used to the stares now, and I guess the girls have had word that I'd be coming here. I take a plate and I'm given sausages with some lumpy-looking mash and a few boiled carrots.

"Thank you," I say, as if it's fine dining not cheap prison food, and I head to the only free table. No one joins me but I'm content to eat my dinner and head back to await my appointment. Yet again, there's little to distract me. There's no telly but I do have my radio, and so I spend the evening listening to that, the old feelings of loneliness hovering close by.

* * *

The next morning, after a very quiet night, my door is unlocked and I'm called to the office.

"Calvey, you've come with a glowing report," the senior officer says. She is a far cry from Lipstick, with short bobbed brown hair and a face devoid of make-up.

Mr Brown must've done my report, not Lipstick, I think with relief. I can imagine what my old SO would've put on that paper.

"Because your report's so good, I'm going to give you the librarian job. It's a nice job and you'll enjoy it more than being a cleaner."

"Oh, but I don't read books," I reply. "Can't you give it to one of the girls who'd be better suited? I don't mind bein' a cleaner."

The librarian role is the plum job in a prison, because it is the easiest and nicest work. Days are spent categorising books, ordering requests from outside libraries, and chatting to people who come in and out. You can usually take a couple of coffee breaks, read the papers and sit at a desk, which is quite a rarity.

"No, Linda, we want you to have the job. Now, bring your washing as the library is near the laundry and you can get yours in before the lunchtime rush."

The screw takes me to the library to show me around. We pass a hairdresser's, the factory, the gym and laundry before we reach the library, where I'm shown the ropes. Briefly, she shows me what to do, but it's all very straightforward. I put books back on shelves, order the ones requested by inmates, and put those aside that will be returned to the library outside that supplies our books. I'm told I have to keep the place clean, and I can bring a flask of coffee with me. I'm thinking this is a nice little number, when the screw reappears after my coffee break.

"While it's quiet, why don't you take your clothes to be washed now? That way, you'll beat the rush from the factory," the officer says before leaving me to get on with stacking some books on new shelving.

That is when I meet her.

I walk into the laundry. There's a line of black and yellow tape across the floor, with a sign saying *Do Not Cross the Line*. Someone is singing inside. It's a happy tune, as if the person is content with their life.

I look over and I see a woman with dark red hair, so unlike the brassy blonde in her police mugshot. I see her thin, high cheekbones and sallow skin.

She's unmistakable.

Myra Hindley looks back at me, suddenly startled. She stops singing.

I keep looking, unable to believe my eyes, but it's definitely her. I'd recognise her anywhere.

Suddenly, the world stops. The air stills. I feel a rush of pure anger unlike anything I've ever felt before.

I don't know what comes over me. Before I know what I'm doing, I march across that line, my washing forgotten.

"You fuckin' bitch! How can you sing when you've murdered innocent children?" Before I can stop myself, my arm propels forward and

I slap her face. The sound seems to echo through the laundry. Myra freezes, her song dying on her lips, and puts her hand to her cheek where the florid red marks of my fingers now appear.

I've hit Myra Hindley square in the face as she works in the laundry room, alone. For a moment, neither of us speaks. My heart is pounding in my chest.

"You'll go back to Holloway for that!" she says. Her voice is low and still has a northern burr, though she's been inside for years.

Her eyes bore into me. Her stare is unnerving and very intense. She looks harsh, like she'd be a low-class madam in another life. I see immediately there's nothing soft about Myra.

"Holloway holds no fear for me!" I retort. I return her stare. It's Myra who looks away first.

Oh my God. What 'ave I done? I repeat over and over again as I storm back into the library. Thankfully, there's no one else about. *That'll be me on report for this. Even though I said I didn't care about being sent back, I don't want to be forced there. If I 'ave to go back to Holloway, they'll add time to my sentence...* Even as I think this, I know I'd slap her again, given half a chance.

I spend the rest of the day waiting for a screw to appear and take me up to the prison governor. Five o'clock comes and still I haven't heard anything, so I go back to my cell. I wash and head to the landing where food is served. Still nothing. I look around but Myra is nowhere in sight. *She must be on south wing,* I think. *Does that mean it'll take longer for them to get to me to punish me?*

That night, I lie in my cell, the image of Myra's shocked face refusing to disappear from my mind. How could I have done that? Even as I recall my hand marks on her face, I feel another surge of anger towards her, and I know why. In the hierarchy of crimes, a child nonce, or murderer, is the very bottom. They are the scum of the earth, which may sound strange, as none of us are angels in here, but that's the pecking order. Robbers, especially big-time gangsters and dealers, sit at the top of the tree, just like in men's prison. Then in between are the girls in for assault, the shoplifters, fraudsters, prostitutes and skag-heads. Beneath them are the nonces. That's the rule. That's how it is, and I don't suppose it'll ever change. Murderers, on the other hand, assuming it's gangland murder, sit somewhere at the top, but inmates are wary of them, and tend to avoid them.

Despite this, there's no defence for what I've done. I assaulted another prisoner. The prison system doesn't care who that is or what they've done. If she reports me, I'm in big trouble.

The next morning, I wake up expecting to see a folded slip of paper pushed under my door and someone banging to tell me I'm locked in until I see the governor. This is how you know you're on report. The paper will contain the charges you're facing. I look down and see there's no piece of paper on my floor. I feel a cautious sense of relief, which is only magnified when I'm working alone in the library later in the day.

The same screw pops her head round the door.

"Just lettin' you know, Myra has her coffee break in 'ere in the mornings and afternoons. Have you got a problem with that?"

I look back at her and shake my head.

"No, if this is where she has it, that's where she has it. It's nothin' to do with me," I reply. It is then I realise Myra can't have said anything about what I did, which strikes me as odd.

At half past ten Myra comes in carrying a cup of coffee. She sits at one of the little tables, unfolds her newspaper, the *Daily Telegraph*, and reads it. She looks across at me. I look at her. Neither of us speaks.

After a couple of days of this same routine, she says: "OK?"

"Yeah, OK," I say, as if all this is perfectly normal.

Again, we say little else. After a week of her coming in to have her coffee break, she becomes a little more chatty. Don't get me wrong, I hate having to breathe the same air as her, but I know I'll be in the shit if I do anything out of line again. I won't initiate any chat though, that would stick in my throat.

"How is it in Holloway? Still a shithole?" Myra says as she browses through some new books that have just come in. I look up and realise she's looking at the psychology section and I shudder.

"Holloway is Holloway," I reply, glancing back down, not wanting to have this conversation with Britain's most notorious child killer.

"What wing were you on?" she asks, seeming not to notice my reluctance to speak with her. I tell her and we say a few more things about the crap food and the constant fights, and I soon realise she has nothing to talk about because she's been inside so long. Later, I ask a screw why Myra is kept inside a relatively relaxed prison.

"Shouldn't she be at Durham in a maximum-security jail?" I say.

The blonde-haired screw, who I have only just met for the first time, replies: "You'd think so, but actually she's safer here. At Cookham, everyone wants to go home. They can see the end in sight, so they won't rock the boat and have more time added to their sentences. When she was in Holloway, Myra had her nose broken by an inmate, so she was moved here.

"People ignore her here. She's as safe as she's going to be."

. . .

Knowing Myra becomes one of the strangest experiences of my life.

She comes in every day, wanting to borrow books. One day she crosses a line but I feel powerless to stop her because of who she is. Myra could make life very difficult for me, and she's got something on me now. One word to the governor and I'd be on report for hitting her, and I'd have time on my sentence. I won't risk that, so I feel like I should do what she asks.

"I've got the name of somebody who don't come in here. Would you order a book in her name for me?"

I look at Myra, knowing this isn't allowed.

"What's the name of the book?" I say, curious to know why she's taking this risk.

"*The Devil and All His Works*," she replies, sending a shiver down my back.

"Alright," I say, believing it will never be approved by the library outside that supplies our books. Myra usually orders romance books such as Mills & Boon titles, which I find really bizarre, but I put this strange request through for her.

A week later the book appears. Myra is delighted when she picks it up. I have a quick look at the cover and see it's all about the fight between good and evil. Myra is creepy. Everything about her reeks of something evil.

CHAPTER 14

COOKHAM

In some ways, Cookham is harder than Holloway.

The boredom is something I hadn't predicted. Of course, the long nights spent in my single cell in Holloway were horrible for their own reasons. They gave me a lot of time to think about my crimes and the regret and remorse I feel towards my children and the victims of those raids. When I was moved to a dorm, things got easier, and I had people to talk to. This place is actually quite dull, even with Myra Hindley washing the sheets. At Holloway there was always a drama or something happening, whereas here it all seems very quiet. People come here when they're getting ready to leave, so they toe the line. There are rarely fights or sirens blasting.

Then, one night, about two months later, it all changes.

Ruby is one of those girls who bounces in and out of prison, or so some of the girls tell me. She bears the hallmarks of a life spent on the game and on drugs. She came in a couple of weeks ago with bruises on her face and the usual grey skin and wild eyes. It seemed she'd settled, as once she'd done her cluck, or detoxed, she was alright. She started work as a cleaner and I didn't really see much of her. She's probably in her late twenties but she has a husband, though I'm not sure if she has kids. I don't like to ask. If someone wants to tell me that's fine, but I don't pry into other people's business.

"'Ave ya seen Ruby today?" one of the girls, a chubby lady called Kirsty, says as I arrive back at the cells after a day in the library.

"No I ain't," I say. "Why, is anythin' wrong?"

"I don't know," Kirsty says. "She didn't look right at lunch. I think she's usin' again 'cos her husband dumped her."

"Oh my God," I say. "I'm sorry to 'ear that."

Kirsty shrugs. She's about the same age as Ruby, but she's blonde whereas Ruby has red hair. She's in for soliciting and shoplifting, and I've seen the two girls hanging around together. Kirsty is higher up in the pecking order than many of the heisters because she only ever shoplifted from Harrods. It's funny how prison works. If she'd been a woman nicking tins from a corner shop to feed her kids, then she'd be one of the lowest, but because she's nicking designer clothes and underwear, she's got a higher status, which is why she talks to me. Anyway, it's nice that Ruby has a friend who's looking out for her.

"Thanks Linda, when she's back from work tell her to come and find me."

As it turns out, I don't see Ruby that evening as I'm busy writing letters to my kids. Mel is now 18, while Neil is 14 years old. It's December 1987 and Christmas is approaching again, my second behind bars, so I'm also writing to family to organise presents for them both.

I settle down for sleep and don't think any more of what Kirsty has said. Hours later, at some point before dawn, a bell begins to ring. Then comes Kirsty's voice. She's screaming something, so I jump out of bed and run to my door to try and hear what she's saying.

"Press yer buzzers! EVERYONE PRESS THEIR BUZZERS!" Kirsty is yelling, and I realise she's asking us all to ring for help. I do the same and press my buzzer, as do all the other girls. Soon it sounds like every alarm on the wing is wailing.

"CALM DOWN! WHAT'S HAPPENIN'?" A member of the night staff shouts seconds later. I can hear footsteps running onto the floor, so there must be more than one screw.

"QUICK! ASSISTANCE! IT'S RUBY! Get into Ruby's cell! She's makin' funny chokin' noises! I think she's tryin' to kill herself!"

Oh my God, Ruby, I think. *Why would you do that to yourself?*

Kirsty has stopped yelling and I can hear the muffled voices of the officers, so they must be inside Ruby's cell.

"Get a fuckin' ambulance!" is the next thing I hear, and then a set of footsteps racing off to get help.

I imagine every inmate has her ear pressed to her door, trying to follow along, willing Ruby to have survived, though I've heard people say terrible things to self-harmers before. In Holloway I heard a young girl called a fuckin' mong because she'd tried to slit her wrists while *EastEnders* was on and everyone got sent back to their cells and missed the episode! Prison is brutal, and often there's little sympathy for those who try to kill themselves as many inmates see it as attention-seeking rather than a genuine act of distress. Depending on a girl's status or popularity, I've heard inmates tell them to fuck off, don't cry 'ere or offer a hug. It all depends whether someone is liked and how far up – or down – the pecking order they are.

The next morning, the wing is abuzz with gossip. Kirsty comes over to me as I eat my toast and sip the Nescafé I've been able to buy.

"Is she alright?" I say.

"I dunno yet," Kirsty replies. "I heard her makin' funny noises and she'd been really depressed for a few days, so I just knew she was tryin' to end it. I was right. She tried to hang herself, but I think they got to her in time 'cos I could 'ear her chokin' as they took her out to the hospital."

"Poor soul," I say. "Life's so hard for some of the girls, and prison just makes it worse."

. . .

One good thing about Cookham is that the visits are more relaxed. The screws let us hug our family and children, and those with very young kids are allowed to have them sitting on their laps. In terms of morale, this physical contact can't be underestimated. When I'm allowed to hug my mum, I feel like a human being again and not just a prisoner. It is, again, just a small thing, but as I've said, it's the small things that really count when you're banged up.

I'm still going from visit to visit to mark out the time. In many ways I recognise that my head is never inside the prison. I'm always looking to my next precious visit or writing letters home. It's what's carried me through the months I spent in Holloway, and through this next stage too. As a consequence, time is passing and I'm starting to get a sense of there being light at the end of the tunnel, though I still have a long way to go. The days pass, the weeks and months too. Every day feels like groundhog day, and what I realise I miss most is daylight. Apart from an hour in the exercise yard everyday, we're inside pretty much all the time, living under bright strip lights. Much of the prison is quite dark, even the library, so we always have to have artificial light, and I find it dispiriting. I miss my little garden and my pots of flowers. I miss popping to Tesco for a loaf of bread or going for a drink in the pub. Such simple pleasures when you think about it! My visits have always been precious, but at Cookham they become an absolute lifeline as it feels like they're all I've got.

My mum and sisters, Shelley and Maxine, are visiting me today. It is a much easier journey for them than travelling into London, so we are all feeling lighter, like there's hope on the horizon. We're chatting about Neil's school when Myra walks in. I clock her, and as if it's completely normal I turn to Mum.

"Oh, Myra Hindley's there, she's got a visitor," I say, without thinking.

I've never seen three people's heads swivel in one direction as fast.

"Don't look!" I hiss.

It's too late. Myra sees my family looking over at her. Gawping at her, actually.

She stares back at them until they turn away. I see my mum shrink a little into her chair.

"Oh my God, how d'you cope bein' in the same prison as her?!" she says.

Maxine shakes her head.

"She looks really scary..."

"What d'you expect?" I laugh. "Of course she's scary. Well, remember me during the week because I 'ave to 'ave my coffee with her each morning and afternoon in the library!"

They all stare at me. I hadn't wanted to tell them so I'd "forgotten" to put that in my letters. I knew they'd worry if they knew.

"Oh my God," Shelley echoes. "How on earth d'you manage that?"

I shrug.

I've met so many strange people and heard so many distressing stories since coming into prison, I've learned to disassociate from them and walk my own path. I've had to do this in order to survive, so whether it's Myra Hindley or Mother Teresa I give them the same courtesy and get on with my job and my journey through incarceration.

* * *

The next day at breaktime, Myra walks in.

"I see you was on a visit," I say. Always best to take the bull by the horns.

It's the first time I've seen her laugh.

"Did you tell your family, 'Don't look now, Myra Hindley's on a visit'?" the Moors Murderess says. Part of me still can't believe I'm here, in the same prison as her, having a casual conversation.

I nod. "Yeah, I did."

Myra smiles.

"I'm used to it, Linda. Everyone must say to their visitors, 'Myra's there', as I'm used to all these heads turning around to stare at me." She laughs, evidently pleased to be the centre of attention.

"I shouldn't 'ave done that," I reply, not sure where this chat is going.

"Don't worry, Linda, I'm used to it, honestly. I wait for all the heads to look at me, then they turn away again and I can get on with my visit."

Myra smiles again and moves away and I'm left with that indefinable feeling she seems to provoke in everyone she comes across. It is a mixture of revulsion, fascination and something else that is hard to pin down. Meeting someone who's done something as horrific as murder children is never going to be easy.

. . .

The months continue in their usual fashion. I work at the library. I see Myra every day. I do as little as I can to chat with her. I keep my cell clean and write letters home. I mix with the girls in the association room. Ruby seems much better. Her husband seems to have called off the split, so there's hope for her. Kirsty has been released, and things carry on. One evening a girl I don't usually talk to walks into my cell during association. I'm sitting on my bed chatting with a young male officer who's new to the wing. He's just introducing himself and seeing if I need anything when this girl, Trace, opens my door, comes in and sits down next to me. We've hardly ever spoken. Just as I'm about to ask what she wants, one of the tougher girls marches up and stands at the doorway. She's glaring at Trace, a prolific thief, who's cowering next to me.

"I've got respect for her (meaning me) so I won't come in there and batter ya, so I'll wait until lock-up. You can stay there as long as you like, I'll be 'ere."

Trace stays where she is while the tough woman, whose name I don't know, stands menacingly in the doorway. The officer doesn't move and so we carry on our conversation, which feels quite strange. Everything carries on as normal except for the stand-off that seems about to take place in my cell.

My flask is sitting on my table. Five minutes before lock-up, the tough inmate jumps forward and undoes the lid of my flask, grabs it and tries to throw scalding-hot water over Trace. Trace reacts fast though, and knocks the other inmate's hand. The water spills all over the screw.

We all gasp. I can see the steam coming off his trousers. Someone outside rings the alarm bell and then I can hear staff running to my cell.

"You're both on report, but I won't mention the water's gone over me," the screw says.

I know if he says the water goes over him that'll be classified as a serious assault, which could go to outside court. The women are grabbed and taken to their cells, to be locked in to await their punishment.

The male officer looks at me and says: "Linda, don't mention to anyone I got water on my trousers. OK?"

"OK," I reply, thinking how decent he is. He knows it wasn't meant for him and he's saving those two from a worse outcome.

* * *

The next morning, my cell door is opened and a screw pokes her head in.

"Linda, you've got to go down the block, you're a witness to the incident last night."

I'm escorted downstairs to the punishment block, or the segregation unit as it's called, where those put on report are questioned and punished.

Prisoners are kept in their cells all the time in this wing.

I step into an office. The governor – a man in his fifties wearing a grey suit – is sitting behind a desk, while on the other side are the two women and various members of staff. They stand this side to stop anyone grabbing the governor.

"Right, Linda, I've read the accounts of both parties, and the staff officer told me his version, so can you fill me in?"

I have to tell the truth, so I say: "Yes, so Trace came and sat on my bed. I thought she'd come in to speak to the prison officer, so I didn't say anythin'. The other woman came and stood at the door. Five minutes before lock-up, she grabbed my flask, unscrewed the lid and went to throw it. Trace knocked it into the air, and my flask smashed through no fault of my own."

"Very well, Linda, we'll replace your flask at the prison's expense. Thank you for your evidence. You can go now."

I'm taken back up to my wing without knowing what the girls' punishment is, but I don't see them for a few days, so I imagine they'll have been kept down the block for that time and probably fined.

CHAPTER 15

OPEN PRISON

"You know the next step from here, Linda, is open prison, you'll be moved to East Sutton Park soon," says the decent male screw. His name is Mr Barlow and all the girls really like him.

"It's nicer there. It's not even like a prison as it's a lovely big old mansion with grounds and much more relaxed rules."

"Oh right," I say, unsure what an open prison is compared to Holloway and Cookham Wood. I guess I'll find out.

The call to leave comes sooner than I think.

I've now been banged up for more than two years, and the thought of being somewhere without such strict rules and with more freedom feels great. It also means the prison authorities are intending to schedule my release, as it's the last stage before being set free. I've served half my reduced sentence, and I know I won't be getting out for a while yet, but even so, I'm looking forward to going there.

Two days later, Mr Barlow comes into the library. I'm stamping out a book for an inmate, another romance novel. Like Myra, the girls all love reading Mills & Boon, which seems strange for a bunch of convicts.

"Linda, you're going on the next ship out to East Sutton Park. You'll need to pack your things as it could be tonight or tomorrow."

"Oh my God," I say, putting down the ink pad and smiling back at the screw. "This means I'm gettin' close to release?"

He nods.

"Yes it does, Linda," he says.

The next day I'm called to reception, where I'm told I'm leaving.

It's the same procedure. I'm taken along the same corridors with the same bleached white lights. I'm put in a cubicle and strip-searched, while my things are searched too. It's all exactly the same until I'm told to step inside the prison van.

I hesitate for a moment.

"Aren't you goin' to handcuff me?" I say to the new screw, who has travelled from East Sutton. She's a kind-looking woman who seems much more laidback than any other prison guard I've come across so far.

"You're goin' to an open prison, why would I put you in handcuffs?" she says with a smile.

I'm so obviously gaping at her that this makes her laugh.

"Oh blimey, this is unusual," I reply. It sounds silly, but sitting inside a sweat box without the feeling of cold metal clasps around my hands, rubbing at the skin on my wrists, feels like a victory of sorts. We drive out of Rochester and eventually down a series of country lanes.

"Bloody hell," I say as the van turns down a long gravel driveway. At the end sits what I can only describe as a stately home. Thinking we must've taken a wrong turn, I expect the van to reverse and head out. Instead, the screw thanks the driver and opens the door.

"East Sutton Park," she says.

There's even a welcome sign at the big double gates at the entrance. The first thing that strikes me is there is no high wall, no barbed wire, no metal fence. The only wall round the perimeter is three feet high, while the windows are all open. Even more astonishingly, there are inmates walking around: women are mowing grass, there are a couple of them digging flower beds on their own. I walk out, feeling strange without having a guard cuffed to me, to find the front door isn't locked.

"You OK, Linda?" the screw says.

"I think so. I can't believe all this..." I reply as we arrive at the reception room. Inside there are no bars on the windows, no locks on the doors.

"Is this what open prison means? No fences and no locks?" I ask.

"Yes, Linda, that's exactly it. The only thing keepin' you 'ere is yourself," the screw says as I'm led to a room for the usual strip search.

"Make no mistake, if you do decide to leave, you'll never get the opportunity to come back. It's still prison, but it's one where you're trusted to fulfil the rest of your sentence with minimal supervision. You might even be allowed to get a job or do voluntary work in the community." I'm left almost reeling. It's the strangest feeling moving from a closed prison, where every movement is scrutinised and controlled, to somewhere like this, which is still incarceration but one that feels more a personal choice. It feels strange to be trusted again, actually it feels wonderful. It's like I'm being trusted to begin rejoining society.

Once I'm processed, the screw leads me to the dorm bedroom. It's a huge room with wood-panelled walls. There are ten beds arranged around the walls like a hospital ward, which I don't like the look of. It's noisy and crowded, and I'm used to having a single cell at Cookham.

"This is the biggest room in the house, and unfortunately, you 'ave to start in 'ere then work your way towards the privilege of a smaller dorm room."

Women are wandering in and out as I check for an unoccupied bed. Next to each one is a little green locker, a small table and chair, and that's it.

Radios playing different types of music are blasting down the length of the room, and for a moment I wish I could be back in my dorm cell with Bobble, Bibble and the other Linda in Holloway, or in my single at Cookham.

This is a madhouse, I think, knowing I have to get used to it. *Oh for God's sake, I can't hear myself think!*

"Good luck, Linda, you'll be startin' as a wing cleaner later today. My name's Karen, make yourself at home," the screw says, walking off. I watch her stop and chat to a couple of women at the other end of the room.

As far as prisons go, East Sutton Park proves to be as far from my experience of Holloway as it's possible to be. Much of the food is grown on site in the vegetable gardens. There are pigs and a farm, with a butcher's shop where women can learn the trade. Women have jobs as gardeners, farm workers and work in the shop, and there's an education block with a hairdresser's, art and computer classes. I sign up for a City & Guilds soft-furnishings course, feeling that if someone pinches me, then this might all disappear. The house itself is beautiful, but I feel sad it has become a prison, one where no smoking or lighters are allowed inside because of the age of the building.

The next morning I wake up to the sound of four or five alarms going off and realise we get up ourselves and get to work under our own steam. This feels like freedom already as there's no screw banging on the door or unlocking my cell.

A young girl with shocking-pink hair and a lip piercing smiles as I get up and head to the showers. Here again, there are no screws watching us in case a fight breaks out. I get dressed and head to the office where I've been told to report. Karen is there and she sends me off to find the cleaners to learn what I'm doing today. I can walk around the prison without a screw beside me, without having to wait for doors to be unlocked or locked again. There's no jangling of keys as I go. After breakfast I begin work and realise I really enjoy looking after such a beautiful building. There are old portraits on the walls and the wooden panelling comes up a treat.

"You're Linda, aren't ya?" the girl with pink hair says. She wanders over from the garden.

"Yes I am. Pleased to meet ya," I reply, wondering if a screw is going to shout from somewhere to tell us to get back to work.

"I'm Reece. I'm new 'ere. Can't say I like it much. I'd rather be back in closed."

"Why on earth's that?' I say, bemused. To me, this is practically heaven after Holloway.

"Dunno. Don't like it. I don't trust myself to stay..." Reece smiles but she seems on edge. I can see she's struggling with something.

"I'm sorry to 'ear that," I say, not sure what advice I can give as I've only just arrived.

A week later, the fire alarm sounds.

"Everyone out!" Karen shouts, running up the stairs to where I'm polishing the banisters. I can already smell the burning.

We all file out and wait in the grounds while the Fire Brigade is called. Reece is nowhere to be seen, but then I catch sight of her with an officer who is marching her up to where the governor is standing.

Another inmate, one of the rougher girls in my dorm, sidles up.

"It was Reece who done it. She hated it 'ere and wanted to go back to closed prison. Stupid cow shoulda just gone into the office and told them she wanted to move. Instead, she's gone and set light to an old wooden chest. Probably could've nearly burnt the place down in the process. It was her who started the alarm, but even so, silly bitch."

I don't see Reece again. Months later, I'm told she got charged with arson and sent back to closed prison. I've no idea what became of her.

. . .

Part of being in open prison is that after a while, once the staff have seen how well an inmate behaves and whether they do their jobs properly, prisoners are allowed to go out for a couple of hours at a time. The first time I'm given this privilege, I've been at East Sutton for about two months. I'm so excited as Mickey's mate Sammy Sapiano, a big blagger (armed robber) who I've stayed in touch with over the years, is in the area and has written to ask if he can see me. I write back saying he can come and take me out.

When the tyres of Sammy's gold Rolls-Royce crunch over the driveway, there's soon a crowd of women looking out of the windows.

"What the hell?" Karen the screw says.

"I think that's my ride!" I say.

"Go for it, girl!" shouts one of the inmates, a young girl who helps in the kitchens.

"That's Sammy, he's so over the top..."

I'm wearing my blouse and skirt, my outfit for visits, when I step out on this late November afternoon. Even though it's chilly, it feels so good to be going somewhere that isn't a prison.

Stepping into that car feels like the kind of normality I'm used to. Sammy is, of course, a gangster, and I'm being driven to Headcorn village in a gold car. I can't explain the feeling of being driven out of there, in something that isn't a metal sweat box littered with cigarette butts. I open the window and feel the air and the weak winter sunshine on my face and I feel truly alive again, for the first time in three years. Sammy takes me to a small restaurant and tells me to order whatever I want. I choose Dover sole with steamed vegetables and crispy golden potatoes. Every mouthful is like heaven. Every sip of fresh orange juice is sublime. Yet it's the enjoyment of being out in the world again which gives me the most pleasure.

"I can't believe I'm free for the day and I can walk into a restaurant and choose what I can eat. I haven't drunk out of proper glass for years now!" I say.

Sammy, who is a dark-haired Italian man with dark brown eyes and a short stature, grins back at me. He's sipping a glass of white wine but I've been told I'm not allowed alcohol, hence the juice.

"I know what it's like Linda. I hated prison," he says. His cockney accent is still strong though he lives in Essex and has done for years. Sammy did 15 years inside for armed robbery, which is how he knew my Mickey. "Mind you, I got the accolade for makin' the best hooch in the prison!"

We laugh, and when we've finished the main course I order a chocolate pudding.

"I know I'm only allowed out for six hours, but it's lovely to think the real world hasn't stopped. Is that a silly thing to say?"

"Not at all," Sammy replies. "Bein' inside means we're entirely away from the world. Of course, it's a surprise, and sometimes even a shock, to think it just carries on without us."

When the Rolls-Royce purrs up the long driveway, the heads begin to appear from the windows again, looking like a row of stuffed animals that usually sit on the walls of grand houses such as this one and making Sammy and I burst out laughing.

. . .

Christmas is a completely different affair compared to Holloway and Cookham. In the other prisons, you get sliced meat cooked a few days before, but at East Sutton Park I'm amazed when a huge turkey is served by the governor. It feels like a proper Christmas and, as we're not locked in, we can roam about, go and watch films or chat to friends. There is a huge Christmas tree and some of the girls are allowed home.

"Sorry, Linda, you're not allowed," Karen tells me a few days beforehand. "But don't get too downhearted, it won't be long before you become eligible for short visits home, and a job too."

This is welcome news. Though my family and children visit regularly, I'm desperate to rejoin them, and to have some kind of normality.

A lot of things happen in a short space of time after Christmas. I achieve a distinction in my City & Guilds, and so I'm allowed to work for two days a week for a soft-furnishings company in Maidstone. The understanding is I won't be paid, but I'll work 10 a.m. to 4 p.m. and begin to re-enter society at large.

After a month or so, I notice I'm the only woman in the company to have a handbag. The prison had allowed me to use one, which was, in itself, a luxury. Then, a couple of weeks later, all these handbags appear by the sewing machines.

"How come you've all got your bags now?" I ask one of the women. She's an outspoken woman with brown hair cut in a sleek bob and long, manicured fingernails.

"Don't take this the wrong way, but we were dead against you comin', love," she says. Her name is Judy and she and I clicked the minute I walked in.

"What d'you mean?" I say.

"I knew you'd be wondering why we've suddenly all got handbags here. When we were told we were gettin' a prisoner comin' to work here, we didn't know what you were in prison for. We decided to lock our handbags away in case you stole them or took stuff out of our bags. Sorry, like I said, don't take offence. We didn't know you then, Linda."

"But I would never do that!" I exclaim. It is the first time I see how much people who've been in prison are stereotyped.

"We were against you comin', but, as it turns out, we all like you. So, we all said, collectively, that we'll put our handbags out like normal. We feel bad that we did that."

I end up really enjoying my time at the company, and they end up offering me a job for when I'm released. I decline, with regret, because I don't want to stay in Maidstone where I know no one. I want to go home to Essex and start my life again surrounded by family and friends.

Spring turns to summer. Most weekends now, I'm allowed to be taken out for a few hours as long as I return before my curfew, which I always do. It seems incredible that I'm coming to the end of my sentence, a fact that is announced to me quite abruptly when I'm hoovering an upstairs landing. It's July 1989, and I know there's talk of me leaving but nothing official's been said yet.

Suddenly, there's an announcement over the Tannoy. "Linda Calvey to the governor's office."

Wondering what they want, I switch the hoover off and make my way to the office.

The prison governor, a lovely man in his sixties who I've barely spoken to, is smiling broadly as I walk in.

"Linda, phone your family. You got parole, which means—"

"I'm goin' home," I finish.

Oh my God, the elation.

"Yes, Linda. You're going home in two weeks."

Those words are the best thing I've heard in my life, apart from being told I'd given birth to a girl, then a boy.

*   *   *

The next fortnight is a blur. Every hour I find myself planning what I'm going to do, where I'm going to travel, who I'm going to see. My sister Maxine and I have already decided to set up a soft-furnishings business. We've even chosen the name – Material Matters – and I'm determined to make a go of it and go straight. I've promised Melanie and Neil I'll never rob anyone ever again. We'll make high-end curtains, and Maxine has already begun collecting orders.

On the day of my release, on August 12th, 1989, I pack up my things: the regulation two outfits (I'm wearing the third), my two other pairs of shoes, including my slippers, and my underwear. It's not much to show for the past three years, but I don't care. Today I could walk out of here naked and I'd be happy!

The time comes to leave. The governor and Karen wave me off, with my £40 discharge grant in my pocket. Outside, Mum and Maxine are waiting for me. We'll travel to my parents' home in Maldon, Essex, where I know my dad, a big strong man, will have tears in his eyes when he sees me. I know I've put my family through hell and I'm determined to do the right thing, go straight and never commit another crime again.

I turn back and the women are all hanging out of the windows, waving.

Before I walk out of the front door, a free woman, I turn to the staff and say: "You'll never see me again."

Karen replies: "We believe you, Linda. I'm sure we won't see you again. You're one of the prison's successes."

I know in my heart I've changed. My new occupation is going to give me a stepping stone to start an honest life. The dark times I've gone through are officially over. Prison has given me a fresh start and I'm determined to live my life to the fullest from now on.

As I step outside, I think of Holloway – the dirt and degradation. I think of Cookham – the boredom and despair. The years of my life ruined. The years that my family has had ruined by my actions. Everything falls away as I squint up at the sunshine. The relief at leaving, at long, long last, is almost overwhelming.

I'll never be back.

I'm a free woman at last.

CHAPTER 16

TT0377, CALVEY

NOVEMBER 1990

The door slams behind me.

I look around. It's all exactly the same. There is food thrown up the cell wall. There is a metal army bed with a thin, stained mattress. There is a small Formica table and chair, and an open toilet. This time, the screaming is worse. Women screech and wail, call out and swear all along the wing. There are sounds of people kicking their cell doors, of hatches slamming shut, of guards shouting and sirens blaring.

Fifteen months after stepping out of East Sutton Park, vowing to go straight and live a decent life, I'm back in the psychiatric wing of Holloway.

This time, I'm on remand for murder.

I've been arrested and detained for the killing of my gangster lover Ron Cook, the big-time blagger, who was shot at point-blank range with a sawn-off shotgun. I know who did it. I recognised him when he stormed into my small kitchen clad in black, brandishing a gun. Earlier that day I'd collected Ron for day release from Maidstone prison and taken him to my home, a newly decorated house in King George Avenue in East London. It turned out that my past followed me through prison and out the other side. I couldn't walk away from the underworld – Ron would never have let me. In fact, he'd already threatened my son Neil, implying he'd kill him if he ever found out I'd been unfaithful. A man like that doesn't let you leave. He carries on controlling your life, even from behind bars.

. . .

It had all started so well. Maxine and I really made a go of it with our curtain company. We had loads of orders and only took on the high-end ones. I loved doing the work, being creative and doing something that added to a person's life rather than taking something away. It all came to a halt when Ron was shot.

I know who was underneath the black balaclava because he took it off, showed me his face and grinned, after he'd aimed the gun at my lover and pulled the trigger. What I don't know is why Danny Reece did what he did. Perhaps he was settling an old score on behalf of my dead husband, Mickey. Perhaps news had reached him that Ron had threatened my son to keep me faithful. As I stare at the cell, feeling like I'm going to retch, unable to take in the fact that I'm back here in this hellhole, I truly don't know.

Danny is my friend. I'd helped him through the death of his son; of course, we knew the same people, were part of that same underworld.

"GET DOWN!" Danny shouted.

BANG went the gun, catching Ron's arm, blood soaking through his jacket sleeve.

"Oh no, Neil!" I shouted, thinking my son was in the house.

"This one's for Mickey Calvey!" Danny yelled before unleashing the shot that killed Ron Cook.

BANG went the gun again, this time splattering blood, skull bone and gristle across my newly painted room. Pieces of Ron's skull rocked on my new terracotta tiles, and his body slumped onto the floor, his head blown apart.

Danny showed me his face and ran. He turned and legged it out of my home, leaving me crouched in a corner, screaming.

For a moment, all I could take in was the smell of cordite, the hiss of blood leaving Ron's butchered corpse. Then all hell broke loose. I ran outside shouting for a policeman.

Now, I admit I've been both a gangster's moll and an armed robber. The Flying Squad shot my husband, and so I've hated the Old Bill since then. I would normally have as little to do with the police as possible, but I was beside myself. What else could I do? A man lay dead in my house.

"HELP ME! PLEASE! HELP ME!" I screamed, grabbing onto the front wall for support. I felt sick. I was hysterical. Fortunately, there was a copper who happened to be passing. When he came inside, the contrast between the bloodbath that was now my kitchen and the outside world seemed ever starker.

From that point everything went into slow motion. The policeman who had rushed over to help me walked outside and on his radio said: "It's 12:28 p.m. It's a murder."

In minutes, blue-light police cars arrived, their sirens squealing. A police helicopter circled overhead. Police officers swarmed over my house, and I was taken down to the local station to give a statement. At first the police treated me as a witness, which I was. They were kind, offering me cups of coffee. They offered me the tests to prove I hadn't held the gun, and I agreed to undergo them, so they swabbed my face and hands for traces of cordite. One of the coppers gave me his hankie to blow into – and this was also taken for the forensic testing. Swabbing is the standard procedure at any shooting. They checked my clothes too to see if there were any gun residues. They saw that there was blood all down my back from where I'd crouched when Danny fired the killing shot. I had to give all my clothes to forensics to be examined, which I did when Terry arrived with a fresh set of clean clothes for me.

Stupidly, I declined a solicitor because I was a witness to a murder, not the perpetrator. They found nothing, the tests came back negative and so they sent me home. Naturally, I lied to the officers saying I didn't know who'd killed Ron, saying he had many enemies. There is a code of honour among crooks. You don't grass, it's as simple as that. It's dishonourable in the underworld, and I was never going to land Danny in it when he'd got rid of a violent gangster, one who was a controlling and violent man. If anything, I was already thinking that Danny had done me a favour, and possibly saved my life in the long run. Ron had said my son's life would be payback if I was ever unfaithful, but that doesn't mean he'd have stopped there. Ron had controlled my life. He gave me money, yes, and he bought me whatever I wanted, but the price was high. I knew I couldn't ever leave him. I also knew that I could never do anything to upset him. He was a violent criminal, a big-time robber who thought nothing of bundling a dead body into the boot of his car. I know. I'd seen it happen. That's why I felt nothing but relief at Ron's death, though the manner of it was horrifying.

Then the Old Bill discovered I was Mickey Calvey's widow and everything changed.

Two weeks later there was a knock at my daughter's door. I'd been staying there since Ron's death as I couldn't bear to go back into my house, to the scene of the killing.

"Linda Calvey?"

A lone police officer stood outside. His face was stern.

"Yes? I'm Linda Calvey," I replied, wondering why he was standing on the doorstep.

"I'm arresting you for the murder of Ronald Cook." The male officer stepped forward; and I stood there, dumbstruck, completely unable to take his words in.

"You're arrestin' me?" I repeated.

"You have the right to remain silent. Anything you say can be used against you in court..."

"What? Oh my God! My kids, what'll happen to them?"

I was questioned under caution at Canning Town nick. By now, I had the duty solicitor next to me. I was stunned, especially when the copper asked me about Mickey.

"Why didn't you tell us that you're the Linda Calvey who caused us so much grief when your husband was shot?" I knew he was referring to the fact I wouldn't sign for my husband's body, and I fought tooth and nail to get the facts of his death changed.

I said nothing to this. If anything, I felt it incriminated them not me.

"You know I didn't kill Ron, because your tests all came back negative," I said.

"Which tests were those?" The officer sat back in his chair.

"The swabs."

"That's funny, none of our officers remember any tests..."

Is this a joke? I thought. Were they really telling me they had no recollection of the swabs I'd had done there only a couple of weeks previously?

"Yes, the ones that showed I hadn't picked up a gun," I said, impatiently.

The officer, his arms crossed in front of his chest, looked back at me and shook his head.

"What's goin' on?" I was starting to panic. "The test results were given to me..."

"Why didn't you say that Daniel Reece had been in your home? We found his fingerprints in your house. We know he was on leave the weekend Ron was in your house. Perhaps you and Daniel planned to kill him together?"

Nothing I said made a difference. My reputation as the Black Widow (a title given to me after Mickey died) was proof enough, in their eyes, of my involvement, so here I am. On remand in Holloway, only this time, at least, I'm an innocent woman.

"Look who's back!" said the screw as I was led out of the sweat box, handcuffed to two officers this time. The reception staff looked at me like they could see a ghost. One of them was the woman who was knitting when I received my first sentence.

"Linda, what are you doin' back 'ere?" said the other screw, the same woman who had processed me five years ago.

"I've been charged with murder," I said, "but I didn't do it."

"Fuckin' hell," she whistled, just like before. "Well, if Linda says she didn't do it, then she didn't do it. Last time, she admitted what she'd done, and said she was guilty, so I believe her."

For that, at least, I was grateful.

"Your number's TT0377, Calvey."

"Well, I didn't think I'd 'ave another number!" I said.

"'Course, Linda. You know the drill," the screw said.

I blinked, unable to comprehend what was happening. It seemed like a nightmare I couldn't wake up from. I was back to being a series of numbers and letters, and not a person with a name.

After going through the same procedure: strip search, belongings searched (this time I had a small bag of things with me), a six-inch bath, I was taken along the ground floor.

"Where am I goin'?" I said.

"Sorry, Linda, but you're back in C1. Everyone who's on remand for a serious charge like yours has to be assessed."

"But you know me!" I said, stung by this pronouncement. "You know I never done it! You know I'm not violent or horrible..."

"It's procedure, Linda. It'll only be for one night, then they'll move you to the remand wing. Good luck."

The screw looked abashed when she said goodbye and walked off.

. . .

I don't think I have ever felt as low as the moment when I stepped back into this cell. The harsh white lights. The filth on the floor and walls. The scratchings of graffiti. The stench of disinfectant and the howls of the inmates. It's all coming back and it's all unbearable.

Last time, I had a different mindset. I knew I'd committed the crime, so even though I wasn't happy with such a big sentence, I knew I had to do the time. This time it's different. I shouldn't be here. I didn't murder Ron and now I'm going to have to wait it out before my trial, which could take a year or more, to prove my innocence.

I sit down on the bed, trying to work out how it all went wrong. For the past 18 months, my sister Maxine and I have run our company and have been making a go of it. Being reunited with my children, Melanie, who is now a young woman of 20 years old, and Neil, who is 17, and then being cruelly separated is such a powerful blow that I'm left reeling. The life I've built has been kicked away – all because the police found out I was Mickey's widow, or so it seems to me. That shouldn't have changed anything, but it did. Everything about them changed. They told me I was a suspect not a witness. They went on to charge me with the killing. I'm in a state of total disbelief, and I'm sure my kids feel the same. I promised them I'd go straight, and never risk going to prison again. The sad truth is, I'd kept my word, but here I am, back in Holloway, and this time I might be looking at a life sentence.

. . .

One thing I'm grateful for is that Holloway holds no fear for me.

I know every trick in the book. I know how the prison operates, and I also know that being on remand for gangland murder, which is my official charge, means I won't be harassed. People will keep their distance, just like before, perhaps more so this time.

I don't sleep much that night, but when the hatch opens and a voice asks me whether I'm normal or veggie I know how to answer.

It has only been two weeks since Ron was murdered, and I sound cold-hearted, but I'm glad he's dead. I was increasingly under his control – and it was only getting worse. It seemed even when I wanted to go straight, I couldn't escape my criminal past. I actually feel grateful for Danny's actions, which is another reason I would never grass him up.

The sight of Ron's blown-apart skull is another matter. The rocking of the fragments of bone in the aftermath, as the shock was setting in, will always haunt me. Every time I close my eyes I see my blood-spattered kitchen, I hear the hiss of the blood as it drains out of his body. I haven't slept a whole night since that day, and I feel like I never will again.

I'm also desperately angry at the system that put me back here, and determined to clear my name, but I know it'll be a long wait for justice. The fear and dread of my first sentence has gone because this time it's not the unknown. Saying that, I arrived with a heavy heart and an absolute fierce determination to proclaim my innocence. I feel like I've been scapegoated for Ron's murder because of my past.

My cell door has been locked behind me. I look up at the small window, my only view the bare outline of a tree bitten by the winter chill.

CHAPTER 17

REMAND

The next morning, I wake up, my eyes puffy from a broken night's sleep, knowing I have to get up, clean my teeth and get dressed and try to carry on. I know I have to show the screws that I'm well and balanced enough to be moved back up to D3 or a working wing where I can wait out my time until my trial. Somehow it all feels much harder this time round. I don't have the same acceptance because I know I shouldn't be here. This knowledge might threaten to drag me down but I can't let it because I have to find the strength to behave as normally as I can.

Once the breakfast trolley has been round, and I've eaten the same miserable meal as before, on the same blue plastic plates, with a cup of water, I wait to be seen. Thankfully, I'm moved back up to D3 before the day is through, which is where I find that prison life goes on much as it did before – except there is one big change.

"What's this?" I say to another girl on remand. She's called Mary. She's a plump woman, who loosely resembles a pig, and about the same age as me. I'm 42 years old now and banged up for the second time. She tells me she is in for importation of cocaine, on quite a major charge.

"Has Holloway entered the 21st century?" I add, and can't help but giggle. In front of me is a mop and a bucket.

"Oh yeah, I'm told it's all different to how it used to be," Mary says. "You don't scrub floors on your hands and knees any more. And you can 'ave as many photos as you like on your pinboard..." Mary hands me a mop.

"Oh my God, progress!" I say.

I'm back to being a wing cleaner, hardly able to believe that any of this is really happening to me. My days fall into the same routine as before: I'm woken up early and unlocked first to help get the breakfast done. I turn on the hot plate, put the tea urn on and take bread into the dining room so the girls can make their own toast. After, my day is spent cleaning except for when I'm helping with lunch, then cleaning again until the end of the day when I eat dinner, clean up afterwards, go around with the supper trolley after an hour of telly, then lock-up. I know the ropes already, and it helps stop me from overthinking my situation.

Another change is that at mealtimes, the kitchen sends up two choices for "normal" and the same for vegetarians. My wage at the end of my first week has gone up to the magnificent sum of £5. At least it's better than 75 pence!

The time goes quickly because I get on with it. All I can think about is my trial, and how this time I'm going to prove that I wasn't guilty. This helps me cope because my mind is focused on getting to that point.

After lock-up is when girls still all bicker and shout from their cells. As before, they drop down cigarettes tied to a dressing gown cord, holler to each other as they do it, while there are still cockroaches climbing up the walls.

"When's Rentokil comin' back?" one woman yells to another.

"Dunno, but they fuckin' need to come again soon. I killed three in my cell today!"

It's the usual madhouse.

* * *

My first legal visit comes round quickly, less than two weeks after arriving on remand.

I'm told to head to the big corridor downstairs where everyone has to go after breakfast to walk either to the gym, to work or education, or to go along for legal visits. I've got an appointment with my solicitor, Peter Hughman, and so I make my way, accompanied by a screw. Again, it's all stop-start-stop-start to get down, through locked doors and past security cameras trained on every inch of the corridors and stairs.

There are screws all the way down this corridor, dotted strategically because this is also where fights tend to break out. That's because this is the first chance of the day to air grievances, and heated arguments and fist fights are regular occurrences. At the same time, some of the women from C1 are brought through after being taken to the gym for half an hour, coming back in the opposite direction to everybody else. It's an incredibly intimidating experience seeing roughly 40 or so women walking along, though, of course, I'm used to it by now.

One of the new C1 girls I see coming back has a bald head.

"Oh my God, how dreadful," I say, turning to Mary. "How could they 'ave someone in 'ere with cancer?" I thought she'd come to prison after chemotherapy.

"Oh her," replies Mary. "She used to be a wing cleaner up where we are. She received a Dear John letter from her husband, ending their marriage. She was so distraught, she started pullin' her hair out. They moved her to C1 not long after."

"How tragic, that poor woman," I say, genuinely shocked. "She needs help, not just be left to become more traumatised in C1!"

There are so many sad stories at Holloway and every single one makes me even more determined to win my freedom.

Down in the booths where legal visits take place, my solicitor Peter is waiting for me. He is wearing one of his usual smart navy suits and he smiles when I walk in.

"Right, Linda, the quicker this year goes the better. It's obvious you're innocent. We've appointed a QC, a barrister by the name of Ronald Thwaites. He is excellent.

"If all goes well, you'll be home in a year."

"A year?" I say, and even though in prison terms this is good news, it's still a year taken out of my life. "I hope so, Peter. I miss my children and I shouldn't even be 'ere."

"It's very hard for you, Linda. We'll do our very best to get you the right result at your trial," he says.

"Oh, I'm not worried about the trial. I'm innocent and everyone'll see that," I say confidently. "I won't go down for murder, but I find the thought of waitin' for the next few months unbearable."

"Like I said, Linda, we'll do everything we can. Now, we need to go over the prosecution's statements..."

I learn that Danny Reece has also been arrested and we're facing the trial together. I hadn't said a word about his involvement, and so it was the police who arrested him because of finding his fingerprints at the scene of the crime. They'd insinuated we were lovers, so I challenged them to dust my bedroom, saying they wouldn't find a single other print there apart from mine and Ron's.

Danny had refused to give a statement and I refused to name the real killer, despite Danny insisting I should name him to exonerate myself. I refused, thinking justice would prevail. How wrong I was.

"I'm happy to go for trial, because then I'll get a not guilty. The police took swabs and said the tests were negative, and I'll swear it on my life. They 'ave no evidence under the sun that could convict me..." I begin to say, and am surprised when Peter shakes his head.

"The police are saying they didn't do the swabs. They're denying there are any missing tests. It doesn't look good for them because it's standard procedure to swab someone at the scene of a shooting."

"I know, they told me when I was questioned. They did take them and someone in that nick will tell the truth!" I reply. "They swabbed my face and hands, and they found no residue or anythin'!"

"Sorry, Linda, they're saying it was an oversight and they should've done those tests but didn't."

Peter stares at me. I blink back at him, unable to comprehend how serious this could be for me. Obviously they'd told me this during questioning, but I thought they were trying it on, trying to get me to say Danny's name at that point and accuse him, which I'd never do.

"So it's my word against theirs," I say.

"Exactly," Peter replies. "So, we'd better make the best defence possible for you. You might want to reconsider your position in not naming Mr Reece..."

I shake my head. "I won't be a witness for the prosecution. Danny saved my son from Ron. If I say anythin', then I'm condemning him to 20 years inside. I won't do that." I am resolute.

Peter shakes his head too but he knows me well enough to see that I won't change my mind.

"The police say there were no swab tests, and they will say that in court. You won't say who did it. This is serious, Linda."

"It'll be fine. The jury'll see sense," I say, though Peter doesn't look convinced.

The rest of the day, I feel stunned. Then things take a turn for the worse.

My cell is next to the wing office, and on the other side of me is Mary.

The next day I hear a screw telling Mary to go downstairs as she has a legal visit.

"A legal visit?" she says, "No, I don't think so. My legals didn't say they were comin' today. Who is it? Can you find out?"

A few moments later, the screw, who returned to the office and made a phone call, comes back.

"It's the police."

"The police! Why the police? I was charged by customs, not the Old Bill," Mary says.

"Will you go and find out what it is, Mary, but keep in mind if you get there and don't want talk to them after they say what they're there for, just get up and walk out." I almost can't believe a screw is giving this advice.

Mary walks off and half an hour later she comes back up. This time she's really flustered. It's time for me to start cleaning and so I begin swabbing the corridor. Mary walks straight up to me.

"Linda, it was your police..."

"My police? Why was my police visitin' you?" I stop mopping and look at her.

"They said to me that they know your cell's next to the office and mine's next to you," Mary says. "They offered to help me out as they said that someone had told them that you talked to me out of the window. They say that someone told them that you confessed."

I look at her, dumbfounded.

"They said what?"

"I know! But I told them that whoever gave them that information only gave 'alf of it. There's no need for me to poke my head out the window as we work together as cleaners, so why would you 'ave to wait until evenin' to talk to me when we're on the landing all day long together?" Mary says. Her face is blotchy red as she speaks. She is distressed by all this, as am I.

"I told them I believe in Linda, and I don't want any reductions on Linda's back. I said: 'You go back where you come from, and tell them I won't be helpin' you.'"

"Oh my God," I manage to say. My heart is beating wildly. It looks like the police are desperate to convict me.

"Come with me," I say, and we march to the office. We tell the officer what happened.

"Fuckin' hell, that's heavy shit," the screw says.

"Look, I want to see my solicitor," I say. "Would you please phone him and tell him to make an appointment to come and see me tomorrow."

The rest of the day is spent going over and over in my head what Mary said. There is no sense in it. Why would anyone lie like that? And why would the police need this obviously fake evidence about a confession if they've got enough evidence to charge me?

That night I sleep very little again, though for different reasons this time.

The next day, I go straight down for my legal visit. I tell Peter what Mary said.

He sits back in the plastic chair and whistles.

"Wow, will she come to court as a witness for the defence to tell the jury she was approached?" I hadn't thought of that.

"I don't know, I'll ask her," I say.

We talk some more and look at who we can call on to give statements in my defence, then I head back up to the wing to find Mary.

"Mary, my solicitor is askin' if you'd do a statement and come to court for me? All you'd need to say is what 'appened and what the police said."

Mary is already shaking her head.

"Linda, I'm not comin'. I've got enough trouble already with my charges, and if I do this it'll go worse for me. I told you what happened, but I'm not goin' to do a statement. They're tryin' to fit me up, so I've got too much shit of my own to deal with."

I can't argue with that.

"It's OK, I understand," I reply. "I'd probably do the same in your position."

From that moment onwards, I'm extra careful with what I say and who I say it to. I look around the staff and inmates wondering who gave that information to the police. It's nerve-racking to think someone in here has it in for me enough to do that, and I've only been here a couple of weeks. Was it a member of staff? Was it another inmate? Frustratingly, I'll probably never know.

CHAPTER 18

TEARS

"Mum, I've got somethin' to tell you..."

I look over at my daughter who is bathed in winter sunlight. She looks happier than she has in months as she sits opposite me in the Holloway visiting room. I've been locked up for almost three months. Same thing, day in day out – but now a ray of hope is poking through the clouds. The room itself is actually a pleasant space. The staff have put pot plants in, a toy area for children and some books on the shelves. There are chairs sitting around a few round tables and the whole effect is quite cheering.

"What is it, darlin'?" I say. "Is everythin' OK?"

My daughter, who is 20 years old, smiles. She has a strange look on her face, half happy, but also half anxious. She puts her hand to her stomach as she speaks, and in that moment I know.

"Oh my God, I'm goin' to be a nan. Am I right?"

Mel bursts into tears.

"Yes, Mum, I'm pregnant, and I'm really happy about it..."

"Oh darlin', don't cry. That's wonderful news, I'm so happy for you. When's your due date?" I feel a sudden wave of emotion when she replies and I realise it'll be before my trial takes place.

I'm thrilled to become a grandmother but I'm choked up at not being able to be there for my daughter at such an important family time. There's no way I'll be allowed to go home and look after Melanie, and I'm pretty sure they won't let me out even at the birth.

"I'm three months gone, Mum. It's early days, but I've decided not to know the sex of the baby. I want it to be a surprise for us all." Mel dabs her eyes with a tissue, but the tears keep coming.

These are the ordinary tragedies of being inside. Life carries on – relentlessly – and there's nothing we can do about it.

I can't help her. I can't do all the things a mother does for her pregnant daughter. I can't go to scans or prenatal classes with her. I can't be there at the birth, and I may not be able to hold my grandchild until he or she is old enough to be brought into a prison, assuming I'm not out by then. I look over at her tear-streaked face and realise I'm crying, too. I also realise that Mel met her dad for the first time in prison when she was a tiny baby. My grandchild might meet me for the first time the same way, and this feels unbearable.

Without thinking, I get up and try to hug Mel but the screw standing closest to me says: "Calvey! No touching!"

"Sorry, it's just my daughter. She's pregnant..." I say, hoping she'll relent.

She is one of the ones that enjoys their moment of power. She doesn't even look at me as she shakes her head. If I'm in any doubt that I'm powerless, then in this moment it comes home to me truly.

I sit back down but I'm shaking. I desperately want to comfort my daughter and also to share in her joy, as any mum and her child would do.

"It's alright, Mel," I say when my daughter's face reddens and I can see she's fighting back anger, too. "It's just how it is. I'm so glad you came to tell me though..."

"Oh Mum, I can't believe you won't be there for the birth. How will I manage without ya?" Mel says, her voice breaking.

I take a deep breath.

"You'll manage because you 'ave to. You've had to manage without me before, and you did. I'll be with you in spirit. I want letters every week from now on, and I want to know every little detail... And don't forget, your family is always there for you."

When it's time for Mel to leave, I wave and make sure there is a smile on my face. She looks so lost and alone in that moment, like a small child again.

"You'll be fine, I know it. You're a tough woman. I love you, darlin'."

Mel waves and tells me she loves me, too.

As I walk out of Holloway's visiting room, I feel my heart sink. Of all the cruelties and punishments meted out in prison, this surely has to be the worst of them. Being separated from family at times like this is agony. The deprivations and lack of privacy, the basic food and living conditions all pale into insignificance next to the tragedy of not being able to hold my pregnant daughter and give her the love she needs. In six months I might be going to trial. Who knows if I'll be a free woman or not? Who knows if I'll be able to hold my grandchild in my arms? I know the wait ahead will be all the more sore knowing about this baby.

. . .

Six months later, as the July heat is setting in, I have a visit from Mum.

She's beaming when she walks into the sunny visiting room at Holloway. When I see her face I just know what she's about to say.

"It's Mel, she's had the baby!"

"Oh my God!" I reply. I want to jump up with delight, then, just as quickly, I want to cry.

"You've got a granddaughter – Samantha – and I've got a great-granddaughter. How wonderful is that?" Mum says.

"And is Mel OK? Is the baby OK?" I ask, at once thrilled for her and devastated that I can't be there to look after the baby.

"They're both fine. The family is looking after them both. There's nothin' to worry about. They're doin' well. They're at home and Mel is already a brilliant mum."

"Send me in some photos," I say, wiping away tears that are running down my face.

"Of course I will, darlin'. Now you just focus on your trial and gettin' out of prison. We'll all be there for it to support ya."

The days can't go by fast enough. Mum sends me in a bunch of photos, and this time I can pin them all to my board, careful not to have any creeping over the edges because that's not allowed. In Mel's arms is a beautiful baby with big blue eyes and a tuft of dark hair. I wonder how long it will be before I can hold her. My heart sinks and I tell myself I must use this sadness to fight even harder for justice.

CHAPTER 19

BLACK CAP

The months following Mum's visit seem to pass even more slowly. I'm on remand, so I'm allowed plenty of visits, and this time it's me pushing chocolate bars through my window for the cleaning party to collect and share out among the convicted. I miss Bobble. She was as good as her word and stayed in touch, and we've been writing since I was charged, but Holloway seems a grimmer, grimier place without her. My legal team finally hear the date of my trial, and it's set for the end of October. By the time it comes around, I'll have been on remand for almost a year. I haven't yet met my grandchild, and so I'm praying fervently that this will go right for me and I'll be home within weeks.

The day the trial opens arrives and I'm driven to the Old Bailey. I'm the only one in the prison van today because most don't go to this court. It's the highest in the land, and it's only used for the most serious cases. My heart is beating wildly as I step out and into the holding area, where I'll be led to a cell to meet Danny and our solicitors to speak before the case begins.

"How are ya, darlin'?" Danny says as I enter. Both Ronald and Peter are there, too, as well as Danny's screws, who are handcuffed to him on either side.

"Never better," I say with a small smile. We share a look of understanding. Neither of us is OK, but we're here, and as long as we're treated as innocent before being proven guilty, then there's hope.

"Linda, you've gotta say I'm guilty," Danny says. He's wearing a dark suit, his hair is shaved back and he looks smart, but there are black shadows under his eyes. His accent is strongly cockney and he sounds gruff, but I know underneath his hard man exterior he's actually got a heart of gold. Except for where Ron Cook's concerned, that is.

"No, I can't say that, Danny. I would never do that to ya," I reply, and see Peter shake his head.

"It's going to be problematic for you if you don't, Linda, you know this," he says.

"Danny saved my son with his actions. Now, whether he meant to or not is Danny's to know. I'll never grass on a friend, especially one who did me the favour of riddin' me of Ron. I won't do it," I say.

Danny nods. He smiles at me and I see that softness of his, the bit he keeps hidden away, the part that still grieves his son. It disappears as soon as it appears.

"Time to go. We've been called," Ronald says, straightening his black robes, and clutching a huge stack of papers.

"Time to go, Danny. Good luck, darlin'," I say. Danny reaches over and takes my hand and then we separate and turn to the door and begin the walk up to the dock to meet our fates.

. . .

"On the charge of gangland murder, how do you find the defendant?" The judge at the Old Bailey's Court Number One says, turning to face the juror who is standing at the end of the jury box.

There is a brief moment's pause.

The packed courtroom falls silent. My family – my mum, sisters Shelley and Maxine and my brother Terry – lean forward in the public gallery to hear better. Even the groups of journalists covering the case stop their scribbling and look up.

. . .

Our trial has lasted three weeks. Over this time, I have heard lie after lie. By the end, I'm convinced I'm the only person in the court who has told the truth about that day. The police asked for protection for the jury, saying I'm a dangerous woman, but the judge refused because the two co-defendants, Danny and me, are on remand. It felt like the prosecution were making a play of creating me as this frightening woman before we'd even started. I pleaded not guilty, and so did Danny, though I knew different.

I've faced hostility ranging from a hangman's noose and the word "murderess" graffitied on my prison van, to screams of "Murdering bitch!" by the crowds who jostle and leer at me while I'm being transported each day from Holloway.

It feels like a dream. Actually, it feels like a nightmare. Never did I think I'd come this close to being found guilty of a contract killing. The prosecution alleged that I paid £10,000 to Danny to carry out Ron's killing. They said that after the first shot was fired, Danny bottled it and so I grabbed the gun and shot him myself.

My words have been twisted, my evidence laughed out of court. When I shouted "Oh no, Neil!" that has been interpreted as "KNEEL!", saying that it was at that moment I grabbed the gun and killed Ron in cold blood. I'm left reeling and distraught. The police claim it was an "oversight" that the swab tests weren't done, but they were done, and my barrister Ronald Thwaites made this very clear. He is every inch a QC, with half-rimmed glasses and a stern expression. His voice is commanding and he has real presence, but will it be enough? It is the word of a convicted armed robber against the Metropolitan Police. I never stand a chance.

Every day, flashbulbs from what feel like a million cameras burst in my face as the world's press photograph me inside the sweat box, arriving and leaving.. I know my stunned face will be interpreted as the blank stare of a killer. I know my bleached blonde hair and lipstick will mark me out as a seductress of men, and therefore guilty as charged. I've listened as I'm painted as a cold-hearted killer, a woman who stops at nothing to seduce and kill men, a queen of the under-world. I'm described as the widow of a notorious armed robber who took up his mantle, a woman capable of killing a man because the pros-ecution says I spent Ron's money while he was in jail, and knew he'd come for me upon his release. All of it is a performance. I wonder if I should've told the police that Ron, far from being the charming lover I told them about, was in fact a controlling, abusive villain. I was scared they'd see that as a motive, but now I wonder if telling the truth about all of it – the fact I knew it was Danny, and describing my relationship with Ron – might've worked in my favour. It's impossible to tell as the days stretch on.

It feels like the stakes are higher than they've ever been and I've been dealt a losing hand. Despite this, every evening back in Holloway I feel optimistic that I'll be going home at the end of this, that truth will prevail and the jury of 12 good men and women will see through the lies. There was a moment where this felt possible when they went out to consider their verdict. The hours passed by. They were still deliberating when the end of the day came, so we were all sent home, which for me was Holloway. That night I lay awake, unable to comprehend what the wrong verdict would bring. Instead, I decided it would all end well and I'd see my children back at home the next day. Hope is a strange thing: wonderful and terrible all at the same time.

12 NOVEMBER 1991

The next day, for the verdict, there is flurry of excitement when the foreman comes out and asks the court a question.

He clears his throat, looking nervous, as well he might when every eye in that court room turns to him.

"If Linda Calvey was standing where she says she was standing when the shot was fired, would she have seen what she says she saw?"

The judge, a kind-faced man called Mr Justice Hidden, says we need a gun expert to answer this question. The prosecution shake their heads, but the police jump up and say, by chance, they have a gun expert with them.

I saw a puff of black smoke and a dull red blaze when the gun was fired for the second time, crouched as I was in one corner. The police expert takes the stand. What he says will stay with me for ever, because it makes no sense to me. He says I wouldn't have seen what I saw. This, despite my expert saying I would have to have had arms eight-foot long to have been holding the gun in the position it was fired from. Makes no sense to me. When the officer, whose name I don't know, says those words, I know it is over. The court room is abuzz with gasps and chatter. I scribble a quick note and pass it to my QC.

Can we question him?

My barrister's reply, written on another note, says: *I know but he's not a witness, he's a professional giving his opinion. We can't question him.*

Was this the final nail in my coffin?

The judge asks for silence and the foreman goes back out. My heart sinks to my shoes. I know from that moment that I am finished.

Twenty minutes later, the jury has come back. Their verdict?

It's all so familiar.

The two screws standing beside me shuffle. Someone in the chamber coughs. Then, the word I had truly not expected to hear again, the one I haven't prepared for, is spoken.

"Guilty," the foreman of the jury says.

Again, there is a cry from the gallery. I recognise my family's voices but I'm too stunned to react. I feel dangerously close to fainting. The chamber erupts as soon as the verdict is given. Lawyers seem to dash here and there. The journalists run out to call in the news to their news desks.

Then, like a scene from a horror movie, the judge reaches for something, places a black cap upon his wig. You can now hear a pin drop, the courtroom is hushed as everyone waits for the judge to speak.

The judge then does something strange. As if this judge knows I'm innocent, he reaches out his arms and says: "You have both been found guilty of the murder of Ronald Cook. There is nothing I can do but pass you directly to the Court of Appeal."

At the time, this is only the second time ever a case has ended this way, with a direct route into the appeals court. To my mind, what he's saying to the jury is, you came back with the wrong verdict! It means I walk out of the dock an appellant, so I don't have to apply to appeal; he's granted it from the bench.

Mr Justice Hidden looks at me.

"The only sentence I can pass on you is life, but I can give you the recommended minimum tariff of seven years."

Why else would he give me such a lenient sentence, approximately a third of what it should be, except to acknowledge what my legal team and everyone around me thinks, that I'm innocent?

I look to Danny. A single tear runs down his face. "This tear is for you, not for me," he seems to be saying. He is given a 15-year minimum tariff.

Melanie is hysterical. I can hear her screaming in the public gallery. I feel like I've been punched in the face by Muhammad Ali.

"Take them down," the judge says.

I clutch hold of Danny's hand until the moment we're led away, down to our separate cells to wait for my van back to Holloway, and his van back to Brixton. Danny looks at me.

"Linda, you'll win the appeal, you will," he says as he is escorted away to the male cells.

My QC comes down.

"Linda, I'm in total shock," he says, shaking his head.

The day before, he'd opened his briefcase and showed me the bottle of champagne sitting inside it, saying that we would drink it tomorrow because we'd be celebrating.

"Listen, I know this is the wrong result, but the judge has already made you an appellant; that cuts down the time it takes to come back to court. We'll be back at court within a year."

"But that's a year I've got to spend inside Holloway, convicted of murder," I say. I'm close to breaking down but I try and hold it together.

He nods. There's nothing else he can say.

In the holding area someone has drawn an arch above the doorway, calling it The Hall of Fame. Both Reggie and Ronnie Kray have walked down those stairs, as well as Dr Crippen, none of whom need an introduction. I'm struggling to believe that I'm standing there, awaiting the van that'll put me back behind bars. Someone once told me that a trial is like a stage, and the best actors win. Well, we'd been the worst actors on that stage and so we'd lost. It feels like the end of the world.

I'm shaking as my brain struggles to take in the devastation. I don't know how long I have to wait before the van arrives. I'm cuffed to two officers this time and, with difficulty, I climb into the metal box on wheels that will take me back. Outside, people are yelling obscenities. Camera flashlights go off. Women are screaming "murderer", and people try and hit the side of the van. The ride in the sweat box is memorable. There is a swell of people jostling and shouting outside the court as the van pulls away.

"Bitch!" someone yells.

"Rot in hell. You deserve everything you get!" another shouts.

*   *   *

Nobody speaks for the length of the journey. I'm too distraught anyway. It's a relief to get away from the precincts of the court, though it's not in the type of transport I was hoping for. In my mind I would've been stepping into my friend Billy Blundell's red Rolls-Royce, heading back with my family. I've known Billy from the early days with Mickey. He is well known as a big-time gangster, a very heavy villain in the East End, but a real sweetie (to me at least) and a good friend of mine. Earlier that day my QC had told me my family would all be in court for the verdict, and they'd arranged for Billy to drive me home. We would have celebrated for hours, then normal life would have resumed. My business could have been started again. My children could have carried on with their lives. All would have been just as it had before. But nothing will be the same again.

Soon we arrive back at the familiar gates, the familiar reception wing, the same stink of sweat, stale cigarette smoke and disinfectant. The same blue metal gates that have to be opened and shut every time we pass through them. The same sickly magnolia-painted walls and blue linoleum floors.

"Linda, I'm really sorry, but you're going to have go down on C1 again for a night. It's the rules if you're found guilty of murder," one of the screws says.

"C1? You're jokin' aren't you?" I say.

"Rules are rules," the screw says, "All those convicted of murder go there because we 'ave to watch you in case you try and commit suicide..."

For a moment, I don't speak. I'm stunned by this.

"I can assure you I won't commit suicide. I'm goin' to be fightin' for my appeal!" I exclaim, but it makes no difference.

All the usual procedures happen: I'm strip-searched again, my clothes are checked, I'm taken to a cell in C1. We go through the grey metal door leading from reception, back along the corridors, through a glazed walkway decorated with colourful designs by inmates. I see none of it. I'm reeling from this latest blow. Another night in C1. Surely things can't get any worse?

* * *

That night, all the usual drama and mayhem is alive around me. It's bitterly cold outside but the cell is warm enough. From my window I can see the outline of the treetop, its branches bare. I lie on the hard bed, my wrists sore from the handcuffs, listening to screams and shouts going across the yard.

"Anyone got any salmon?"

"I have. I want one back t'morrow though!"

"Alright, thanks."

I look up as a pink dressing gown cord dangles down past my window. I can't take anything in. I'm living in a nightmare and I can't believe this is happening to me.

Though it's more than a year ago now, I think of Ron's shocked expression as my front door was kicked in and Danny burst into my kitchen. In my mind's eye, I see him reaching for a gun, which he didn't have on him because I'd just picked him up from Maidstone prison. I see the anger turning to fear as Danny raised his gun.

Why did you do it, Danny? I think to myself. *What good did it really do? The two of us have life sentences as a result. How can this be any better than the alternative?*

The only hope I have now is my appeal, which is already being launched after the judge directed my case to the Royal Courts of Justice.

I go over what has been said in court. They said Danny fired the first shot. They said I fired the second, but Danny did both. He fired the gun. I never touched it, yet the evidence showing this had vanished.

My QC questioned the Murder Squad, who had my bank statements. He asked if I'd drawn £10,000 out. They said no, but stated I could've borrowed it. My QC asked if they found £10,000 on Danny. Again they said no, saying he could've hidden it. It all seemed so surreal. When my QC asked how they came up with a figure of ten grand, as there was no evidence I gave money and there was no evidence Danny received any, they said that in the East End the usual price for murder is £10,000.

My QC told the jury this was fiction presented as fact.

I don't know how the jury thought I was guilty. It simply doesn't make sense. I never thought I'd be back down here. I lie looking at the ceiling, listening to the sounds, wondering how on earth this has happened to me. I'm totally numb.

Even so, in my heart I pray that sense will prevail. I just have to get through the next 12 months. Again. I think of Neil, who is still mourning his father deep down. I think of Mel, who went off the rails with alcohol while I was doing my first sentence. She only told me this when I was released, and so I worked hard to try and rebuild our relationship and give her the love she'd missed from me. I worked so hard to bring my broken family back together over those 18 months I was free. I could weep with frustration and sadness, knowing they'll go back to their respective homes tonight with the knowledge their mother has been convicted of the worst possible crime.

CHAPTER 20

LIFE

My attitude towards my sentence is very different this time.

When I was convicted of armed robbery, I knew I had to face the consequences of my actions. I was pragmatic. I didn't make a fuss. I got on with it, and learned that's the best and easiest way to do time. Not so now. Now I'm beside myself with anger and outrage, frustration and sadness. I've been through a lot in my life – my Mickey's death, Ron's murder, and now a life stretch due to a miscarriage of justice. I know in my heart I'll have to accept this jail term eventually or otherwise be crushed by the system, but for those first few hours and days I can't. Even though I'm moved straight back to D3 the next day and everyone (including the staff) is commiserating with me and welcoming me back, I can't settle. Every second feels longer. The place seems bleaker. As each set of bars shuts behind me, walking through the prison I notice the harshness of the lights, the yellow walls, the colour of tobacco stains, the hideous linoleum, the smallness of my cell, the continual stink of boiled cabbage on every wing, the petty arguments and tussles between the girls. I didn't used to mind being woken up as it meant another day was over, but now the sound of staff banging on cell doors grates. Everything irritates me. I have to shut myself down again so that I don't become a target for bullies. My feelings have to take a deep dive downwards, and they'll have to stay that way for the length of my term. It feels like an impossible task this time.

The only thing I won't dampen down is my anger at the establishment that put me here. This hatred burns in my chest night and day. I know I'll fight tooth and nail to get myself freed, whatever it takes. We all know that prisons aren't full of innocent people; yet I didn't do the crime I'm doing time for. Where's the justice? Where was my evidence?

Back up on D3, I'm taken to my cell.

"We keep it for ya in case you're convicted," one of the screws says. She has the decency to blush as she says it.

"Right," I say, my heart sinking as I look inside the cell I left 24 hours ago to go to court, hoping and praying for the right verdict. I'd given away all my bits in case I got a not guilty: my radio, my shampoo and a jar of Nescafé. All of it lies neatly on my bed, returned to me by the other girls on the wing because they've been told I got a guilty verdict so won't be leaving any time soon. I feel like crying.

I sit down heavily and though I'm touched by the kindness, especially a note written by one of the girls saying, *We're so sorry, Linda*, I can't shake the despondency that comes over me.

As I line up for clean linens, it feels like I've never been in a prison before. The staff all assumed I'd be set free. They're all surprised to see me. The girls on the wing are kind. They come over and chat, saying how shocked they are. I nod and thank them, but I find I can't bear each second that passes inside this concrete, harshly lit jungle.

This time, I notice a lot more, including the bullying.

I think because I was always thinking about my life outside prison during my first sentence, I got on with my own work and didn't really pay attention to what was going on around me. Then, while I was on remand, I was focused on the trial and feeling hopeful I'd go home, so, again, I kept my head down and got on with it. I can't do that this time, because I shouldn't be here. I've suffered a gross miscarriage of justice and now I must wait to right the wrongs from that court room. The blinkers have come off and I start to see more of the chaos around me, and it isn't a pretty sight.

I can see the women who prey on the newly convicted, particularly those who haven't been on remand. They come in "green", which means they have no clue how it works here.

Cigarettes and drugs are the main currencies as there's little money. So, when girls come onto the wing with ciggies given to them on a visit or sent in, you get the tough women circling them. This is what's happening to a new girl called Lucy one mealtime not long after I arrive back. She's in for three months for soliciting, and she has a brand new box of Marlboros. One of the women who looks a bit rough sidles up to her in the canteen when all the bits that people are allowed to buy are handed out.

Please don't do it, I think as I see the woman, who is in for assault and burglary, walk up to Lucy. *Stand your ground from the beginnin'.*

I know what she's going to do. She's going to demand she gives her a ciggie, and that's when all hell breaks loose.

"Give us a fag, go on," the woman says, nicely at first.

Don't do it...

The new girl opens her packet and hands her one, probably thinking it's the right way to make friends. It isn't.

As soon as that one has walked off, then her mate, another butch-looking woman with tattoos everywhere, walks up.

"Give us a fag, then. You gave my mate one," she says.

Lucy frowns but she hands one over.

"Let me have a ciggie," comes another of the same gang.

"And me. Why won't ya give me one? Don't ya like me?"

"What's the matter with me then? Give me a ciggie."

And so it goes on, until the poor girl who is only just starting her sentence finds she has no cigarettes left and she has been intimidated.

From now on that girl is going to have so much trouble. Once someone knows they can bully a girl, they won't stop.

The only way to deal with bullies is to just stand your ground from the off. What Lucy should've said (and what I would say if I smoked) is no, these are mine. I worked for them.

Bullies prey on weakness. From the minute they get that first cigarette, they know they can intimidate her.

It winds me up watching them but there is little I can do to help. Lucy has to find her own way, even though it's going to be hard for her.

* * *

Each day passes somehow. I write to my family. I keep my cell clean. I do what I'm told, but all the time the questions keep beating against my brain. Did someone set me up? Did the police deliberately lose the evidence of the swabs that came back negative, or had they really mislaid it? Did I get convicted because of who I am rather than what they thought I'd done? There are no answers. Not even from my legal team. When I walked out of my first sentence, vowing never to come back, I thought I'd never see the inside of a prison again, yet here I am, and this time I'm in for life.

My legal visits happen every week and Danny is allowed to write to me and my solicitors to work on our case with Ronald Thwaites.

There is a mountain ahead to climb, though. We go through a list of names, everyone who spoke in court, every witness who took the stand, asking those who lied to the court to retract and correct inaccuracies. It's a long shot, but I'm convinced someone somewhere will relent and help me.

Among them is Ron's nephew, a man called Paul Pemberton, who was governor of The Widow's Son pub in Bow. On the stand he swore that I'd been overheard saying "I could kill you" to my boyfriend one night. This in itself was true, yet it was a joke, and one I thought would be perfectly obvious to the jury. When I said it, I remember I was laughing. I didn't laugh when the prosecution used my words in court. I understood that Ron had lent Paul money to buy the pub and wanted it back. In my mind, Paul had a stronger motive to kill his gangster uncle, because that way he wouldn't have to give the money back. This was my understanding of the situation, anyway.

All I need is one person to say I got it wrong and we can then build a case to present before the appeal judges. Peter writes letter after letter for me. Someone will help us, surely?

. . .

Two months after arriving back a convicted murderer, I'm called into the wing office.

"You're goin' to Bullwood Hall," the screw says. "You'll be nearer your family there and they won't 'ave to queue for hours to get into the visitor room for visits with you."

"Oh," I say. I hadn't expected to be moved so quickly.

"You'll stay there until your appeal."

"Alright," I say. One prison is surely much like another, but it's disconcerting to be moved to another prison when I'm only really beginning to settle into my sentence at Holloway. I don't know anything about Bullwood Hall and, again, it's the feeling of having no control over where I'm sent that feels upsetting. From my experience, one prison is much like another unless it's an open prison, so it makes little difference. I'm glad it'll make things easier for my family, and so this becomes a point of hope, making the transition easier for me to swallow. Really, I don't care where they put me. I just want this all to end so I can clear my name and go home.

. . .

HMP Bullwood Hall is a smaller prison than Holloway, and was once a young offender institution. We drive down a tree-lined road towards the sprawling buildings that sit on a large estate. There's razor wire looped along the top of the high metal gates. I'm processed in the same way, with a strip search, a sandwich and a prisoner pack with a heavily starched sheet, a towel, the usual prison-issue scratchy blanket and a pack of toiletries.

I'm shown to my cell, taken along shabby corridors, where the magnolia paint is peeling off the walls and the bright blue linoleum on the floors is scuffed. The brick walls of the single cells are painted dull grey and there are no radiators, just heating pipes running along the walls, which gives the place an old-fashioned feel. It's also the first place I've been to that is "slop out", which means there are no toilets inside the cells.

Walking into my cell and seeing a large potty is a bit of a shock.

"Bloody hell! I exclaim. "It looks very undignified!"

"You'll get used to it," the rather brusque screw says. She hasn't said much on the way over here in the sweat box.

"I don't think I want to get used to it!"

The screw shrugs. "Overnight you can buzz if you need to go to the toilet. We can let one person out at a time to go to the loo. You can then come back and shut yourself in."

"Oh right," I say.

I soon discover this is open to abuse by inmates. That first night I buzz to go out to the toilet as I'm not happy about using a potty like it is Victorian times.

"We can't let you out," one of the night staff says through my hatch. "One of the girls is already out."

It turns out this girl buzzes, then refuses to go back into her cell, so the rest of us are left crossing our legs until they can put her back in.

"Get back in your cell, you bitch!" someone shouts further down the corridor.

"I want to use the proper toilet, get your arse back in your cell!" yells another.

The next morning I'm horrified to discover that we have to carry our potties to the sluice room.

"This is vile!" I say to one of the other inmates.

The stench in that room is unbelievable.

The next shock is breakfast. I'm woken up at 7.30 a.m. by someone rattling the door and opening my cell hatch.

There's no canteen, so we have to eat in the lobby as there are only about 40 inmates on each floor, 20 cells running down each side of the length of the corridor, which is used as the association area too. Compared to Holloway it must be half the size or less. The food is more like school dinners than anything else. There is grey lumpy porridge for breakfast, which I refuse to eat, and mashed potato with a cheap cut of fatty meat and boiled vegetables. There's a smell of cabbage soup that lingers even though it's never on the menu. It's all quite bizarre, but there's little chaos. It's much quieter than Holloway and, again, I find it pretty boring! I'm allowed a radio in my cell but no telly. Just like Holloway, there's time in the evenings in the association area to chat to other inmates, then we are all locked in at 8 p.m. and the lights are turned off.

When the girls go on hunger strike to try and improve prison conditions, I join in. Two days into the strike, the Tannoy announces that those who will not eat will not have their medicine. It soon stops everyone. Everyone except me and about three other women who are not taking anything. When prisoners go on hunger strike, the rule is they have to walk past the food and decline it. When I walk past the lunch, which is liver and bacon, I say no, thank you and walk on though my stomach is growling. Looking around, I realise that everyone else is tucking into theirs while I am starving. *Blow this*, I think. I rejoin the lunch queue and this time walk away with a tray of food. Liver and bacon has never tasted so good.

I spend nine months in total at Bullwood. Every eight weeks I'm allowed to have a meeting with my solicitor, Peter, to discuss my case, and my appeal, the date for which has been given. I'm lucky. Danny and I will go to the Court of Appeal a year after our conviction, which is quite quick, and only because we jumped the queue by leaving court as appellants.

I don't really mix much with the other girls at Bullwood. I'm just waiting for the time to pass to find out if my case can be thrown out and my freedom obtained. I don't become friendly with any of the screws either. I just live for my visits from family and for the next stage of this nightmare, which surely must end soon.

CHAPTER 21

APPEAL

A few days before my appeal date in November 1992, I'm sent back to Holloway Prison because they can't drive me to and from the appeal court and Bullwood Hall each day, it's too far.

If I'm honest, I'm happy to be back in London and I'm filled with anticipation and hope for the outcome. They can't keep me. There was no evidence to convict me on. It was all hearsay and conjecture, and I'm convinced the judges will see the truth and set me free.

Little has changed at the women's prison. I've only been back on the wing for ten minutes when an argument breaks out between a Jamaican girl and a mixed-race inmate. I don't hear the beginning of the row, but they're squared up to each other in the corridor as we make our way to work or education.

"Shut the fuck up, n****r!" the mixed-race woman says.

"Oh look, 'ere comes trouble," the woman standing next to me says, nudging my elbow. There is a growing feeling of excitement as the tension mounts. Locked-up women are angry and frustrated. Many of them proclaim their innocence, many are traumatised or withdrawing from hard drugs, so it's a tinderbox ready to explode at any moment. It's clear it's about to.

Women stop walking and begin to loiter around the assailants, choosing their side and making gestures or shouting insults from the sidelines. It's like two boxers squaring up in the ring.

"What the fuck did ya call me?" the black girl spits.

"You heard me, n****r..."

Someone whistles a long slow note. Someone else says, "Fuck me, did you 'ear that?"

We're all waiting for the inevitable fight.

"At least I'm not a no-nation bastard like you!" the black woman says. Her friends behind her are cat-calling and staring out the other woman. "You ain't a black so you don't belong to us. You ain't a white and you don't belong to them neither. You don't belong anywhere."

Before the mixed-race woman can answer, several screws run from all directions to stop it progressing into a fistfight.

As I continue on my way once the crowd has been broken up and everyone sent where they're meant to be going, I realise I've never heard anything like that statement. What a strange thing to say, and how bleak it must be to hear that. I can't imagine not belonging. More and more I realise there's a huge difference between my world and that of so many others. I belong with my family, wherever they might be, but our hearts and my roots are always in the East End of London. I class myself as an East Ender. That's where I grew up. That's where I lived with Mickey and my children. I know where I'm from and who I am. I'm a cockney through and through, so the thought of not belonging is very strange. In some ways this incident reminds me I have so much to live for and aim towards. It lifts my heart, which is odd considering it wasn't a pleasant thing to see and hear.

The night before my appeal begins, I give away all my possessions again: my slippers and shoes, my prized radio (my only real possession inside), and my toiletries to girls who have run out. I give my radio to a girl who's just come in and has absolutely nothing. She is a very sad case and I feel sorry for her the moment I hear her story, though I hear it from another inmate. Her father is a drug addict, her mother a prostitute and addict as well. Macy was pimped out by her dad and also became hooked. It must be one of the most tragic stories I have heard since stepping inside this rathole of a prison, apart from that of beautiful Maria who died at King's Cross Station, most likely knowing she'd never get her kids back because of her drug habit. Macy's child is in care and she looks ravaged by drugs. Her clothes are tatty and dirty, her teeth are already bad even though she is young, perhaps 25 years old, and her hair is lank. The same, repeating story for so many young women.

Danny and I have been able to write to each other in order to prepare for the appeal. He's urged me time and time again to tell the court what really happened that fateful November day back in 1990. I still won't consider it though. Rather I do the time and fight for my release than do anything that'll shame me and my family. Really, if Danny wanted to be sure I wouldn't be convicted, perhaps he should've pleaded guilty himself, but even then, who's to say I wouldn't have been convicted?

Anyway, my legal counsel say it's too late to offer an alternative version of events. Peter says it would look like Danny and I are lying to get me freed, which is frustrating, but I can see why the judges would think that.

During this time Danny and I become close. We write to each other every week and I count him as a good friend, even though his friendship has brought me a long jail sentence.

* * *

The day of my appeal dawns.

I feel excited. My family will all be there and, if all goes well, I'll be going home with them tonight. They've handed an outfit into reception for me to wear at the hearing. Last night one of the girls blow-dried my hair as there is something new in Holloway – a hairdresser's! This causes a great deal of excitement in the prison, and I was taken down and given a treatment to make sure I look good for my day in court.

My stomach is churning as the two screws who are accompanying me – the plain-faced one from reception whose name is Pauline and a kind-faced lady with a ready smile – attach my handcuffs. The metal feels cold against my skin but, today, I'm undaunted.

"Good luck, Lin!" shouts an inmate who is cleaning the reception area.

"Good luck, Linda, hopefully we won't see you again," says another screw who is doing paperwork at the reception desk and smiling.

"Thank you, I don't mean to be rude but I hope so too," I reply.

My heart is beating wildly as we move off and out of the prison gates. Soon we draw into the back of the Royal Courts of Justice and I step out into the London air. I breathe it in. This is my home city. This is where I belong. Perhaps now I'll be a free woman again.

I'm cuffed to Pauline as we walk into the court precincts. I'm taken to a cell where Ronald Thwaites and Peter Hughman are waiting for me.

"Hello Linda, take a seat. We both feel this has been the most unfair trial we've ever been involved in," Ronald says, peering over his half-rim glasses.

"You should be going home today, and we know you shouldn't have been convicted in the first place, but ultimately, it's up to the judges and the evidence we put in front of them," Peter adds.

"But it must count for somethin' that the judge referred us straight to the appeals court?" I say.

"We'll find out," Peter replies. They leave and I'm left twiddling my thumbs, staring at yet another blank wall.

"'Ave a look at that while you're waitin'," says Pauline, handing me her copy of the *Daily Mail*. I start to flick through, wondering how long I'll have to wait.

"Thank you, darlin'," I reply, though I'm too nervous to read.

"We're sure we're goin' back without ya today," she adds, smiling.

. . .

It doesn't take long for my case to be called. An hour or so later, I find myself stepping into the dock with my two screws. Next to me is Danny, with his two screws, and we share a smile briefly.

I look around. My family is there in the viewing gallery: Mum, my sisters and brother Terry. They're all looking nervous. There are three judges sitting on the bench, who listen as my legal counsel go through my case, highlighting the obvious flaws and saying there's been a miscarriage of justice. It seems things are going well, and it seems that way to my family too as they smile over at us.

At the end of the day, after hearing all the evidence, the judges say there are certain aspects of concern. My heart leaps. Could this be the moment I'm freed? I exchange a glance with Shelley who shows me her crossed fingers, but then the judges continue.

"As there is no new evidence put in front of the bench to overturn the conviction, we have no alternative but to deny the appeal."

Deny the appeal? Are they joking?

There is a shocked gasp from the court.

Terry, my sisters, Melanie and Neil all turn their faces to me. I shake my head, not knowing what's happened. Everyone thought I was going home, and this is like a second punch in the face. The judge has passed us straight here. He knew we'd been wrongly convicted. How can this be happening?

In some ways this is more devastating than getting sentenced in the first place. This time I'd worked so hard with my lawyers, and believed that the mistakes and "oversights" would be reviewed and the decision overturned. I really thought I had a chance.

Emotions collide inside me. I feel like I'm going to retch, or faint, or scream. The hopes and excitement come crashing down and it's truly devastating. Why did the judge at my trial bother to send us to appeal, if this is what we needed to win it? Why have we wasted all this time hoping I might go free, when in reality it could never be? Without new evidence, my case is sunk. We should never have tried.

"Oh my God, Linda, we really thought we were going back without you today," Pauline says as I stumble out of the dock, shocked to my core, wondering what went so wrong. I'm trembling and I can't speak to reply to her. Danny bows his head as he's led away, and I know he'll be feeling devastated for me as well as for himself. I shake my head, my thoughts too jumbled, my head too full of shock and anger to process anything that's happening right now.

Both Peter and Ronald are beside themselves. We barely get a moment to speak back in the downstairs cell before we're told the court is closing and we have to go outside.

"We'll speak soon, Linda, once we've had a chance to reflect and talk things through."

"Alright. Thank you both," I say, though I'm bitterly disappointed.

"Linda, we've missed the prison transport so we've had to phone up and ask for a van to come and get us," Pauline says, looking at me awkwardly. I don't think anyone knows what to say to me, I'm still so shocked.

"Oh right," I say, barely able to take anything in.

In seconds I find myself standing out the front of the court on the pavement as the court is closed. People come and go, tourists and lawyers, young people clutching coffee cups as they leave work and head for the Tube. It's surreal being out in the normal world, yet still being so far removed from it.

"I'm not lettin' her stand on the street with handcuffs for people to gawp at," the kindly screw says to the other screw. "We know you're not going to run."

In a move that astonishes me, she unlocks the cuffs and takes them off my wrists. I look like a normal person now, except I'm standing with two prison guards. It takes half an hour for the sweat box to arrive, but it feels longer. I watch people go past, not giving us a second look. *I should be walkin' about doing the same, and not goin' back to prison,* I think. Even though I'm not cuffed, I still feel intense humiliation being outside and part of a world I'm shunned by.

The van arrives and I'm almost relieved to step into it. Once inside I'm cuffed again to Pauline and we head back to Holloway. I don't think I've ever felt as despondent as I do when the gates slide open and we are, once again, back inside the prison.

"Oh my God, you're back!"

"What are you doin' 'ere? We thought you was goin' home!"

"I'm so sorry, Lin…"

Everyone is very nice to me but it can't soften the blow. When my cell door is opened (they kept my cell for me until they knew the outcome), all my things are back on my bed again: my slippers, my shoes, clothes, toiletries and even my radio. I've missed dinner, so I'm brought a sandwich from the kitchen, which I can't swallow I'm so upset.

* * *

The next morning I'm unlocked early to help with breakfast, just as before. I'm wearing my white overalls, just as before. I switch on the hot plate and the tea urn, just as before. I'm hugged so many times that morning, but my head is just not there. My head has flown off with my family, back to Chigwell where they're all based now.

When I go out into the communal areas, even the rougher inmates are sympathetic to my situation.

"Babe, you shouldn't be 'ere, what bastards they are," says a heavily tattooed woman with a shaved head.

"It's not right," says another, a large black woman with hair cut in a sharp bob.

"Thank you darlin'," I say but all I can think is: *Where do I go from here?*

My solicitor has booked a visit for later in the day, and so I try and get through as best I can until then.

"I'll be honest with you, Linda. I don't know where we go from here. Unless new evidence comes to light, or someone from the police offers an alternative version of the missing swab test results," Peter says, "there's little hope."

I could weep at those words.

"For God's sake, I've got another five years to get through..." I wail. "I've got to live every day in 'ere hopin' that somethin' will come up that will set me free?"

"Basically, yes, Linda." I know there's nothing Peter can say that will make me feel better.

Alone in my cell that night, I feel thoroughly despondent. Is this ever going to end? Am I ever going to prove my innocence? Usually, I don't allow myself to dwell on things, especially questions such as these with no answers. Tonight, I can't help but sink a little further into despair, knowing that tomorrow I'll have to pull myself out again. You have to live each day with good grace. I have to make myself cheerful again and do my best to get through. What other option is there? In terms of bad situations, this doesn't get much worse. Banged up. The years stretching ahead of me.

．　．　．

Two weeks later, I'm called to the governor's office. The governor, who has replaced Mr Brown, looks shifty. I soon find out why.

"I'm sorry to have to tell you, Linda, but I've had a memo from the Home Office. They've said there was a mistake in your sentencing and you should've been made a Category A prisoner from the start of your sentence."

I look back at him.

"What d'you mean?"

"Linda, you know what a Cat A is? It's the highest security category for an inmate. It means your charge is extremely serious and you represent a danger to the public."

"But I don't!" I say, stung into defending myself. "I'm no danger, you know that."

"It doesn't matter what I think, Linda. They've instructed us that you're now to be classified as a Travelling Category A prisoner. This is not something we've ever had to deal with before. What it means is that as soon as you leave the grounds here, on a visit or a transfer, we'll have to move you immediately to Durham, which is the only other Cat A place for women."

I've heard about Durham. It is notorious as a men's prison for only the worst and most hardened criminals. Then I remember what someone told me about it there. The prison has a small section for women, housing the child molesters, paedophiles and killers.

"Oh my God, I'll be in with all the nonces! This is so unfair! It's disgustin'! How will my family come and visit me if I'm all the way up north? It's so far away for them."

"Because you've been in prison for more than two years now, and been well-behaved, there's no new justification for making you Cat A – and so they've made a category for you, the Travelling Cat A. The moment you go outside these prison gates you become a Cat A and you can only go to a Cat A prison. You'll have to go to Durham. I'm sorry but rules are rules and there's nothing I can do about them."

"You can't do that to me, I should be in Bullwood Hall so my family can visit!"

The governor shakes his head.

"There's nothing I can do about it. You're being sent to Durham H Wing."

Somehow, things are getting worse and worse for me.

I don't understand why. I've never been on report. I haven't caused any problems. I've always worked. Basically, to my mind, I haven't done anything to justify making me a Cat A. The staff, who all seem as shocked as I am by this latest ruling, let me have couple of extra visits before I leave. My brother Terry comes in and, later, makes contact with my solicitor, asking what can be done. It's always the same answer. Rules are rules. Nothing can be done. We have no control over prison procedure. The girls rally round, arguing with staff, saying I shouldn't go up there, saying it's not right, and they agree, but it's the decision by the Home Office, and what they say goes.

Months later, with a heavy heart, I pack up my stuff. I realise that Holloway, with all its madness, its chaos, its cockroaches and rats, has been something like a home to me, and I'm desperately sad to say goodbye.

CHAPTER 22

H(ELL) WING

The day I'm due to leave arrives three months after my failed appeal. I'm heading up north to begin the next stage of my sentence.

Three staff have driven down from Durham to pick me up and take me hundreds of miles away. I'm being driven in a prison van but it is not the normal sweat box. It's a metal box with no windows, and I'm double-handcuffed. One set of cuffs is attached to both my hands, the other is attached to one of my hands and one of the screws. As we drive, one of the officers speaks into a walkie-talkie, giving our position in terms of police districts every few minutes. The whole thing feels like a strange dream, but of course it isn't, and this is how it's going to be for me from now on. I'm a high-security prisoner, and this is the way a Cat A inmate is transported.

My God, what's happenin'?, I keep thinking as we drive, halfway between tears and laughter at the ridiculous manner in which I'm being treated. *I'm no danger to anyone, why are they doin' this?*

Somewhere on the motorway, I realise I really need to pee. We haven't stopped, but I'm becoming desperate, so I plead with the screws to let me get out somewhere and go to the toilet.

At first they say no, as there isn't another high-security women's prison we can stop at.

I have to beg them before they make some calls. Eventually it's decided that we're allowed to stop at a Cat A male prison on the way, so we make a detour. I have no idea where I'm going, but we draw up at the gates of another prison and we're taken to the punishment block.

"We have a problem," the screw I'm cuffed to says. "This is a male prison, so we can't take you to reception. The only place we can go is where the men are in solitary 24 hours a day and can't leave their cells."

"Oh right," I say, totally bemused at all this fuss over me wanting to go for a wee.

I'm escorted out, still cuffed, and I'm taken to the toilet. Afterwards, I'm walked to a cell, as it is now lunchtime and they're sending me a sandwich from the kitchens. Outside the cells is a sign saying *No Graffiti in Cells – anyone drawing on the walls will not be allowed back until it is cleaned.*

Despite this, I notice a piece of graffiti on the cell wall. It is a cartoon drawing of a face peering over a brick wall with the words *Charlie Bronson was here* written underneath it. I have to laugh. I can't believe I am sitting in Charlie Bronson's cell! I turn to the screw and say: "Oh I see you didn't make my Charlie clean the wall then."

Without glancing in my direction, talking as if I'm not there, the screw says: "If she's a friend of Charlie, no wonder she's a Cat A..."

Being a prisoner can feel like being invisible. We're shunned by society. We're treated as less than human by some prison staff, and often screws talk about us as if we're not there. I laugh, though, as it's good to see a familiar face, even if it is a cartoon version. I've known Charlie by association for many years. Both Danny Reece and Brian Thorogood knew Charlie, so he knows of me too, as they've all been inside at the same time in various prisons.

When the time comes to leave, my spirits are lifted slightly, but as every mile takes us closer and closer to Durham – and further away from my family – I become distraught.

This isn't right, it's so unfair, my family are all in Essex, and it'll take them hours to drive up to visit me. *Why can't I go back to Bullwood? Are they doin' this to punish me?*

My thoughts churn over and over, and I could weep when we finally see the sign for HMP Durham. The sky is overcast. It's a freezing cold, blustery February day, and the clouds hang grey and heavy over our heads as we step out. I shiver, but I can't pull my coat round me as my hands are cuffed.

"This way," one of the screws says, and we walk to the reception, which is as bleak a place as any I've been to, with harsh lighting, cigarette butts everywhere and unsmiling staff. As this is a men's Category A prison, meaning it is the highest level of security, the women's part is deep inside the grounds. Unlike Holloway, which is built like a hospital, Durham is a foreboding, austere-looking Georgian-era jail. Here are housed some of Britain's most dangerous and volatile inmates, all serving sentences. I'm surprised, therefore, to be greeted in a friendly way by the staff once I'm processed and taken through locked doors, security cameras recording every movement, the clanging sound of barred doors closing behind me down long, bare corridors. The stop-start motion I'm now so familiar with is even more disrupted here. Each set of iron-barred doors is opened and locked again behind us. Each corridor has security cameras trained down on us, and there seem to be more guards here than I've seen anywhere else, almost as many as the inmates. At every turn the lights are harsh, the walls are painted sickly yellow and blue, while the floors reflect the bleached white lighting. H Wing is an old part of the prison. There is no reception area for women, so I am taken straight there. It is late afternoon by the time I'm left standing in a small room, clutching hold of my pillowcase containing my few things, wondering where on earth I've landed.

. . .

Durham H Wing is unlike any other prison I've ever been in. It had been condemned as a men's prison, then it was turned into a facility to house women who can't mix with the rest of the prison population: paedophiles, child killers, bombers, murderers, as well as helping to reintroduce male Cat A prisoners to more traditional rules in the main prison.

"Hello Linda, how are you?" a plump screw with hair scraped back off her face says, not unkindly.

"To be honest, I'm not 'appy. I don't want to be 'ere," I reply.

"We guessed that when we found out you came from the East End," she says, nodding. "It's a long way away from Holloway."

"It's not a problem for me," I say. "It's for my family. They'll 'ave to travel a long way to come and visit, and I don't like thinkin' of them 'avin' to do that."

"I understand, Linda. You know you can save up your visits then go back down to London and have them all in one go. They'll let you take a month's worth of visits over a week or so at Holloway. Why don't you suggest that to them?" The screw points towards a cubicle before I have a chance to finish.

I sigh. Time for yet another strip search, which I submit to with as much grace as I can muster. I'm tired, and pretty upset, but I don't want to start on the wrong foot, however much I don't want to be here.

The L-shaped wing is three floors high. I look up and see netting strung across each level. It's the first time I've been in a prison with this. It's designed to stop people committing suicide or throwing someone over.

"That's the governor Mr Smith's office to the left. Next to that is the principal officer, Mr Atkinson. Next to them is the senior officer. If you have a problem, go to senior. If they can't resolve it, go to the principal. If he can't resolve it, go to Governor Smith, but do it in that order.

"You're not locked in by day, only between 8 p.m. and 8 a.m. You'll find it very easy-going here, you can even cook your own food."

This is very different to HMP Durham's reputation as a tough, uncaring place housing only the most violent prisoners.

As we walk, two women nod at me. They're both young, probably in their twenties, and look attractive. I nod back wondering what they're in for. They don't look like nonces, but then again, everyone said I didn't look like an armed robber so I've learned you can't judge a book by its cover. Still, the whole experience so far has been far from deserving of its nickname "Hell Wing".

"Walk around, and see which cell you'd like," the screw, whose name is Alison, says.

"Aren't you goin' to tell me which one's mine?" I say.

"You're only the 15th inmate on this wing, and we're built to take 40 women, so you have a choice," Alison says. "Some of the rooms overlook the cathedral and some the yard, while others look onto the street. Take your pick... any that haven't got a card on the door are empty. A cell is a cell, but there are different views."

"Thank you, I'll 'ave one that looks onto the outside world. I want to be reassured that the world is still carryin' on as normal."

It feels really odd to be inside a prison that isn't overcrowded. I'm so used to women being crammed in dorm cells, or queuing for linens or a shower, that the empty feel here is quite daunting. The actual cells are all the same: tiny with a small single bed, a table and chair and a pinboard. I step inside my cramped new home and realise there is a door to the side. I open it and almost shout with surprise. It is a toilet and a sink! *A cell with an ensuite, things are lookin' up at last,* I think. Later the same screw tells me that when the prison was given its refurbishment, they knocked out every second cell and put in a private toilet and door. To have privacy after all this time makes me feel strangely emotional.

"It's better than Holloway, for sure, but I won't be 'ere long," I say to Alison after choosing where I'm going to sleep. I'm goin' to speak to the governor and tell him I 'ave to be moved back down to London because I'm too far from my family."

This raises a few eyebrows. There's another officer in the wing office who glances over at Alison.

"Linda, I would get unpacked. I don't think you'll get moved any time soon," the woman says.

"I won't unpack, I'll be goin' back. When I explain, it'll all be OK," I say, resolutely.

* * *

The next morning the knock on my door wakes me up.

"Morning, Linda," a different screw says. "If you go downstairs, you can get your breakfast."

"OK, thank you," I say, feeling more than a little nervous. I have no idea who I'm about to meet, or what their crimes were. I get dressed into joggers and a sweater and make my way across the corridor and down the stairs. A few other women are about, but not many.

Down on the ground floor, there are little tables on landings where people are already sitting. It's obvious to me that each person or clique has their table and I should be careful not to sit in someone's place. This is important in prison. You don't know who you might offend just by taking their chair or sitting where you shouldn't. It sounds ridiculous but prison can make people really territorial. People say, "That's my seat", "That's my table" and say to their friends, "We'll sit 'ere". It's the one thing girls can actually choose. Everybody on a wing knows where everyone's seats are, and no one presumes to sit in someone's chair. It isn't the done thing.

Durham feels very different to the other prisons. Already I can see that women have placed tablecloths on tables to mark out their space where they'll eat breakfast. Having a tablecloth has been unheard of so far. I can also see china plates and real crockery on the tables, meaning prisoners don't have to eat off prison plastic.

I wait for a while as women with bowls of porridge or plates of toast sit down together or at separate tables. There is one empty table left and so I help myself to some toast with a scraping of margarine and sit down. Once I've eaten I head back up to my cell, figuring this is the safest place to wait for my next instructions. It doesn't take long for the screw to come and find me.

"Mr Smith will see you now in his office."

"Thank you," I say, steeling myself for an argument. I'm determined to buck the system and get myself sent back.

After knocking, a voice says, "Enter".

Inside, sitting at a large wooden desk is a handsome blond-haired man in his forties.

"I've been waiting to see you," he says.

"I don't want to be 'ere, this isn't fair on my family," I begin, thinking I'll have to fight hard for my wishes. He seems to ignore me completely, which throws me off my tracks.

"Would you like a coffee? The percolator is on..." He smiles and gestures towards the bubbling coffee machine.

My heart leaps. Real coffee! It has been a long time since I've drunk filtered coffee.

"Yes please, I'd like that," I say.

The wing governor makes two cups of coffee and puts them both on the desk. He then gestures for me to sit, and he does the same, his elbows on the desk, smiling at me. This isn't what I expected at all!

I'm still going on about how angry I am and how unfair the system is, and he just watches me, the smile never leaving his face, letting me say what I want to say.

"It doesn't matter to me which prison I'm in – a prison is a prison – but it matters to my family..."

Eventually I stop and breathe.

"Linda, I'm not going lie to you, and pretend to get onto the Home Office," Mr Smith says. "They've made their decision and I can tell you now, they won't change it. This is where you're going to be for the fore-seeable future."

"But I didn't do it and I shouldn't be 'ere."

Mr Smith takes a sip of his coffee. I can feel my heart beating. Am I in trouble for speaking out?

"Look, I could send an email to the Home Office, but it's pointless. The reply will be that you have been allocated here in Durham for the next part of your sentence, which might be long time. You're going to have to reconcile yourself to being here. I'm sorry, Linda."

I can feel tears welling up in my eyes.

"This is disgustin'. I don't even want to be here with all these nonces, all these child killers and perverts."

Mr Smith puts down his cup. His expression changes to a frown.

"Not everyone on the wing is a 'nonce', as you put it. Ella and Martina aren't..."

"No, maybe not, but I believe the rest are," I say, feeling like I'm pushing my luck. I wonder if the women who nodded to me when I arrived might be Ella and Martina.

"Can I give you piece of advice, Linda?" Mr Smith sits forward again.

"OK," I say, begrudgingly.

"If I could let you go back to Holloway I would, but that's not going to happen. There are only 15 of you here on this wing, a very small number of people. When you meet each one, I strongly advise you to take them on face value. Don't think of their crimes. Instead, think of them as someone you've just met, and who you don't know anything about.

"If you start thinking what they're in prison for, it'll drive you insane. One thing I will say is that we are forward-thinking here.

We try our best to make life easy for you women. Both myself and Mr Atkinson are progressive and believe the sentence you got is your punishment, so there's no need for us to make it harder. Look, all the women here objected to you coming because they didn't want a gangster and armed robber on the wing, so it works both ways. I've said the same to them."

"But I don't want anythin' to do with killers or child molesters," I say, still horrified at the thought of living among women who've committed these crimes. I can see what he's saying though, and how the other girls would object to me, thinking I'm a killer.

"Well, you won't have anyone to talk to, then."

"Oh right," I say, trying to take it all in. I sip my coffee and the bitter flavour calms me down. I can see this wing governor is a bit different and I want to hear what he has to say.

"We allow as many clothes as you want, as many pairs of shoes as well. You can have your own bedding, your own curtains and other knick-knacks. We want you to live as comfortably as you can while you're here. It might surprise you to know that we also allow you your own cutlery, but I suggest you get it engraved so you know which is yours."

By now I'm listening intently.

"D'you mean I'm allowed to 'ave my own china plate, bowl and cups as well?" I say, incredulously. "I saw girls with their own stuff at breakfast but I thought it was a privilege or somethin'."

"Yes, that's exactly what I mean. You can ask your family to send you nice things. I won't make life any harder for you here than it has to be, and I ask the same of you. Accept the fact you're here and don't make any enemies. Try and make the best of it, Linda."

I nod, feeling a little lost for words.

"OK, let the staff show you around now. During your time here, you'll never go off this wing because it's a male prison. The only exception is when you need to see a dentist, which is over on the male side.

I can let you have anything you want, but I can't let you go where you want to go. Are we clear?"

Mr Smith smiles over his desk at me. I finish my coffee and smile back.

"Crystal," I say.

CHAPTER 23

REGGIE

One of the staff, a rather beefy looking screw with long dark hair pulled back in a pony tail, shows me around H Wing.

"You're allowed to buy food, so give the staff shopping lists and they'll go to Sainsbury's and get your shopping. All the meals are cooked on the men's side, so don't have rice, don't have custard, definitely don't have mashed potato..."

"But why?" I ask.

"Work it out yourself..." she replies, grimacing.

"Oh my God," I say, choking. Nothing else needs to be said.

There is not much to see as the wing is small. The visiting room is tiny compared to Holloway, with four or five little tables and chairs, and has curtains.

"You can bake your own cakes and biscuits to give to visitors," the screw, who is called Shannon, says. "You can bring your own nice tea and coffee, make sandwiches. It can be quite homely here."

"I won't 'ave any visits 'ere," I say. "I'm goin' to save them all up and when I've got 15 or so, I'll go back to Holloway and 'ave them there."

"OK, you can do that." The screw shrugs.

She opens a door to reveal the exercise yard, which is shared with the male Rule 43s, which are the vulnerable prisoners (VPs), who could be grasses or have challenging circumstances. They're segregated because of the risk of attack if kept with "straight" inmates in the men's wing exercise yard. I look out and see the concrete space has been left in a pretty appalling state. There are cigarette butts everywhere and litter, along with lots of spit and some suspicious-looking residues on the benches.

I shudder.

"Let's move on," Shannon says, that same grimace on her face.

"Here are the baths and showers. Here is the gym where you can do step aerobics. And here is the workshop where you can do pottery classes and soft furnishings. The things produced are sold. That's where you'll be working, Linda."

I brighten up a bit at this.

Later, at lunch, the two women who I'd seen when I arrived beckon me over to their table.

"I'm Ella," says the blonde-haired woman.

"And I'm Martina," says the other, both very attractive young women with strong southern Irish accents.

"I'm Linda..." I begin to say.

"Oh, we know who y'are." Martina smiles. "But d'you know us?"

"I don't," I say.

"We're political prisoners. We're fighting against the oppression of the British Empire. We came here from Brixton and we've fought very hard to make this place endurable. Did you know there used to be slop out and we were locked in 23 hours a day?"

"I didn't know that," I say.

"Do you exercise?" Ella says, she pushes her plate away.

"I don't. Is that what you're into?"

"Sure we are, come and train with us. We're allowed an hour in the yard, so we go for a run. Keeps us sane." Martina smiles again.

"I'd like that. I've always wanted to get fit," I say.

We make a plan to meet at the yard. I watch them walk off, both chatty and very confident. Later one of the screws I don't recognise sidles up to me.

"Your new friends, did ya want to know who they are?"

"I suppose so," I shrug, wondering what agenda this guard might have.

"They're members of the Irish Republican Army..."

"The IRA?" Now I'm listening.

"Yep. And they were somethin' to do with the Brighton Bombing. Both given life for planning attacks there and in London. They were only young. I think Ella was 26 years old, and Martina just 23."

"Blimey," is all I can say.

"Yeah, so watch out for them..." The screw walks away, whistling.

I don't judge anyone. I don't know much about the IRA but I do know that there are many sides to an argument. Obviously I don't believe in bombing innocent people, but I also have enough understanding to know that in their own minds they're fighting for a cause. I can see the staff and other inmates are wary of them, but it doesn't intimidate me.

Live and let live is my new motto, and one I've been told to live my life in Durham with, so that is what I will do. Even so I hear some disturbing things about some of the inmates. Myra is not the only child killer in the UK, though if you look at the headlines in the newspapers for the past 20 years, you would think she was. There are women who have killed their own children who are occupying cells inside this wing. They can't be talked about or named in the press because the cases concern their own children. It's sickening being here, but I know I have to get by somehow and try to put this knowledge to the back of my brain or I won't survive.

. . .

One week after being transferred to Durham, I'm woken up by a screw saying: "Linda, you've got a letter."

An envelope is pushed through my door as the cells are open all day.

"Thank you, darlin'," I say, jumping out of bed and grabbing it. Getting post is a highlight of the day, despite the fact it will have already been opened and read. Living under surveillance is a strange thing. We're always watched. Our letters are read. Cameras record every movement. Everywhere there are eyes looking at us. I suppose I must've become used to it by now as I hardly notice the fact the envelope is open. It is stamped with HMP Maidstone and I wonder who's writing to me from there.

I fold out the letter. The handwriting is scrawny and hard to read.

"Reggie Kray, I can't believe you've written me a letter! After all this time..."

I first met Reggie back when I was 19 years old and taken out on the town by my cousin Pat and her partner George. They took me to a plush club in the East End, one of the Krays' haunts. Everyone turned to stare as Reggie made his way across the crowded dance floor to greet us. He would have stood out anywhere. Wearing an immaculate tailored navy suit, with dark hair Brylcreemed back off his face in the popular style and a cigarette between his lips, he looked suave – and immensely dangerous. I was drawn to him immediately.

He shook George's hand and with a smooth smile said: "Who's this young lady then?" To my delight, he was looking at me.

"Reg, this is my cousin Linda," Pat said. "Linda, say hello to Reggie Kray."

Well, I could've died on the spot.

We locked eyes and I smiled.

"Hello Reggie, I'm glad to meet you," I replied.

He looked me up and down, smiled broadly and took hold of my hand. Kissing it, he turned to Pat and said: "She looks very refreshing, does your Linda."

I blushed at that, knowing I was surrounded by sophisticated women dripping in diamonds and wearing heavy make-up. I was a teenager, with my one good dress from Roman Road Market, and up to that point I'd lived quite a sheltered life.

Of course, I knew about the Krays. I grew up only streets away from them and their names were bywords for power, influence and violence in the East End. I have to say they've always been courteous and charming to me, so I never saw any of that side of things.

Looking down at the scratchy writing, I wonder how Reg knows I'm here, but then I remember that my brother Tony and friend Billy Blundell are now serving time together at Maidstone, so they must've spoken about me there.

Dear Linda,

I was so sorry to hear what happened to you. It may seem like you'll never get out but you will. Just be brave.

I'd like to ask if I can call you?

Reg

It is not a long letter by any means, but I'm thrilled to receive it. I write back immediately, saying he can call me, and hand it into the office for the screws to read. Both of them stare after me when I walk out, which makes me chuckle. It seems even now the name Reggie Kray is one that leaves people fascinated and repelled.

A week later, I receive his call. Phone calls are a new part of prison life. I've done all my communication so far via letters or visits. Here we're allowed two 15-minute calls a week as there's a telephone on the wing.

"'Allo, Reg Kray 'ere." His voice is so familiar, softly spoken with a real cockney accent.

"Hello, it's Linda Calvey 'ere," I reply. There's a moment's silence before Reg bursts out laughing.

"There ain't many people who do that, who'll answer me with their full name," he says. "How are ya copin'?"

"It's alright, 'ere, Reg. Not as bad as its reputation, but I think that's because they've made lots of changes. It used to be terrible," I reply.

"I've been in Durham. We may 'ave been in the same cell, just think of that!"

I giggle at that.

"I lost my appeal, so I'm stuck 'ere," I say.

"I know, Linda. I'm sorry to 'ear that. Listen, we don't 'ave much time, but can I call ya regular?"

"Of course you can, Reg. That'd be nice," I reply. There is something reassuring about his voice and manner, a taste of home perhaps. I've never been frightened of the Kray twins. They have an incredibly violent reputation but they have only ever been gentlemen to women. We finish the call and already Reg feels more like an old friend than a familiar name in the underworld.

A few days later I'm peering out of my cell window when I see a screw carrying a large basket of creamy white roses with long stems.

"I wonder who those are for?' I shout out to Ella and Martina.

Minutes later the screw is standing at my cell door with the flowers.

"These are for you, Linda."

"Oh my God!" I cry, amazed to see such a beautiful display.

The card tucked inside them simply says: *To Linda Calvey from Reggie Kray.*

Ella and Martina look at me.

"Looks like someone's got a soft spot for ye," Martina says, nudging Ella, and they both giggle.

CHAPTER 24

IRA

Danny walks into the small room used for legal visits. He's been brought from Whitemoor Prison to spend a week at Durham so we can work on our case. I think both of us know we're clutching at straws, but we spend hours poring over lists of those we'll write to, asking them to speak up for us or shed new light on our case.

"I can't see who's going to turn around and say 'We lied in court.' I'm sorry, but I don't want you having false hope, either of you," Peter says, looking at the list of names we've produced.

I've been at Durham for six months now, and this is the second time they've let Danny come for a legal visit. We've hit dead end after dead end. Every letter our solicitors write for us is either ignored or we get a dispiriting reply saying nothing. I don't think either of us wants to give up – and yet we haven't really moved on at all.

Peter sits back in the chair. His coffee is cold and we've spent all morning going around in circles, trying to think of new names, other contacts we could approach.

"You're going to have to accept that, until something changes, there's nothing more we can do at the moment. You should know as well that they won't let you carry on having legal visits together for ever."

"What d'you mean?" I say. "Why can't Danny keep visitin'?"

"I don't think there are any hard-and-fast rules, but as there's no new appeal or evidence to work towards, I can't see they'll let you continue indefinitely."

Danny looks over at me. He's wearing a grey sweatshirt and sweatpants, and he runs his hand over his head. I know he's doing this for me, to try and make up for the sentence I'm serving because of what he did.

"I see," I say, as the meeting comes to an end, and I wonder if this means my fight for justice is over.

. . .

By now, I'm working in the prison pottery, making cups, jugs, vases and teapots to sell in the gift shop. Time moves on, and I have a lot to think about, but one day, as I'm hand-glazing a cup, one of the girls, Mary, a murderess who killed her own children, sidles up to me.

"I've got some news, Linda. Three guesses who's joining us on H Wing."

"I don't know. Why don't ya just tell me, I can see you're dyin' to," I reply, turning the cup around to check for smudges. Mary is one of the girls I can't bear to be around. It was one of the screws who told me what she did, killed her own son and daughter for no reason, and has since shown no remorse, and I wish I didn't know. She's creepy and I usually stay away from her.

"Oh Linda, you're ruining it... Oh go on then, I'll tell you. It's Myra Hindley. Can you believe it?"

I put my cup down and stare back at Mary.

"I know Myra from Cookham Wood. I've got no problem which prison she's held in. Now, if you've got nothin' else to say, then I need to finish this as they're being fired this evenin'."

I look down at my cup. On one side is the H Wing symbol – a dove breaking free of its ball and chains. *How ironic*, I think, and now Myra's joining us. Well, I'll be steering clear of her as much as I can.

. . .

Nine months after I'm sent to Durham, Myra arrives from Cookham Wood. She's now very ill with osteoporosis and other health conditions and looks terrible. The first day I see her in the yard, she looks sickly yellow and is unable to walk very far. She sits at the far end of the yard on her own with a screw nearby, smoking one cigarette after another. She nods to me, and I do the same back but I don't go over. I don't want to be known as someone who might be friends with Myra Hindley.

"Bloody hell, what's she doin' 'ere?" says one of the girls.

"She's been moved up 'ere but I don't know why. Prison policy I guess," I reply, not paying much attention.

"Fuckin' cunts!" A male voice roars from a cell window beside the yard, making us all jump.

"Show us yer tits!" comes another.

"You dirty bitches!" comes yet another.

Accompanying this bad language is a spray of (what I hope is) spit. The men really are disgusting, and this is standard behaviour from those whose cells overlook our exercise yard. Both Ella and Martina are doing laps of the perimeter of the yard, while I'm catching some late winter sunshine. It's November and it's cold but the sun is quite bright today, which has put us all in a good mood. Both women appear untouched by the privations and limitations of incarceration in a Category A prison. They're steadfast in their views, and though I don't agree with them or what the IRA does, I can't help but admire their unwavering belief in themselves and their cause.

Both were treated pretty harshly during the first part of their sentence in Brixton prison, or so they say. Strip-searched five or more times a day, kept in solitary for months at a time and under constant surveillance, they say it was horrendous for them. They both say they received this treatment because they were held as political prisoners, not as criminals. I don't dare argue with their logic. Despite the tales they've shared, they both appear untouched by the brutality of the system.

They've also both taught me to use exercise as a way of getting through prison time, and I'm surprised to find I enjoy jogging and aerobics.

"Keeps you mentally strong, as well as physically," Martina says as she passes me, grinning.

As soon as Ella, who has long blonde hair and a slim figure, and Martina, who has long auburn curls, appear they get a mixture of wolf whistles and obscenities thrown down at them.

"You should wash your mouths out!" I shout up, laughing at the men who I'm sure will throw a few obscenities my way as well.

Before anyone can answer, there is a sudden, loud noise, followed by a scream of pain. We all look round to see Myra shrieking in agony. I can't see why because the lurid coloured kaftan she has taken to wearing hangs over her body, but it looks like she'd been trying to get up from where she was sitting and had fallen and broken her leg in the process.

"Everybody in! Now!" shouts a screw who comes running out into the yard.

Ella, Martina and I sprint over to the door, but as we go we hear the screw saying: "It's OK, Myra, we'll call an ambulance."

Minutes later there is the wail of an ambulance siren, but weirdly no one appears for Myra who has been left out in the yard with male inmates hurling globules of spit and some seriously nasty abuse down on her.

"Why aren't they takin' her?" I say to Ella.

It's Martina who replies.

"There's been an overdose on the wing just now. The quiet one who never says much. She's OD-ed on heroin I think."

"Oh my God, poor girl," I say. "I expect she's the priority and they'll 'ave to take her off before they can get Myra."

Eventually, the ambulance does indeed leave, its lights flashing, the sound of the siren wailing in the distance now.

Myra is left outside in God knows what agony for a couple of hours. I can't imagine there are many people in the prison who feel much sympathy for her. None of the guards stay with her because she clearly can't run off. I almost feel pity for her. This is as far as I can extend my empathy. It's difficult to sympathise with a woman who helped torture and kill small children, even as she is spat and jeered at by the men who have cells overlooking the yard. On and on it goes with no let-up. She is universally hated and feared, and as soon as she shows weakness they come for her like a pack of hyenas.

. . .

While in prison I become friendly with Kate Kray, Ronnie Kray's ex-wife. She writes to me and visits regularly, which is nice because I've told my family not to come up. It's a five-hour drive each way, and so they have to leave at 5 a.m. to get to me for the morning visit, then when they leave at the end of the same day's afternoon visit they have another five hours on the motorway to get home. I've stopped them coming so I can just save up my visits and every few months go down to Holloway to have them there. As a consequence it can feel lonely and so Kate's visits are a welcome respite. She tells me she wants to write a book about me, and asks if she can interview me, which I agree to. She is due to come and see me on the following Saturday, and I'm looking forward to a good catch-up, finding out what's going on in the outside world. Despite the notoriety of her marriage to Ron, she lives a straight life.

An hour before the visits, Martina and Ella stick their heads around my cell door. I'm listening to the radio to pass the time before I see my friend.

"So, they won't let us have visits with our husbands at the same time..." Martina begins.

"Because we're political prisoners and a threat to state security," Ella continues.

"Right," I say, wondering what any of this has to do with me, but pleased to see them anyway.

"So, there's been a mix up and Paul has been sent here at the same time as John..." Martina says.

"And they're not allowed to visit us at the same time, so they had to go and see the governor."

"Oh right," I say, looking over at them both framed in the doorway. The passion and energy of the two women is undeniable, though I have to remember they were part of a conspiracy to bomb coastal towns of Britain, including the Brighton hotel bombing. Their husbands, Paul Kavanagh (who was jailed for the Chelsea Barracks bombing that killed two people) and John McMullen, another member of the IRA and bomb gang, have both served time, though John has since been freed.

"They're not allowed to say a word to each other, can you believe that?" Martina adds.

"The governor was great about it, though. He said that as long as they don't speak, they can visit us at the same time, or so Paul told me."

"It was an oversight, apparently," Ella says, "but because the governor knows John has come from Ireland especially to see me, he's allowed it to go ahead."

The outside world has come sharply into focus with meeting the two IRA women. Being locked up has meant an almost complete separation from the wider world, except for reading the occasional newspaper or hearing news on my radio. Even at visits, we're all more concerned with talking about family news than anything happening on a larger scale, and so hearing Ella and Martina speak about Ireland and the ongoing peace process, and what it might mean for them, and this visit, is a strange reconnection with a world I'm not currently part of. I've never followed current affairs, but being in prison means we don't really get a chance to.

I know enough about their situation to know that the peace process is in the advanced stages, and neither of the women is going to be here much longer, which is why I assume the rules have been bent for them.

"I'm happy for you both," I say. "I've got a visit from my friend Kate today, so I'll see you in the visitin' room."

The visiting room is crowded but I soon see Kate's blonde hair and big smile. She is a bubbly, chatty woman and someone I really like. Kate comes over and we sit together, opposite each other at a table.

"Security is really tight today," Kate says a little breathlessly after we've said hello and I've poured out a coffee for us both.

"What d'you mean?" I reply, stirring a spoonful of sugar into the hot liquid.

Just then, I see Martina's husband Paul and Ella's husband John walk in. They glance at each other, walk over and, without a word, they shake hands and nod. It strikes me as strangely honourable to see these two men, who are both members of the same terrorist organisation, do the right thing. There are double the number of screws watching us all today, and I guess it must be because there are four members of the IRA together in the same room. Quite a surreal moment.

CHAPTER 25

ROSE

Back in the yard a year has passed since Myra's injuries and she is back from the hospital wing recovering from breaking her leg in the yard. I don't know why she was able to injure herself so badly when she tried to stand up, but she has osteoporosis and her health is very poor. I can't say any of us has missed her.

Ella and Martina have been moved to a prison in Ireland as part of the peace process, and it was hard to say goodbye to them. They were my friends, and I've missed their fizzing energy and unbreakable spirits. Durham feels an isolating place. These months have been some of the hardest for me since being banged up for the second time, and without my IRA friends there's little to feel joyful about. The months seem to last for ever, but they creep ever onwards. There's no news on my case, and Danny and I have been told that our visits can't continue.

At our last legal visit, Danny and I rake through every name we've collected over the years and mark which ones we've written to. There aren't any new leads and no one has replied to say they could help us. As the visit comes to an end, Danny reaches his hand across the table and holds mine.

"Linda, I'm goin' to miss these visits," he says.

"I am too, darlin'," I reply.

"Listen, I've had a thought about the visits. What would ya say if we got married? That way we can carry on with visits and work on our case, and they won't be able to stop us," Danny says. "'Ave a think anyway."

"I will," I say, feeling grateful for his suggestion. It seems like a neat solution. We both desperately want to carry on trying to find that bit of evidence that might free me. How bad would it be to do that? Prison is like living in a small bubble. By now I'm so cut off from the outside world that I can't see further than the extent of the prison walls. I don't consider this might be a decision that could backfire on us, and make me look guiltier than I did before.

I mull it over, but there's bigger news on the wing: a woman called Rosemary West is being sent here on remand.

"Myra's not the only one makin' people nervous..."

"What d'you mean?" I say, a few days after Danny leaves, asking me to think his proposal through. I turn back to an inmate called Sheila, aged around 40, who is wearing a grey set of joggers and sweatshirt and has her mousy hair scraped back off her face. Sheila is serving 18 years and I have never asked what it is for. I've always taken Mr Smith's advice and I keep things light and friendly. I never ask what anyone is in for, but sometimes they choose to tell me. She is one of the people I get on with on the wing, though she is a tough cookie and I wouldn't mess with her.

"Didn't ya know? Rosemary West is comin'. She's the one they say committed all them murders, including her own daughter."

"Oh my God, the frumpy one with the glasses. She's comin' 'ere?" I say, almost whistling.

I'd seen her image on the front of a tabloid newspaper left in the association area by a member of staff.

Sheila nods.

It turns out the prison is alive with gossip. Some of the girls tell me that Rose West is arriving any day now. How on earth they know this is anyone's guess.

For obvious reasons, no one wants her here. We've all been following the case in the newspapers. There is no such thing as normal life in a prison. You can plod along, keeping your head down and getting on with your sentence, then everything changes in a flurry of new inmates and the exit of other inmates being moved to different prisons or ending their custodial sentences.

The next day Mr Smith appears on the wing, showing around another man, who is smartly dressed and has a posh accent.

"Who's that?" I say to one of the screws.

"That's Rose West's solicitor, Leo Goatley. He's in to have a look and see if it's safe to have her stay here..."

I raise my eyebrows.

"Really?"

The screw smiles.

"Yeah, Linda, it's very unusual, but then she's an unusual case. She's as high profile as Myra."

At that exact moment Myra walks along the wing with a cup of coffee.

We both stare at her as she goes, neither acknowledging her. As she walks past, my fellow inmate Sheila says under her breath: "Piece of shit!"

Rose turns up and, lo and behold, in a queasy turn of events, she becomes bosom buddies with Myra. The pair of them are sitting at a little table on the landing with a red-and-white checked tablecloth, looking for all the world like they're a pair of old women sitting outside a bistro. Their heads are together and they are chatting and smiling together.

"Oh my God, she's nothin' like I expected. She looks like someone's maiden aunt!" I say from the other side of the space. Everyone is looking at them with a mixture of fascination and disgust.

That afternoon I have a call with Reg. He's been ringing me every two weeks ever since that first call, and we're firm friends now.

"You'll never guess who's 'ere!" I say.

"Go on, Linda, tell me, though I think maybe I can guess. I read the papers, too!" Reg chuckles at the end of the line.

"It's Rosemary West, the one in the papers, who helped kill her own daughter," I say. "She's come to Durham and we're on the same wing together. Myra's 'ere too, so it'll be somethin' to see those two evil twins make friends."

"Oh Linda, you do make me laugh," Reg says. "If we was out of prison, I'd take you out for the most expensive meal of your life and we'd put the world to rights."

"Yes, we would, Reg. Perhaps one day we'll get a chance to," I say, knowing they'll never let a Kray out on the streets again.

I soon have plenty more stories to tell Reg. Within days of dumpy Rose West arriving in Durham, the rumours have already started.

"They've started an affair," Sheila tells me. "Fuckin' birds of a feather, Lin. What d'you expect?"

"I agree, look at them. Thick as thieves. How can they stand each other?" I say.

We both look over at them: Myra, with her purple-red coloured hair and a brightly coloured kaftan, sitting next to Rose, with her prissy cardigan, tweed skirt and large glasses, knitting as she always seems to be doing. Their heads are together and they're both laughing.

"What I'd give to 'ave a camera right now." A male screw sidles up behind us. "That picture'd be worth a fuckin' fortune!" It is quite normal for male staff to work on the wing, because Durham is a men's prison. In fact, the majority of screws are male here.

We all laugh, which makes Rose and Myra turn our way.

I shudder. I can't help it.

"Look at them, havin' tea, like they're two aunts on a day out. It's disgustin'," I say, walking off.

For the rest of the day, the wing is in uproar. No one wants Rose here. Having Myra is bad enough, without another evil murderess turning up and ruffling everyone's feathers.

As each day passes the sight of them becomes more grotesque. They're in each other's company constantly, eating breakfast, lunch and dinner together, taking their tea breaks together, walking around the exercise yard together. I try not to pay any attention to them, knowing they both seem to thrive on the notoriety of their bizarre friendship.

Then, just as suddenly, within a month of Rose arriving, her and Myra's friendship, if that's what it was, ends abruptly. Neither seems to be able to stand the sight of the other. Whatever it was they fell out about is kept from us, but how does anyone have any privacy here?

"What's goin' on?' I say to the same screw who wanted the camera to take that picture. I don't know his name as he is not often on the wing.

He shrugs. "A lovers' tiff?" he says. "Can't stand the sight of either of them, so it's best they've stopped whatever it is they were up to."

"Oh my God," I reply. "You can't make this stuff up!"

From that day, Myra and Rose avoid each other at every turn. Whatever strange friendship, or relationship, they embarked upon has ended and they both continue serving their sentences without speaking to one another, which is quite hard to do as there are only 20 prisoners on the wing now. I make sure I avoid them both.

Meanwhile, life in prison moves relentlessly onwards; 1994 becomes 1995. Rose's trial comes around in October and we're all on tenterhooks to know what happens. When she's given life without parole, there's a collective inhalation. We're stuck with her, though the result isn't a surprise.

* * *

I look only far enough ahead for each trip down to Holloway to spend a month there catching up on all my saved visits. I've learned to shut down my emotions and become like a robot, showing no weakness that someone else could try and exploit. I get up. I wash. I dress. I work in the kitchens, making sure to keep the best bits of food aside for us cleaning girls. I'm polite to the screws. I count the days in between each trip to London. I write letter after letter and spend my nights alone in my cell listening to the radio. Somehow, time moves on, and most importantly I manage to keep going. I'm still convinced somebody will proclaim my innocence one day, and this hope is what sustains me, though my solicitors have nothing new to bring to the judges.

I'm managing to put aside the anger and frustration of being convicted for something I didn't do and focus on getting through this. It's taken me five years to accept this sentence and though I fight it through letters and legal visits, I know the score. No one's going to let me out any time soon, so I buckle down. It's not always so simple for some of the other women on the wing, particularly those with mental problems and unstable personalities.

· · ·

Sitting with a couple of friends eating breakfast on the landing of the top floor one morning, I notice one of the girls has not come out of her cell. She usually sits opposite me at a nearby table. The girl, called Debbie, is doing life for a terrible crime. At face value she is a surprisingly "normal" person, someone who I would've felt like I could chat to in a shop or supermarket, perhaps. But I've avoided her ever since someone whispered to me in the lunch queue what she'd done. You'd never guess her crime, though I expect that's the same for most of us in here.

Before I get a chance to say something about Debs's absence, one of the girls who usually sits with her gets up from the table, saying: "She'll miss her breakfast. I'm just goin' to check on Debs."

The girl, who is a young woman with short hair whose name I don't know, pushes open her friend's cell door.

"Oh my fuckin' God!" The scream reaches the far ends of the corridor.

"Oh God, what now?" I say, though I had an instinct something might be wrong.

"Oh my God! Oh my God! Get help, quick! I think she's committed suicide..."

All hell breaks loose.

Suddenly, Principal Officer Mr Atkins appears. He runs up the stairs.

"What's wrong?" he shouts.

"She's tried to commit suicide but I don't know if she's dead or not... She's left letters for her kids on the bed..."

Hearing that makes my heart sink to my stomach. However bad it is in here, feeling bad enough to leave your kids like that is just horrendous.

Mr Atkins goes inside. By now, no one is speaking. All the usual noise – people bickering, a few girls laughing and various shouts of "You fuckin' didn't" and "I'll get that cunt when I'm out" – all vanishes, leaving just the scene that is unfolding before our eyes.

A few minutes later the principal officer comes out.

"It's OK, girls, she's not dead but she needs help as she's unconscious."

There is a sigh of relief but tension still runs high. The friend is now crying and women look shocked.

Mr Atkins takes out his radio.

"I need Healthcare immediately. I need a nurse, this can't wait until you've done the meds. I've got an attempted suicide. No, this can't wait. Get here now, please..."

Five long minutes later, a nurse wanders in with a distinct lack of urgency. We are all waiting to see if the girl will survive, willing her to despite what she has done. If she dies, then her children will be left without a mother, which is yet more tragedy in their lives.

"Where is it?" The nurse speaks brusquely. I notice she doesn't say "she".

"Up on the top floor. Come now," the officer says, leading the way, taking the stairs two by two. The nurse follows behind him and goes into the room on her own. We are watching every move the senior staff are making. I've never known the wing so hushed.

The nurse comes out a minute or two later and locks the door.

We all glance at each other. Why has she done that?

"What have you locked the door for?" Mr Atkins is as puzzled as we are.

"Well, she's nearly dead, so there's no point helping her," the nurse replies and starts to walk away.

The principal officer looks like he's about to burst.

"What the fuck are you talking about? If she's nearly dead, then she's still alive!" he practically shouts back at his Healthcare staff.

This is when the hierarchy of the prison becomes confusing. Even though a principal officer is technically above a nurse in rank, they are still not able to call an ambulance unless agreed by Healthcare. It's a strange rule, and one that is breaking down in front of our eyes.

"Yeah but by the time an ambulance gets here, she'll be dead, so I'm going to leave it."

Our heads swivel from Mr Atkins to the nurse, who is a sour-faced bitch, back to the officer.

"Call an ambulance," he says.

"No, I won't," the nurse replies. Her eyebrows are almost touching her hairline.

"Oh my God, I can't believe I'm hearin' this..." I whisper to no one in particular, but a few of the girls nod in response.

"It's disgustin'," says one.

"She's a fuckin' murderer," says another.

"I'll get someone to come and collect her later," the nurse adds.

Mr Atkins looks at the nurse as if he cannot believe what he's hearing either.

"I'm telling you, call an ambulance. Now," he orders.

The nurse shakes her head.

"I refuse," she adds, as if we were not here.

"Then I'm going above your head and I'm calling an ambulance now."

We all know that if it was an ordinary screw standing in front of the nurse, they would have no choice but to respect her decision.

Within minutes we hear the scream of a siren. The whole wing is standing around watching this play out. I know some of the girls will not be sad to see this woman go, but I know the rest cannot bear the thought of the kids being left without their mother, however mentally unstable she is.

The crew run up to the cell, and minutes later she is carried out on a stretcher and wheeled to the ambulance.

The nurse walks out as if this is all an ordinary day, seemingly unperturbed by the chaos she has created. I often wonder about the medical staff in a prison hospital. I have been lucky enough never to have been ill while in prison, but some of the stories I hear, of bullying nurses, mishandled medication and staff who don't appear to give a shit, make me wonder if some of the most disturbed people inside are actually those who are meant to care for the women.

I often think to myself that it's astonishing what really goes on inside our prisons. If most people knew of the abuse and neglect, the stealing, thieving and rackets that are run inside, many of which are instigated or facilitated by members of staff, the country would be in uproar.

The rest of the day is spent dissecting the events of the morning. Mr Atkins is hailed a hero for standing up to that bitch of a nurse, let alone for the possibility he may just have saved the girl's life.

We have no news of her condition and after two days the wing is starting to settle down, albeit sadly as we're all assuming she didn't make it.

Then, at the end of the second day, she walks in with a screw, bold as brass, and is taken back to her cell, alive and not nearly dead at all.

"You're our hero, Mr Atkins, you saved her life!" one of the girls says as he passes, which makes him smile.

"You really are. We love you," says another, which makes him laugh this time.

The next day, one of the girls is unwell and Healthcare is called again.

Lo and behold, the same nurse walks back onto the wing as if nothing happened.

"My God, how does she 'ave the nerve to come back 'ere?" I gasp.

"Fuckin' hell, she's back. Who's she goin' to try and kill this time?" someone else says.

As far as we are aware, no disciplinary action is ever taken against the nurse. She carries on working on the wing. I wonder if she hears the whispers of "bitch" from the inmates as she goes about her tasks, but it seems to me, even if she does, she wouldn't care. Prison hardens people. Many of the staff are as institutionalised as the girls. They have to wear a uniform, live in a set routine, and they even have an officer's mess, just like the army. Prisons like Holloway and Durham are bleak, brutal places and, in time, it is my theory that the people who work in them (as well as the inmates housed inside) become just as bleak and brutal. I'm sure there are many who choose to work in the prison service out of a sense of duty and to help transform the outcomes and lives of those who are incarcerated, and we should applaud them if they do. However, many seem to be simply there to do a job, which is a difficult one at the best of times, and do it without too much humanity or care.

CHAPTER 26

BAD IDEA

When my daughter Melanie announces she's getting married, I immediately put in an application to be taken to her wedding. I've been sent back to Holloway to have the visits I've accumulated over the past months. It's while I am back here that Mel shares her exciting news.

The app is refused. I'm utterly distraught. The prison governor turns down my application, saying I can have a video of the day and a slice of cake. I feel this like another punch in the stomach. Of course I don't let my family know that I'm devastated by the news. I write to Mel and my mum, telling them I'll be there in spirit and to save the top tier of the cake for me.

The wedding takes place on a Saturday. That evening, I'm sitting in my cell listening to all the usual sounds from the women in the prison, thinking about Mel's day and trying to pull myself out of the fug of gloom that's descended upon me.

We're all locked up, as it's a weekend and so the staffing levels are low. My hatch is opened and a screw peers through.

"Hand me your flask, Linda," she says.

"It's alright, I've got water for the night, but thank you," I reply, not paying much attention.

"No, Linda, give me your flask…"

I look up.

The screw nods and so, a little bemused, I hand over my flask. We're given hot water each evening so we can make ourselves a tea or coffee overnight in our cell.

She walks off and returns a few moments later.

"Here you go, Linda, now you can toast your daughter tonight."

My hatch shuts.

I unscrew the lid and take a sip. It's neat vodka, just like when my appeal failed all those years ago.

How kind of her… I think to myself. There are many ways the inmates and staff get around the rules. I've heard of screws bringing alcohol inside bottles of lemonade or squash, bringing it in with their packed lunch. Prisoners have to pay staff for the privilege, but it's a common way of getting contraband inside the prison. Drugs are smuggled in inside people's mouths on visits. Just like with Maria, when they kiss the drugs are passed over and the inmate swallows the package and regurgitates it later. Drugs can also be smuggled inside in the heels of shoes or lobbed over the walls inside tennis balls. I've heard of drug works (i.e. syringes and needles) being wrapped inside a new baby's nappy before attempting to smuggle them in through security. How terrible is that?

When I visited my gangster boyfriend Ron in prison, I used to put a small flat bottle of vodka in between my cleavage. I would unscrew it then go and get him an orange squash. Then I would lean over to kiss him and pour the bottle into his cup.

Even though it's illegal, that vodka in my flask is a small act of kindness, which I'm incredibly grateful for. That night, which could've been one of the bleakest banged up, is still sad, but I'm touched by the screw's action and determined that, one day, I'll make it up to my daughter.

.   .   .

Perhaps it was Mel getting married, or perhaps I've finally lost my mind in prison, but when I return to Durham from Holloway I put in an app to marry Danny, half-expecting it not to be granted. After all, they wouldn't let me out to see my own daughter get hitched, so why on earth would they let me marry the man I was convicted alongside? Astonishingly, the governor approves it and the date is set for 1 December 1995, just a few short months away.

I don't have any romantic feelings towards Danny, and if he has them towards me then that's for him to say. The reason I've done it is we've grown close as friends, and it's the only way we'll be able to carry on with our visits. If it buys me time to spend trying to put together my case for freedom, then it's a good thing, surely? Life in prison isn't all chaos and drama. Much of it is boring and repetitive. The idea of a wedding is something to look forward to, to celebrate, as celebrations are thin on the ground in Durham.

When I tell the girls on the wing they're ecstatic. Even so, I can feel alarm bells ringing in my head, though I try and ignore them.

* * *

"Don't do it, Linda. It's a bad idea, it makes you look guilty!" my mum says as she sits opposite me.

"I know what you're sayin', Mum, I hadn't thought of it like that. OK, I'll speak to Danny. He'll be OK about it. I'm not really sure why we were doin' it anyway, except he thinks he's tryin' to make things up to me and we know it's the only way we can carry on with our visits," I reply.

"Linda, darlin', please don't get married to Danny Reece. If you walk down the aisle with him, everyone'll think you really were in cahoots all along."

"OK, Mum, I won't," I say, smiling back at my mother, hoping I'm reassuring her.

After the visit, I go back to the wing and start to tell the girls that the wedding is off.

"You can't do that, Lin!"

"It's the most exciting thing we've had in 'ere, please don't change yer mind!"

"Lin, you 'ave to get married, we've asked the kitchens to make a cake and have a party afterwards."

That evening, I sit in my cell, pondering what to do. My daughter Mel has sent in her wedding dress for me to wear, and as I touch the white lace and the beautiful shimmering silk of the dress, I think: *It can't hurt, can it? It's a bit of fun and excitement for the wing, and it might be a nice day. Surely there's no harm in goin' ahead, especially as everythin' is now agreed and sorted, down to the prison priest comin' over...*

Ignoring the nagging feeling in my gut that this isn't right, I write to Danny and say we should go ahead because it gives us the time together we need to keep fighting. The women on the wing are ecstatic.

At the same time, Reg proposes during our next phone call. This comes as a surprise, I have to say, but then again, he sends flowers after every conversation we have, so perhaps it isn't so unexpected.

"Reg, I've got some news," I say. It's an autumn day and it's only just over a month until my wedding day.

"Linda, can I stop ya there. I wanted to ask if ya might marry me..."

Well, I'm not expecting to hear that.

"Oh," is all I manage to reply. This feels like it's come out of the blue despite his attentions.

"That doesn't sound good. Sorry, Linda, I don't mean to embarrass ya. Forget I said anythin'," Reg replies.

"No, it's alright, Reg. It's just that I've agreed to marry Danny so we can carry on our visits. I don't think they'd ever let me out of prison if I married a Kray twin, sorry Reg," I say, hoping this doesn't upset him.

"No, I'm sorry, Linda. Many 'appy congratulations to you and Danny. I see ya point about your freedom. Let's forget I said anythin'. Anyway, how's Rose doin'? Any more gossip?"

We chat away, but life feels quite surreal at the moment, because Reg's proposal isn't the only one I've had this week. Charlie Bronson has been writing to me. He writes to say he's moved regulary to different prisons and is largely in solitary confinement, so I'm unsure where to send anything anyway. Each letter contains a proposal for the "Black Rose", as he's taken to calling me. I've never met Charlie. He's well known in my circles and most of the male crooks I know have met him or are friends with him. He's a dangerous man, yet his antics make me laugh because he knows they're insane and he does them anyway.

．　．　．

When the wedding day dawns, someone does my hair, while another inmate puts make-up on me, and I forget my worries and concentrate on having a good day. I'm helped into Mel's dress, feeling like a child going to a party dressed as a princess. All of Durham H wing walked to the chapel, which is housed in the men's part of the prison, and wait for Danny. I have a reception table groaning with non-alcoholic fizz, cakes, sandwiches and even confetti and two bridesmaids, both dressed in black because of me being the famous Black Widow. To be fair, the two who accompanied me in the service were both convicted of murder, so the black dresses felt appropriate!

We say our vows and drink a glass to each other. Danny doesn't say much and I wonder if he's starting to regret our decision to go ahead too. We're not entitled to conjugal visits, and anyway, our relationship has never been that way. Perhaps he was as bored as we all were with prison life and wanted something to plan, or perhaps, in his own way, he feels that he's making up for the fact that I'm serving life for the crime he committed. Whatever the situation, Danny is a hardened man, a killer, though a dear friend, and now my husband. We know that after the short ceremony, I'll go back to my wing. He'll go back to Whitemoor and life won't be much different, except we'll be able to continue the three-monthly meetings.

One thing is certain, we've bought more time for visits to discuss our case, but it isn't the only thing we've brought to our door...

"'Ave ya seen the headlines, Linda?" Mum says, shaking her head when I'm back in Holloway for my family visits a month after the marriage.

"They've slaughtered you in the press. They're sayin' the Black Widow has married her contract killer! This'll make things harder for ya to get out!"

Mum's right.

I wince as she speaks.

"I shouldn't 'ave done it," I agree, "But it's done now, and I can't do nothin' about it. The press'll find somethin' else to write about. They always do," I say, but I admit I'm feeling anxious at the reaction.

"Why did you do it?" my mum says, sitting opposite me in the visiting room. "You both look guilty as hell of Ron's murder now."

"I know, I don't know what I was thinkin'," I reply. I can't disagree. I've been so removed from the real world, living inside this small prison environment, that I really hadn't given much thought about how the world would view Danny and I getting married. It sounds naïve, and perhaps it is, but there's nothing I can do about it now.

"I think I thought, bugger it, they think I'm guilty anyway, so why care what anyone else has to say..." My voice trails off. It's a weak argument. My mum just looks at me in the exasperated way she does. Her blonde hair has gone mostly white now, but she has the same loving – if frustrated – expression on her face she always did.

"I'm sorry, Mum. It was a stupid thing to do, but it's done now and we 'ave to make the best of it. I got carried away, especially as there's never been a weddin' in the chapel in Durham Prison. Don't forget that with the lack of new evidence, we were runnin' out of reasons to be able to meet up to talk about our case. Gettin' married was another way we could legitimately keep our visits goin'. I know none of it makes any sense to anyone outside of these walls."

I think I've also been starved of fun. When Kate Kray also sent in her wedding dress, a peach and cream dress she wore to marry Ronnie, I'd shown it to Mr Smith, who enthused that he would bring his camera in. At the time I was thinking of cancelling, and so he'd said he would take pictures of me in my "never-got-married" dress. If only I'd stuck to that, I wouldn't be facing what feels like the world's condemnation.

CHAPTER 27

GOLDFISH

My wing governor at Durham, Mr Smith, is always kind to me.

Staff often say to me, "Linda, go and ask Mr Smith for us because he'll let you 'ave anythin'." It could be something for the recreation room, or permission to organise a small birthday party. Anything I ask, he would say yes, as long as it is me doing the asking.

When he announces he's leaving, we're all devastated, not least me. We organise a party for him, with canapés from Sainsbury's and bottles of non-alcoholic wine, and he is such a gentleman that he insists on having a dance with each inmate, coming to me last.

"There's something I want to show you, Linda," he says with a smile when the record finishes. "Come into my office."

I follow him inside. He takes out his wallet and pulls out a photograph. I'm instantly puzzled.

"What are you doin' with a picture of me?" I say, and even as I speak my brain is telling me the photo looks a little bent and is not newly taken. "I don't remember that dress…"

I look up. Mr Smith is smiling sadly.

"You won't remember that dress because it isn't you."

I look over at him and realisation begins to dawn.

"It's my wife who died. I couldn't show you this while I was still working here, but that's why I've always had a soft spot for you. When you first walked into my office, I thought I was looking at a ghost."

I look down again at the photograph of the smiling woman. She has the same cheekbones, the same smile as I do.

"I'm so sorry for your loss," I murmur, but I feel a little shaken up. There is nothing stranger than life – especially on a prison wing.

* * *

A couple of weeks later, not long after Mr Smith has left, my son and daughter come for a visit. Mel brings Samantha, my first grandchild, and Neil brings his baby daughter, Mia, who was born just before my wedding. After I've asked them all about school and nursery, we settle back into our usual chat.

"Have you got a pet?" Sammy, who is now four years old, asks, taking a bite from her KitKat.

"A pet?" I reply, smiling. "What d'you mean?"

"Oh, I told her you'd said some of the girls have budgerigars in their rooms so ever since she's been sad that you don't have one for company," Mel says, smoothing down Sammy's dress as she sits at the table in the visiting room.

"I'm not sure I want a budgie," I say. "They create a terrible mess and you 'ave to keep cleaning out their cages. Anyway, I don't like the idea of a bird in a cage, it isn't right."

Joking, I turn to Neil and say: "Perhaps I should have goldfish!"

"A goldfish! Yes, Nan, get a goldfish!" Sammy is delighted by this thought. I laugh and say: "OK, I'll put in for one and see if I'm allowed, if it makes you happy?"

"Yes, Nan," Mia squeals, giggling.

Expecting to be refused, I put in an app, but, to my surprise, the new governor, who is a very strict man, agrees – with one condition: there have to be two fish in the bowl. I can't have one on its own.

The next time I get a chance to call my family, I ring Neil and tell him to come back with a tank and the fish, and all the bits they'll need.

The following week, Neil and Mel arrive. They're late coming through security.

"Is it busy out there?" I say.

"Well, it's not too bad but you ain't goin' to believe it, Mum." Neil shakes his head.

"Believe what?" I say.

"They only put your goldfish through the X-ray machine!"

"Go on, no they didn't!" I laugh, thinking he is having me on.

"They did, Mum! We had to put the tank through and then the fish in their bag of water!"

"Poor things," I say, though I don't think too much about it.

After they've gone, and the usual lump in my throat and sinking feeling in my stomach subside, I start setting the fish up in their tank. I put the goldfish in carefully. They seem happy enough, swimming around. Neil bought lots of little rocks and pretend treasure chests for them to look at. I sit and watch them for a while, thinking how peaceful they look. Most of the women on the wing have a budgie, and you can hear the squawks and ruffled feathers as you pass by the cells. I've never really thought about having a pet, but I'm already finding the sight of the fish and the gentle trickling sound of the water in the tank quite soothing.

This doesn't last long.

The next morning, I wake up to see them floating on top of the water, clearly dead. I go straight to the wing governor to complain.

"I'm really unhappy about my goldfish…" I begin.

"Why, what's wrong?" the governor says, barely looking up from his computer. He wears a dark suit and has a frown on his face.

"Come and look at them," I say.

The governor follows me up to my cell.

"Oh my God, what's happened?" he says.

"They were perfectly alright until your staff put them through the X-ray machine!"

"I don't believe any of my officers did that," he says, turning around to face me.

"Yes they did, my son told me when we was on his visit yesterday," I reply. "And someone needs to replace them. They've only been here for one night."

"Come down," he says, and together we walk back to his office, where he picks up the telephone and dials reception.

"Who was on the X-ray machine yesterday? Can I speak to them, please."

There is a pause, then he speaks again.

"Did you put two goldfish through the X-ray?"

I hear the person at the other end say: "Yeah."

"Why did you do that?" the governor says, his tone not happy at all.

The person at the end says: "Checking for drugs."

"Checking for drugs? Anyone who's clever enough to put drugs into a two-inch-long fish deserves to have them!" the governor shouts, and puts the phone down.

"Sorry, Linda. I'll order you two more fish and the prison will pay for them. Is there anything else?"

"No, that's it, thank you," I say.

True to his word, a couple of days later I'm called to the wing office and given two new goldfish.

"This lot haven't been X-rayed," the screw says.

"Well, thank God for that," I reply. "They might last longer this time, then."

I take the fish and place them in the water, which I have replaced, as well as cleaning out the tank. When I sprinkle some food on the surface, they rush up and gobble it all down greedily.

"I'm gonna call you Reggie and you Ronnie," I say, and I see my reflection smile back at me from the glass side of the tank.

CHAPTER 28

BACK TO HOLLOWAY

When I'm called to the wing office and told I'm leaving and going back down to Holloway, I'm thrilled. Despite the fact I've been allowed small luxuries in Durham, I only really care about seeing my family more often and am elated.

By now my cell is like a little gypsy caravan. Over the years my family has sent in a few nice bits: I now have pink silk curtains, a pink silk duvet, a big ornate photo frame with my daughter's wedding picture proudly displayed, and lots of ornaments, alongside Reggie and Ronnie the fish. It isn't much, but it makes my cell feel homely.

"Come on girls, who wants what?" I say, handing out my things. I know I won't be allowed to keep them at Holloway, because it's only at Durham that inmates are allowed these comforts. It will be back to having a bare cell with just the bed, table, chair and toilet. The only thing I keep is my radio, everything else is shared out, except for my clothes and shoes.

I don't know why they're suddenly moving me, but I have a suspicion. Throughout my time here, I'm regularly asked to do prison courses. These are courses about offending behaviour, looking at how people can change. It has always been my argument that as I didn't do the crime I was convicted of, then I have no offending behaviour to correct. I have refused every course on this basis, which doesn't go down well. I know that if I'd taken those courses they might have taken time off my sentence, but it would've meant I'd have had to agree that I'm guilty – and I can't do that. I kept saying that as I'm not guilty I shouldn't have to take the courses. To do so would admit guilt and there is no way I will do that.

It doesn't help that I'm associating with some notorious crooks while I'm inside, Reggie being one of them, and Charlie the other, which I know makes me look like I'd rejoin the underworld if I was released. There's been no talk of my release date even though it should've been mentioned by now because I've served more than five years including my year on remand. My solicitors say they're pushing for this, but there's nothing new to report.

My punishment for this refusal to do the courses is to be sent down to Holloway, which is silly because it's exactly where I want to be in order to make life as easy as possible for my visitors.

Everything is just the same. I'm strip-searched before I leave Durham. I don't think I'll ever get used to the humiliation of a complete stranger – or worse, a screw who knows me – looking me up and down. I've heard of girls being told "Oh, you've put on weight" and comments like that, which is not nice to hear, and actually quite disturbing as it demonstrates an unasked-for intimacy.

My plastic bag containing the bits I'll be allowed to take to Holloway is searched again, and finally I'm placed in the same two sets of handcuffs, one holding both my wrists together, the other attached to a screw I don't recognise. The cuffs are cold and too tight and I know I'll be left with sore wrists by the end of the day.

The journey back down to London is uneventful, but as I'm still a Cat A Travelling prisoner, another screw gives our location every few minutes or so via a walkie-talkie.

When we arrive I step out awkwardly with the screw I'm cuffed to, and I'm almost pleased to see the familiar building.

Once inside, it is the same procedure again.

"Alright, Linda. Back again!" says one of the staff.

"Yeah, I am. I'm happy to be 'ere. Durham was too far away," I reply, smiling.

I'm strip-searched again. My bag is checked again. I'm led to the holding room again. Then I'm taken straight up to D3, passing through the same locked and barred doors, under the same security cameras, until we reach the wing. The corridors are still just as shiny, the metal and concrete surrounds just as intimidating.

At least they didn't take me down to C1, I think. *That's a blessing.*

"Good luck, Linda," the screw says and heads back down to reception.

"Back again," says one of the inmates, a woman I recognise from my last stay here. She works in the kitchen, while I'll be a wing cleaner again. I left before we had a chance to speak, but there was something about her I knew I was going to like.

"Yeah, 'ere I am, back in Holloway." I smile. "I'm Linda."

"I fuckin' know who you are!" the woman says, laughing. She looks like a character from a Dickens novel. She has blonde hair pulled back in a ponytail and a wicked smile. She is the same age as me and she has a definite twinkle in her eye.

"I'm Sue. Anythin' you want thievin', I'm yer girl. I know all the fuckin' rackets in 'ere, all the cons. You stick with me, girl. In fact, why don't ya come and work in the kitchens with us girls? We got some fuckin' things goin' on, I can tell ya."

I smile at this sudden development. I feel like I've known her for years already, though her continual swearing might take some getting used to.

"Yeah, I will. I'd like that," I say, and so, later that day, I'm moved to the kitchen to be a baker, while Sue is on wash-up. It is here our friendship begins in earnest.

"I'm from a big fuckin' crime family in South London. This is my sister-in-law, Veronica," she adds, and I smile at the woman standing next to her.

"We're goin' down to the stores. Loads to fuckin' nick there. They've got 12 Dualit toasters, the expensive ones, which I'm goin' to fuckin' nick, you watch me."

I shrug. "I'd like to see you try."

"Come fuckin' on then," Sue says, winking.

"She's Cat A. She'll be out of bounds down there," Veronica says.

I know what they mean. If I'm caught down in the stores, near the prison gate, I could be transferred back up to Durham. It's strictly out of bounds for me. I'll have to wait until they've done the deed, and hope they all get away with it.

Later, Sue, Veronica and another inmate, a large, extremely tall woman called Big Jill, burst into my cell during association.

"We was like fuckin' naughty school girls. Inside that store there was fuckin' boxes of everythin': sheets, towels, toothpaste, knickers. You name it, it's fuckin' in there!" Sue says.

"Well, it ain't now," Big Jill says, laughing.

"Too fuckin' right." Sue grins, her beady eyes jumping everywhere. "Them boxes were stacked to the ceilin', Lin, half of it meant for the officers' mess!

"I wanted them irons and them toasters, and I said I'm goin' to get them out the fuckin' nick. I'm havin' them all," Sue says.

"I told her, ya can't fuckin' 'ave them, you silly cunt," says Big Jill. She is taller than most men, with muscles to match, and is a kung fu expert. Someone told me she was in the Israeli army and can load a semi-automatic machine gun in seconds. No one messes with Big Jill, who they also call Big Bird. I have no idea if anything said about her is true. There are so many gossips and bored inmates making up stories about people, it is hard to know what's true and what blatantly isn't.

"So, we packed a few bits inside a rubbish bin and headed back to the officers mess," Sue says, looking very pleased with the day's events.

"What about them toasters?" I say. "'Ave you decided to leave them?"

"Course I ain't!" Sue says. "I'm goin' to 'ave them toasters out of this nick." She grins with pure wickedness and I can't help but laugh.

"Well, I don't know how you're goin' to do that!"

The next evening, Sue marches up to me to give me the bag with the stolen orders in.

"We done it," she says. "All 12 Dualit toasters and the irons. All picked up by my family outside the nick."

"Oh my God, how did you do that?" I giggle, pouring water into the tea urn.

"We had them out of the boxes, and put them in rubbish bags. That Big Jill is an arsehole. She kept prodding the bags as we walked to the bins, and they went DING DING. I told her to get away from me and fuckin' stop it 'cos the screws would work out what we were doin', but she wouldn't fuckin' stop. We told that screw Maud we was collectin' the laundry. She's always tryin' to get us nicked, I can't stand the old bag. I can tell by her smarmy face that she wants to get me nicked and strip-searched.

"We took them rubbish bags out two at a time. I got all them toasters and 11 irons!" Sue is cackling with laughter now.

"We said we was takin' the rubbish from the officers' mess. We put it in a hidey hole, and got family to come up and go to them bins and get the gear out and take it home."

"Oh my God, you didn't!" I laugh.

"We did, Lin. We slaughtered that officers' mess too, and the stores. We took everythin' – riot boots, drinks, Mars bars – everythin'. You should've been there when the screws came into the stores to pick up the empty boxes of toasters. 'It must've been the fuckin' night staff,' one of them said, so we got away with all of it!" Sue is doubled up laughing now.

Later, I discover that Sue has access to all the staff uniforms and badges, their passes and all the paperwork which is kept in the officers' mess. We could have escaped easily! Naturally, Sue nicks all that stuff too.

"Lin, you can still get in on the action. What we can do is: you can take the fuckin' orders, and we'll nick 'em from the store, then you can hand them out on the trolley in the evenin'."

"Yes, I can do that," I agree. "And no one's goin' to grass us up and risk losin' their contraband." I nod enthusiastically. Anything to get one up on the system.

It's all planned. Sue will nick stuff to order from the stores, then we'll sell it to the girls on my evening trolley run, punting it around the wing under the noses of the screws. We'll be paid in chocolate bars, cigarettes or tobacco, and sometimes money, then we'll share out our spoils at the end of each evening. For a long time now, prison has felt difficult, isolating and hard. It's a relief to find some partners in crime, though I know it's a risk getting involved. I take it anyway. I've always been a risk-taker, convinced that everything will work out OK. Even though I have plenty of evidence that it absolutely doesn't, I can't resist joining this little gang and having some fun.

. . .

Life becomes even more surreal. One day, I'm mopping the landing when a screw walks over.

"TT0377, Calvey. Phone call for ya."

Puzzled, I walk over to the office.

"Linda, there's a phone call for ya," another screw says.

"But we don't get calls in 'ere?" I say, really confused now. Normally, we have to book a time for a call on the landing phone with a screw listening in to the conversation. This must be important.

"You can 'ave this one 'ere..."

Why is the screw smiling at me? What is going on?

"Who is it?"

"It's Charlie Bronson," she replies.

I pick up the receiver and his familiar voice, always a decibel or two too loud, says: "Hello, Black Rose."

"Hello Charlie," I reply. "How are ya?"

He starts to laugh.

"I've come into the office to take a hostage for you."

A door slams at the other end of the phone and I hear Charlie shout: "You're all my hostages!"

"Charlie, what's goin' on?" I say. "What are ya doin'?" Is this some kind of joke, or has he really locked people in a prison office with him?

"Black Rose, they let me in the wing office to call you, and now I've taken everyone in 'ere hostage!" He sounds delighted with himself. He's practically whooping with joy. If I heard him right, Charlie has managed to get himself into the wing office to make a phone call. Charlie can be very persuasive, by his own account, and has lucid periods of sanity and remorse, which is perhaps why they'd thought he was well enough to ring me.

"I've told them they've got to set you free, and I'm not lettin' them go until you're released."

There is a slight pause as I work out exactly what I can say to this. Obviously, I don't want people being held hostage for me, and if Charlie decides to fight my corner vocally, I'm lost indeed.

"What 'ave ya done, Charlie? Please don't get yourself into trouble on my account. Look, it's OK, it's really good of ya but I don't need any hostages today. I'm alright. I don't want to go home today because my solicitor says they're goin' to set me free soon. We're goin' back to court in a few weeks..." This is a blatant lie, but I have to say something so those poor people can be allowed to leave that room. This is becoming more bizarre by the second. The screw's eyes are as wide as saucers as she listens to this play out.

"Please let them go, I really don't need it."

"Oh right," Charlie says. He sounds a bit deflated. "You don't need any hostages today."

"I really appreciate what you've done, but honestly, I really don't need it..."

I can almost hear the sighs of relief from whoever he has inside that room.

"OK, it's your lucky day! Black Rose doesn't need hostages today. To say thank you to her, we're all goin' to sing 'He's Got the Whole World in His Hands', but we're goin' to change the lyrics and say 'sawn-off shotgun' instead."

After they have finished singing, he adds: "Black Rose is so classy. She's got red varnish on her fingernails and gold varnish on her toenails... How classy is that?"

Where's he got that from? I think, trying not to laugh as the people in that room echo "very classy".

"I'm goin' to go now, Black Rose, so you won't hear from me now 'cos I'll be going down to solitary for a few months."

"Oh Charlie, I hope they'll be kind to ya," I say.

"Don't worry about me," Charlie says, putting the phone down. I am left standing in the wing office, staring back at the screw who is looking at me, laughing.

CHAPTER 29

HOOCH

Making hooch is a normal part of prison life. Everyone does it if they can, though it's closely guarded by those who manage to make it. People hide it in the weirdest places to avoid detection from the screws, who confiscate it on sight. I think the strangest place I know of is inside a toilet cistern, where Big Jill hides it, which isn't very hygienic. It shows the lengths inmates will go to for an illicit drink in the evenings.

Now I'm working as a baker, I have access to lots and lots of yeast, as well as tins of fruit. The perfect recipe to make prison alcohol. The only problem is none of us has ever made it before, though we all think we know how it's done. It's Big Jill who insists she knows what to do.

I smuggle out the tins of fruit and a large block of yeast from the kitchen store cupboard, which I attempt to cut in half. As I do so, a plume of yeast powder coats the kitchen, which we have to hurriedly clean up so the screws don't guess what we're up to, laughing as we scrub the surfaces.

Sue pours the contents of the tins into a large container, adds the yeast, then screws on the lid.

"Shouldn't there be a hole or somethin'?" I say, not at all sure we are doing this correctly.

"Nah, just stick it somewhere warm where the screws won't find it, it'll be fine." Big Jill grins, looking around the kitchen.

"How about the boiler?" Sue says, so Big Jill takes the container over to where the boiler sits in a large cupboard and places it behind the system.

"How long do we leave it for?" I ask.

"It needs a few days to ferment, but I'm not sure exactly how long," Big Jill replies, shrugging and walking off back to her job as a cleaner.

It doesn't take long before we find out.

That afternoon, I'm making bread while Sue is buzzing about, her eyes darting everywhere, doing goodness knows what. Somehow, she always seems to give the impression she's up to no good.

Without any warning, there is a sudden BANG!

"Oh my God!" I shout, thinking a small bomb has gone off somewhere. Or perhaps it's the start of a riot?

When nothing happens, we all look around, and it's then we see that there's tinned fruit and fizzing liquid everywhere. It's the smell that really stands out.

"It stinks!" Sue shouts.

"Oh my God, what happened?" I say.

A screw runs in to find the kitchen covered in the disgusting mess that was our first attempt at making hooch.

"Who did this?" shouts the screw.

"I don't know," Sue and I echo, looking at her with our most innocent expressions on our faces.

The officer looks between us both. She starts to say something but stops, turns around and marches off again.

"Clean it up!" she says as she goes. Luckily for us, it's a decent screw or we'd have been put on report. When she is safely out of earshot, we dissolve into laughter.

"I knew we should've put a hole in it somewhere!" I manage to say between giggles.

Sue is bent double, almost crying with laughter.

"You was fuckin' right!" she manages, before starting to laugh yet again.

It takes a good ten minutes before any of us can compose ourselves enough to begin the clean-up job, gagging as we do so with the stench of that horrible mixture we'd created.

"I was right, now who's goin' to tell Big Jill?" I say, looking over at my friend, who begins to laugh all over again.

Sue is a terrible influence on me but she has made prison life a hell of a lot easier.

Over time, we perfect the art of making hooch, and thankfully we never cause another explosion. At night our wing is more like a pub than a prison, as hooch is drunk in every cell, and the girls get more raucous along the corridor as the nights wear on.

* * *

The days pass. The outside world keeps moving on without us. I've been inside for almost seven years if you count my time on remand. Seven years of slops for dinner, of light deprivation, of isolation from society. Seven years not being able to make my own dinner or open a locked door myself. Seven years of screws watching me night and day, of security cameras and barbed-wire fencing, of prison vans and saved-up visits. I could weep but what would be the point? It won't get me home any faster.

One morning, I get up and switch my radio on and realise they're talking about Princess Di.

It must be her birthday, I think as I pull on my white overalls, ready for another day in the kitchens. I keep listening as I get dressed, until I realise they're talking about her death. I stop what I'm doing. I think I must've misheard, but no, they're definitely talking about her death in a car crash in Paris.

"Oh my God," I mutter, slipping into my trainers.

Shocked and desperate for more news, I head to the kitchen to meet the other inmates to begin preparing the breakfasts. In all my time in prison so far, it's the only time the television is allowed on in the kitchens outside of the association session in the evening.

Screws are standing with us as we watch, in horror and grief, the terrible news that this beloved lady has died in a Paris car crash. Even though I'm banged up, I realise I'm witnessing history along with everyone else outside these prison walls. It is incredibly strange to be here, watching the events unfold, not being able to speak to my family or friends about this momentous event.

The day is really odd. Lots of the girls are crying and we're all devastated by the news. A week later, the whole prison stops to watch Diana's funeral. I've never seen anything like it as inmates and screws crowd around the telly, and join the rest of the world in saying goodbye to such a loved woman. I feel sad that I can't be in London to watch the procession, and my heart goes out to William and Harry as they walk with their father behind the coffin. Such an incredibly tough thing to go through, yet it serves to bring everyone at the prison together. There are no fights today. No one is kicking off or trying to rob a green newcomer. Everyone seems to be grieving for the loss of her, even though none of us ever met her and never will. I feel my separation from the outside world keenly. Even though we've watched the funeral on telly, just like millions of other people, it isn't the same as being at home or in an office and watching it, or attending the event in London. I already feel trapped, of course I do, but today I feel it even more acutely. I want to be witnessing history rather than hidden away inside Holloway, with only the supper trolley and another night listening to the radio to think about.

. . .

A month later, when the grief at Diana's death is passing, Sue has been released, and is surely back to her old ways, just as if she had never been inside. I miss her and her antics but I'm glad she's free. One day, my name is called over the Tannoy. I wander up to the office and find a huge parcel waiting for me.

"What's this?" I say.

"'Ave a look," says the screw. "There's no name on it so we don't know who sent it to ya. It's passed security though..."

I put my hand in to find it's full of silk knickers of all sizes and colours.

"Oh my God, what's this?!" I say, astonished.

"Fuckin' hell, you've got some proper posh friends out there," the screw says, touching one of the pairs. We look at each other and the penny drops.

"Sue's up to her old tricks again, then," she says, her eyebrows raised.

I shrug.

"Let's share them out," I reply, starting to look through them. There must be 60 pairs of designer silk knickers in this box. "I'll take some for the girls on the wing, and you can 'ave the rest," I say, wondering if the screw is about to confiscate the lot as contraband rather than a gift. They are obviously stolen. All the labels are still on them.

Without a word the screw takes the remaining pairs. It seems we've come to an agreement. This is probably what's most shocking about prison. Some of the screws are as bent as the inmates. Accepting stolen goods is all in a day's work, or so it seems.

"Thank you," I say, hurrying along the wing, my arms filled with beautiful silky knickers. I pick out a few pairs, then make sure I have enough to distribute on the wing tonight as I do my trolley rounds.

CHAPTER 30

NEW HALL

"We're movin' you, Linda, and the good news is they've dropped the Travelling Category A status, so you can go to a smaller prison," the screw says. He is new on the wing and I believe his name is Mr Jordan, but I don't pay much attention. I'm preoccupied with thoughts about why my release date hasn't been set yet.

"Right," I say. "Thank God! I'm assumin' I'm goin' to Bullwood as they've dropped the Travelling Cat A crap?"

It seems obvious they are going to start to send me to less strict prisons, as I've served my seven-year minimum tariff even though there's no sign of my impending release.

"No, Linda, you're goin' to New Hall, up in Wakefield."

For a moment I'm stunned. I've been called to the wing office and I'm standing in front of the screw, unable to breathe.

"I'm what?!" I exclaim eventually. "You can't do that! My family will 'ave to travel up north again. It isn't right!"

The screw shrugs.

"You know that when they've made a decision, that's it. You'd better get used to the idea quickly as you're goin' in the next couple of weeks, as soon as a cell is free."

"But that's a fuckin' young offenders institution," Big Jill says. She is days from release and I can't help but feel envy for her being able to go home and return to her life outside these walls.

"A what? Why on earth would they send me there?" I say.

"The Home Office has a sense of humour..." is her reply.

I ask for a legal visit, and a few days later Peter Hughman comes to see me. We're back down in the shabby rooms designated for this purpose and I feel distinctly gloomy.

"Actually Linda, I've got some good news for you. We're going to apply to the Criminal Cases Review Commission (CCRC) to get your case reviewed, saying a miscarriage of justice has taken place.

"We're still protesting your innocence, and it's time they gave us a timescale for how long your 'life' sentence will actually be. You've served the seven-year tariff set by the judge, so we need clear direction. Hopefully, I'll have some good news for you soon."

This is welcome news, and when it's time for me to leave Holloway again, I feel bolstered by the news that *something* is happening at last.

When we finally arrive at New Hall, I step out of the prison van and into the reception wing of the prison and young offender facility, which means it holds juveniles as well as women. A young screw walks over. She has small eyes that narrow as soon as she sees me.

"We've heard about you coming up here."

"Oh right," I say, not sure what she means by this.

"We won't stand the likes of you up here," she says in a thick Yorkshire accent.

"Stand what?" I reply, genuinely bemused. The journey has taken six long hours and I'm hungry and tired.

"You cockneys all think we're thick," she sneers.

She is eyeing me as she speaks, as if testing my reaction.

"I don't know you so why would I 'ave an opinion on you?" I say. I don't blink. I hold her gaze until she looks away.

She sniffs, before speaking.

"Let's go through your stuff then," she says, gruffly, already shoving her big hands into my plastic bag.

She finds nothing I'm not allowed. Then she looks up at me.

"You can't have your earrings, the hoops are too big."

"Fine," I say. I'm not going to argue. I take them out of my ears and hand them to her. "So, what can I 'ave instead?"

"Studs or small hoops," she says. The she looks down at my necklace and her eyes light up. "You can't have that necklace."

"Oh yes I can 'ave my necklace, so I won't take it off."

"No, you can't. Take it off now."

I'm beginning to lose my patience. This woman has it in for me, but I won't back down.

"Yes I can."

"You're only allowed religious necklaces up here, so take it off, Calvey."

"Yeah," I reply, "and I'm allowed this...".

"No you're not!" The screw is starting to shout now.

She doesn't intimidate me. I've faced up hardened crooks and held my own. This screw, as obnoxious as she is, is no threat.

"Yes I am."

It's obvious to everyone that an argument is building up. A voice shouts from the office: "What's going on?"

The screw shouts back: "She won't take her necklace off!"

A head appears from the doorway. "Why not?"

"Because I'm allowed it," I say, robustly.

"She's not allowed it! It's not religious..." the screw starts to say.

The woman who poked her head out of the office steps out and walks over, her black shoes squeaking on the linoleum floor.

"I 'ave the Star of David around my neck," I say, showing her.

The woman looks to the screw, frowning.

"It's a religious necklace, she's allowed it." And she stalks back to the office, leaving the screw silenced.

"What did you say about what we think about you up 'ere?" I add, staring her hard in the eyes, knowing she'll be on me like a tonne of bricks from now on.

Worth it, though, I think as I keep staring, knowing yet again she'll be the one to look away first.

Overall, it is clear that New Hall Prison isn't going well.

Once I've been through the usual checks, a young male officer walks up. He is smiling and actually seems to be really nice.

"I'll take her across to the wing," he says, cocking his head at me, gesturing for me to follow him.

I find I'm laughing along with him as we go, which is a surprise.

"You know they're going to try and slaughter you up here, the staff and the inmates," he says, conversationally.

"I'd guessed," I say, and we both burst into laughter again.

He shakes his head eventually.

"She's not a good one to make an enemy of."

"Do I look like I'm bothered?" I retort, grinning. "It'll take more than a jumped-up screw to upset me!"

He laughs: "I know who'll end up winning and it won't be them."

We walk along the corridors of yet another prison. It's all very similar: the same long clean corridors, the same security cameras at every angle, the same barred doors to be unlocked and then locked again after we pass through. The place smells of bleach and sweat, like every other prison, and everything is painted the same pale yellow as all the others. New Hall is a bleak place, just like all the others, but I get to the wing in fairly good spirits. It doesn't take me long to realise I'm by far the oldest female on the wing, and the only cockney!

The girls are all just that – young women in their teens and early twenties in for thieving, soliciting or drugs. The next thing I notice is the number of fights. Holloway is chaotic and there's lots of bullying, but the fighting tends to happen in the yard or when we're all put in the long corridor on our way to education, the gym or work. Here, there seems to be a fight every few minutes or so.

"Oi you fucking slag! Get yer own fucking works!"

"Back off cunt! I don't want your gear neither!"

There is the sound of a tussle and then the inevitable scramble of screws to break it up.

"Right! You're both going to the punishment block!" a voice shouts.

"See if I fucking care!" shouts a woman's voice.

"Bitch! Yeah, you fucking get her!"

"She's trouble! She's a fucking cunt!"

A girl pokes her head around my cell door. I've unpacked and am now waiting to be seen by the wing governor.

"It's mental in here," the girl says. She must be no more than 20 years old, and has black hair, pale skin and a tattoo that runs up her thin neck.

I smile.

"After Holloway, it's a piece of cake, I'm sure," I reply.

The girl nods.

"I'm Dana."

"Hello darlin', I'm Linda," I say.

She comes in and sits on my bed beside me.

"They say you got life," she says, chewing the end of a lock of hair. She seems a nervous type but nice enough.

"That's right," I reply. "What are you in for?"

"Soliciting. I'm in and out. Those wanker pigs have it in for us working girls. I'm always getting nicked."

"What a shame, darlin'." Inside, I'm thinking, why on earth would this young woman choose a life working the streets – but then again, I doubt she ever had a choice. So many working girls don't. I don't judge them. We all have to survive somehow, and so many of the women I've met in my years banged up were left to fend for themselves by the care system or a broken family.

Just then a different male screw walks past the door.

"Hello, John," she calls out, and gets up as if to go to him for a chat.

The screw stops, turns to look at her, clearly startled, then blushes bright red.

"John?" the girl says.

Immediately he hurries off, leaving the girl standing in my cell.

"What's that, one of your punters on the outside?" I say without thinking, then realise that's exactly what he must be.

The girl looks back at me.

"I wouldn't mention it again if I was you," I say. What I mean by this is she'll only get herself into trouble if she tells the staff that one of them is a punter from when she works the streets. It won't go well for her. He'll deny it and she'll be in the shit. In prison it's best to shut your mouth and concentrate on making as little fuss as possible, even though it's very unfair.

Later that day, when I've had my tour and been given my job as a cleaner, I find I'm standing next to John in the dinner queue.

"And you get paid to lock her up," I say so that just he can hear. I can't resist, even though I could get in trouble for that remark. I'm not some little girl in my twenties; I'm 52 years old and I'm not cowed by their authority.

Again, his cheeks go bright red.

"I don't know what you're talking about," he says, coughing with embarrassment.

The double standards in the criminal justice system are all too glaring. Why is it that girls get banged up for soliciting but their punters don't? Why is it that men like John walk free, work in responsible jobs, while the girls they procure for sex pay for it with their freedom and reputation? It's disgusting. Yet another failure of the system we're so proud of in this country. Of course, I have no proof that this man is a punter, only this girl's word for it and I have only known her for a few hours, but the imbalance of power is obvious to see.

.   .   .

The next morning I join the queue for the showers and am horrified to see female screws lining the shower room.

"What's goin' on?" I say to someone who is standing next to me.

"There's so many fights, we have to get showered with staff standing in with us," she replies.

"They do what?" I almost choke.

I've never been in a prison where we all have to line up naked in front of staff and be watched while we get ourselves clean.

"It's degradin'!" I exclaim.

The inmate shrugs.

"It's how it is. They're always at each other. They use soap wrapped in towels as weapons, or put razors in their toothbrush bristles to bring in here. It's why the staff now watch everyone."

In all my years inside, I've never come across women inmates with weapons. Granted, there are lots of fights over girlfriends or drugs, but no actual handmade weapons. For some reason, it's not something women seem to do. It's the men who create objects to cause harm or for self-defence. This is the first time I have heard of it inside a women's jail, and even then I still haven't seen anyone brandishing anything worse than their fist or boot.

"It's like another world in 'ere," I say, whistling.

When it comes to my turn, I make it clear that I don't like this system, even if it is for my protection.

"It's like bein' strip-searched again," I grumble.

Even so, it's amazing how quickly something that feels bad becomes normalised, especially in prison. After a few days I barely even notice the screws or the fact I'm stark naked in front of the other girls.

The bullying I see in New Hall is some of the worst I've witnessed inside the prison system. A lot of the teenage girls are tearaways who've had hard lives, and there is a lot of stealing and forcing new girls to give up their "canteen". Just like Holloway, you get given your canteen once a week. This is the stuff you want such as cigarettes or face cream, which you go and pick up from the shop. The weak ones get their stuff taken off them before they've even left the shop. At times I step in, especially if I know one of the women doing it. I remind them that they wouldn't like it if their kids ended up in that situation, having their stuff nicked off them, and most of the time the women say: Oh, alright Lin, and they give it back. I say most of the time, because the bullying is rife, and there is little one individual can do about it. Prison is tough. New girls are targets, especially when they're young. The harder women can sniff out weakness, which is why I've always stood my ground.

CHAPTER 31

ADDING TIME

There is a knock on my cell door.

We're all locked up as it is a Saturday lunchtime and staffing levels are low, as usual. The cells run down each side of the landing and the place feels very open. Every inmate can hear the sound of someone walking up to a door and knocking. I know every set of ears will now be pinned to their doors to listen in and find out what is happening.

"Linda, are you decent?" It is the voice of the senior officer, a pleasant enough man who is good to the girls.

"'Course I am," I reply, wondering why he's here.

There is a short pause.

"Would you like to come to my office? I have a bit of bad news to give you..."

It might be my imagination, but the place seems to hush as everyone tries to listen in. My heart skips a beat. My family? Has something happened to my parents? My brothers and sisters?

"Oh my God, something's happened to Mum or Dad!" I say. "Or is it my children?"

"It's not your family," the SO replies, "but just come to the office and I can tell you there."

My heart swoops to my stomach. Relief instantly washes over me. I exhale then reply: "Whatever it is then, it's not that bad. I'm not worried, so just tell me now. I'm not comin' to the office."

There's another pause. It all seems a bit ludicrous, having this important-sounding conversation either side of a locked metal door.

"Can I open your door?" the officer says.

"Yes, that's fine," I reply, getting up. I was lying on my bed listening to the radio. I turn it off and try to mentally prepare myself for whatever might be coming next.

The door opens and the SO steps inside.

"Linda, I'm so sorry to tell you but I've got this memo come through from the Home Office..."

I look at him. He looks devastated. Behind my back, I cross my fingers and wait for the bombshell I know is about to go off.

"Linda, they added eight more years on to your sentence, making your minimum term 15 years."

As he says it, I hear an audible gasp, as everybody's reaction is echoed right around the wing.

I find I can't reply. My head buzzes, my brain seems to go into freefall. This is bad news. This is terrible news. Obviously, I have known for a while that I'm not going home anytime soon. I've known for months that something was afoot, because no mention has been made of my release even though I've served my seven years – and more. My solicitors have been frustrated as hell by the inaction of the courts. Well, now I know why.

"How will you do it?" he says. He is a tall man, and he seems to be peering down at me though I am standing opposite him. For a brief moment I feel like I'll faint, but I force myself not to, to retain my grip on myself. I've survived this far, I'll just have to dig a little deeper and survive the rest. Even then, I have no guarantee they'll let me out after the 15 years has expired.

"I suppose I'll do it the same as I did the last lot," I reply, my voice croaky as I process the clashing emotions that are hitting me right now. I feel like I've been punched in the face. I feel sick and giddy. My legs have gone to jelly. Fifteen years. It's a very long time in total.

"Er, Linda. Do you want to come and talk about it?"

"Will that alter the situation?" I reply, looking him in the eyes. He glances away, clearly uncomfortable with this new outrage.

"No, I'm sorry Linda, it won't."

I shrug.

"Well, what's the point, then?" I say, sitting back down on my bed. I can hear people starting to chatter along the wing, as they pass on the news.

. . .

The worst part of it is telling my kids.

My son and daughter, and their kids, are due to visit me next week. I decide to wait until I can tell them in person, as they deserve more than a phone call. I know that it'll kill me to keep this from them until then, but I know how upset they'll be.

The week passes in a blur. All the girls rally round me, saying how sorry they are and what bastards the government are to do this to me. I'm grateful for their words, but none of it goes anywhere near to comforting me.

Mel and Neil walk into the visiting room with my grandchildren. I hate them having to come into a prison to see their nanny, but today I'm just so grateful to see them. We get ourselves a coffee and some biscuits for the kids, and as they chatter away, flicking the pages of colourful books or playing with their toys at the table, I realise now is the time to tell my children this latest blow.

"Listen, there's no easy way to tell you this..." I start.

"Tell us what, Mum?" Neil says, grinning down at Mia who is sitting on his lap. She's four years old now and a little poppet.

"They've added another eight years on my tariff. I won't be eligible for release until 2005..."

Both Neil and Mel turn to me, their faces looking thunderstruck.

Then they both burst into tears.

"Listen, I knew I wasn't goin' home anytime soon. Seven years came and went, and there was no news, no changes to bein' inside a closed prison. Because I won't do any of the 'offending' courses, which I'd have to admit I did the crime to complete, I always knew I'd be penalised. It's worse than I thought, though. It's just like starting my sentence all over again."

"Oh Mum," Mel says, tears streaming down her face. I'm crying too now.

"I'm not doin' a course to say I committed a crime when I didn't do it. So now, they've done this to punish me. We could see I hadn't been progressed to an open prison for my release, so I was expectin' somethin' like this. Even so, it's a long time to add onto my sentence."

"I don't believe it. How could they do this to ya?" Neil joins in. He too is weeping.

I shake my head.

"They can do what they like and we 'ave no control over them. None whatsoever. There's nothin' we can do..."

"'Ave ya spoken to your solicitor?" Neil adds.

I nod.

"I saw him the day after they came and told me. He says there's nothin' we can do except accept it, and keep tryin' to find someone who'll support me."

It's a gloomy visit. We all try not to be too upset in front of the children. It breaks my heart to see their innocence and love inside a prison visiting room, and I wish yet again it doesn't have to be like this.

CHAPTER 32

DEVIL'S ADVOCATE

DECEMBER, 2002

I'd be lying if I said the weeks and months after the devastating news were easy. They weren't. I sank into a pit of despair for a while and I really saw why some women take drastic action and end their lives. Prison can seem endless, and utterly hopeless at times. Of course, I'd never kill myself. I've got my family to live for, and I damn well wouldn't have given the Home Secretary the satisfaction of becoming yet another prison suicide statistic. No, I got myself out of it by vowing to myself that I'd be a free woman one day. That vow has carried me through the last four years since my sentence was extended, and yet I'm still in prison. I've been inside for more than 12 years now, as it's the end of 2002. Then, I get a visitor.

"My name is Giovanni Di Stefano from Studio Legale Internazionale. I've heard of your case and I think I can help."

A very smart-looking Italian man wearing shaded glasses and a pinstripe suit has come to see me alongside a new legal team. I've been moved to Highpoint Prison in Suffolk and have been here a couple of months. Highpoint has been generally uneventful, except for the fact that I'm still locked up, still waiting for my release.

I look over at my new young solicitor, Julian Hardy, standing next to him.

"Mr Di Stefano wanted to see you. I think one of his clients who is working with him here has said you were interested in meeting him?" Julian says.

"Oh right," I say.

"Hello Linda, it's a pleasure to meet you at last." Giovanni takes my hand and kisses it. I can see his hair is receding, but he has such a charming, confident air that I'm quite drawn to him.

"So can you help us?" I say. I'm referring to both myself and Danny.

"Linda, I have looked at your case, and it is my opinion that you should not be in jail. Please let me help you. I will fight for your freedom, I promise you."

I catch something in Julian's gaze. Perhaps it's a trick of the green fluorescent light throwing down harsh shadows, but it seems like he doubts this man's words.

Despite this, my heart leaps in my chest.

"Anythin' you can do for us would be fantastic," I say.

We run through my case from the start. This Italian lawyer makes a few notes in his neat handwriting, nodding his head and flashing smiles as I speak.

After he leaves, I turn to Julian.

"He seems very charming," I say.

Julian looks back at me.

"He does..." he replies. "Don't hold out too much hope, Linda. Let's see what he comes back with, OK?"

"OK," I nod, wondering how much hope I've had to drop during my incarceration.

· · ·

Months later and there is a flurry of excitement on the wing when I announce my news, which Julian tells me during another such visit.

"Linda, you're goin' back to court. You'll be represented by our legal team, but we've managed to get you a hearing to challenge the Home Secretary's failure to pass you to the parole board," Julian says, beaming.

"What does that mean?" I say, smiling back.

"It means we're challenging David Blunkett himself."

When I let this news out, the girls are stunned.

"Blimey, Lin, let's hope you'll be celebratin' a victory. You might be free in a matter of weeks!" one of the screws says.

"Fuckin' go for it, Linda!" an inmate says.

"You'll win. You shouldn't be 'ere," says another.

I hope fervently they're right.

* * *

Frustratingly, we have to wait until October 2003 for my case to come to the High Court.

My family send me in a new outfit for court and when the day comes I feel butterflies in my stomach.

I really could be goin' home today, I think to myself as I follow a screw down through the prison to the van that will take me to the High Court.

When I step into the dock, I see my family are there: Mum, Mel (who is heavily pregnant with her third child), Terry, Shelley and Maxine. It's as much as I can do not to burst into tears at the sight of them. Of course they still all visit me. They've never let me down, and I feel as much part of my family now behind bars as I would if I was a free woman, but seeing them today seems different. There's a real sense of possibility in the air.

I'm represented by my counsel, Alan Newman QC, and what he says takes my breath away. He accuses the Home Secretary David Blunkett of being in breach of the European Convention of Human Rights in not referring my case to the parole board, and asks the court for permission to challenge him. My QC insists Mr Blunkett is acting unlawfully.

I've been in prison for 13 long years now. Every appeal has failed. Every time we've reached out to those who spoke against me during my trial, those efforts have resulted in nothing. This feels like the last-ditch attempt to gain my freedom. Everything is riding upon today. The stakes have never felt higher. I can feel a trickle of sweat down my back and my heart is pounding in my chest. The air in the court is stuffy and crowded with the usual reporters, family and onlookers, as well as the legal teams that buzz round in wigs and swishing black cloaks.

I know it won't be a walk in the park. My friend Kate Kray's book about me, which was published a year ago, has proved a sticking point with the authorities. My solicitors have told me that they're using the book to say that I still have links with the criminal underworld. Well, it would be hard not to! I've grown up in the business of crime, most of my friends were involved at one time or another. They have now retired and are living straight lives, which I had started to do before I was wrongfully accused and convicted of murdering Ron. It seems harsh to penalise me for the connections I made back then and the friends I've made through the years in the gangster world, but there it is.

The original trial judge had set a minimum tariff for retribution and deterrence at seven years. The Home Secretary saw fit to more than double it, increasing it to 15 years, with no guarantee I'll be released at that point. The tariff is the minimum period served before being eligible for a parole hearing and possible release. The problem is that even after serving the minimum, a parole hearing doesn't happen straight away. It can take a year or more to get that hearing, and then release is actually the second part of the sentence. Upon release, lifers have to report to the probation services, and then as time goes on, and with good behaviour, the rules are relaxed, even though there are restrictions on travel or associating with certain people.

I have not even got to the end of the first part of my sentence, the custodial part, so goodness knows when the government will see fit to release me. My counsel goes on to say that in November last year, the House of Lords ruled in the case of Anderson that it was incompatible with human rights laws for the Home Secretary to set tariffs for mandatory lifers. After that case we had asked the Home Office to refer my case to the parole board, which it had refused to do. My legal team asked for leave to apply for judicial review.

I look over at Mel and she returns my gaze. I manage a smile but my eyes fill up with tears that I have to blink away. I feel desperately sorry for her, heavily pregnant in an airless courtroom, watching her mother try to challenge the powers that be. This is no life for my daughter and grandchildren. My children have not had a mother for 13 years, my grandchildren have not had their nanny. Will that all change today?

. . .

It turns out, nothing changes. I don't walk free. My request is denied.

I stumble away, still in custody, still unable to hug my family, and am taken back to prison. I know it is over. I know this was my last chance at freedom. David Blunkett has said I must wait for new legislation to pass through Parliament, which could take another three years, by which time I will have served my extended sentence anyway. It is a huge blow on top of all the others over the years.

Afterwards, I ask to speak to Giovanni.

Surely he must be able to do something?

My request is denied. Apparently, he too is under scrutiny and may not be a qualified lawyer after all. This feels like yet another slap in the face.

"It looks like it was all a pack of lies," Julian says. "It looks like he has never had any form of legal training though he claims he's working for Harold Shipman and the like. The irony is he's quite knowledgeable on law, but anyway, he's not available and it's definitely for the best."

Could life be any more surreal?

I don't think I have ever felt so low as when I step back inside the sweat box, heading back to Highpoint. Leaving the courtroom I glance back at Mel, who has tears streaming down her face. I know the system has failed her, and failed us all. I also know that I was jailed originally for my lifestyle, for being an armed robber and Mickey Calvey's widow, for mixing with gangsters and being a dangerous woman. I didn't do the crime I was convicted of, but in their eyes at least it didn't make me any less guilty. If I could turn back the clock, back to that newly grieving widow, I would do so. I would take another choice. I would throw away Mickey's sawn-off shotguns and I would find another, legal, way to feed my small family. I would bury my desire for revenge beneath my love for my children, and never let it resurface. I can't change the past though. I'm still living with the consequences of it – and so are my family.

I'm devastated as we drive away from the court. I don't notice the press pack or the onlookers, all trying to get a glimpse of the Black Widow. I only remember the stricken look on my children's faces as, yet again, we lose another court battle.

CHAPTER 33

TRIFLE

"Hi, I'm Tracy," says the attractive woman working out next to me in the gym.

"Hello, I'm Linda. You been 'ere long?"

I don't recognise her but I instantly like the look of her. She has long blonde hair and a twinkle in her eye. She is on the running machine, but slows it down to chat.

"Oh, everyone knows who you are, Linda." Tracy smiles.

"It seems they do," I reply, smiling back at her. "You on remand?"

Tracy nods.

"Yeah, I never thought in a million years I'd end up inside. I got caught fair and square, though, with a lorry load of puff on the M25!"

"Did you really?" I say, giggling. "Well, you were bang to rights then." We both laugh.

"I'm from Romford, they call me the Essex Girl on the remand wing."

"My family live in Essex now, though we're all proper East Enders," I say, feeling as if we already have a lot in common. As I've said, prison life is a microcosm of the external world. Friendships are made quickly amid the simmering tensions and conflicts across the prison yard.

"My trial starts soon..." Tracy looks downcast now. "I hope they don't go too hard on me."

"I hope not as well," I reply, my heart sinking. It is not like me to lack optimism, but my latest ordeal has taken the stuffing out of me. I feel knocked sideways and am finding it hard to lighten my spirits and just get on with my term. My failed High Court challenge was only a week ago. If Tracy senses my gloom, she doesn't say. She is facing her own, I can see that. We chat amicably and decide we like each other.

After that, we meet as often as we can in between her legal visits and our working hours, so when Tracy tells me her trial is starting and she has to travel to Chelmsford every day, I immediately start working out how I can help her.

"I'll do your washing each night, and get your clothes ready for the next day in court," I say, knowing how the usual things – preparing food, washing clothes, etc. – can feel like scaling a mountain after a long and stressful day in the courtroom. As the trial begins, I make sure Tracy has a meal saved for her each evening, usually a salad or something light. I lay out her clothes for her and bring her the food when she gets back so she doesn't have to fetch it.

The weeks pass and Tracy, who was initially buoyant at the start of her trial, believing that things might go well, is becoming more despondent. The night before the final day of the hearing, we speak in her cell. I take her the quiche I saved for her and a coffee and put them down on her table.

"Thanks darlin'," she says, but I can see she's struggling with the thought that things will not go as well as she'd hoped with the jury.

"Try not to worry too much," I say, but I know words don't count for much.

"Listen, Lin, it's my last day tomorrow. If it goes badly for me, if it's a big 'un, tell the girls to stay in their cells and don't come and see me."

"Alright," I say. "Good luck, I'll be thinkin' of ya."

. . .

The next night, I think about my new friend as I serve the dinner, hoping for good news, though I have a sinking feeling in my stomach. I ask the screws if they've heard anything, but they shake their heads.

I'm back on the wing when Tracy arrives back from court. I ask the girls to wait in their cells and see her the next day. I wait for her to come on to the wing, and we walk straight into her cell.

"I got a big whack. Ten years, Linda. Ten fuckin' years! How am I goin' to do that? And all for a bit of puff!" She is crying now. It's the first time I've seen her break down. She is usually one of the more chipper inmates, with a ready smile and a laugh. Perhaps because she thought she might go free, or get a reduced sentence. Whatever it was that was keeping her positive and uplifted, it has gone now.

She is sitting on her bed staring at the wall. I go straight over, shutting the cell door behind me so no one is in earshot.

"Oh darlin', I'm so sorry," I say, pulling her into my arms. "You'll be alright, honestly, you can do this. Listen, if you want to cry, you cry. There's no shame in it. That must be a real shock."

I don't think anyone was expecting a sentence as long as that. Ten years is a long time, especially for a cannabis-related offence. I believe it is still only a Class C drug so the judge has obviously gone hard on my friend to make an example of her, to deter others.

Tracy doesn't reply at first. Eventually, she wipes her eyes and turns to me.

"I've cried now, I won't cry again. Don't say nothin' to the girls, don't tell them I've cried."

"Course I won't, though there's nothin' wrong with bein' upset, anyone would be with how things turned out. Listen, Tracy. Nothin' and no one can put us down. We're alike, you and I. We can face it all."

. . .

For a few days Tracy is less bubbly than usual, but as I thought, it doesn't take long before she bounces back and adjusts to the new situation she finds herself in. It doesn't take us long to think about how we can run a racket together. In some ways meeting her, and helping her go through what she has, helps me to overcome my own regrets and sadness. I start to feel alive again as the days pass. Running a racket has been the last thing on my mind, but suddenly I feel like my old self – able to take a risk, do something that undermines the unfair system we're in, and have a few laughs along the way. I am not saying this is the best way to behave, far from it, but I don't care. The system has robbed me of my liberty and denied me justice. Anything I can do to undermine it is fine in my book.

By now Tracey and I have the personal laundry and the servery sewn up. We're well placed to chat to everyone and take orders.

We start charging people chocolate bars and cigarettes to do their washing for them if they want it done more than once a week.

"How much should I charge her?" I say, talking about a particularly rough inmate who neither of us has much to do with. She's in for aggravated assault, so we usually steer well clear.

"We don't like her, so it's at least one Mars bar for each wash, if not two," Tracy says, pouring detergent into a large industrial washing machine.

"Alright, I'll tell her when I serve her at lunchtime. Leigh's a right bully, she's one of the ones that's always pickin' on the new girls, that one, so this is our revenge."

At lunchtime I dollop a portion of cottage pie onto her plate.

"What's this about payin' ya to do our washin'?" she says, gruffly. She is built like a brick shit house with muscles that would rival any man's and short spiked hair.

"Well, we're not exactly askin' for anythin' except when you might want your washin' done again in the week. You know the rules, they're strict when it comes to the number of washes we're allowed..." I don't look up at her. She is hovering now as I spoon another portion onto an inmate's plate.

"How much are ya chargin'?" she says, coming straight to the point.

"Two Mars bars or five fags if you want to do a second wash. Double that if you want two extra washes."

This time I look up and smile.

"We're so busy, you see. It's hard to fit in extra washes, but if you make it worth our while…"

Double for you, you bully.

"Oi, move," shouts a screw from the back of the queue, meaning Leigh, who is still standing by the serving hatch holding everyone up.

One of the more bizarre prison rules is that inmates can't put their knickers in the washing machine. No one has ever explained to me why, but that's the main laundry rule, that and the fact that prisoners are allowed only one wash every week.

"If you want yer knickers in, that's another Mars bar," I hiss at Leigh, who is only just turning away to scowl at the screw.

Later that afternoon, as I take some of the laundry orders to Tracy, we giggle over the idea of charging to shove a few pairs of pants inside the machines. My friend comes back up with me to help prepare the dinner, as one of the girls was released earlier today.

When the food comes up from the main prison kitchens, there are two large trays of trifle. It looks like the most heavenly dessert I've ever seen in my life. The top wobbles with fresh cream and is liberally covered with coloured sprinkles.

"That looks good," Tracy says. "Come on, let's keep one of them trays and eat it after."

"What? We can't do that, someone'll guess!' I say.

"No they blinkin' won't. Don't worry, we'll hide it at the back of one of the fridges where no one looks."

Tracy grabs one of the trays and marches off to the fridges. I look around but no one else has arrived yet to help serve the meal, so she is able to find a space somewhere in the far reaches of one of the huge fridges, behind the big cartons of milk, without being seen.

It's an awful thing to do, really.

Pudding, though a small luxury, is a highlight of many people's day. Taking the lion's share for ourselves and leaving the other prisoners with smaller portions is not exactly justifiable, but we're not thinking things through.

"Tight gits, there's not much pudding today, is there?" one of the inmates says in the queue.

"Oh, I know," I agree, trying not to giggle at the thought of the massive trifle waiting for us. "They only sent up one tray. The other never arrived."

Everyone grumbles as I dish out the smaller servings.

If I feel a pang of guilt, it is soon replaced by greed for that delicious-looking dessert.

When everyone has finished, and we've tidied away everything, washed all the plates and bowls and are sitting down to eat ours, we skip straight to trifle, completely ignoring the pallid-looking shepherd's pie floating in grease.

Tracy brings it out with a flourish, as if it's a wedding cake.

"Oh my God, it's huge!" I say, laughing.

"Come on, let's dig in. We fuckin' deserve this!" Tracy grins.

We sit there, thick as thieves, stuffing our mouths with the trifle we told the girls had never arrived.

We giggle as we eat, the mixture of custard, fruit jelly and cream rendering us silent.

I don't laugh for long.

After half the pudding has gone, I'm feeling distinctly queasy. I look over at Tracy and she looks the same. I try to keep eating because by now I feel so guilty about putting it aside and depriving the others.

"Oh my God, I can't eat no more," I say eventually, pushing my bowl away.

"You can't stop, Lin! What if someone finds the evidence!" Tracy says, shovelling another spoonful into her mouth.

That makes me laugh.

"I don't think that's a crime we need to worry about, Tracy…"

We look at each other.

Tracy has a smear of cream on her lip. I look down at my bowl. The mess of pudding has definitely lost its appeal.

I watch Tracy as she demolishes the lot.

Hardly able to walk, we get up and make sure the tray is hidden under the rest of the rubbish and food waste, before leaving the kitchen. I don't think I've ever felt as sick as I do that evening. Talk about karma.

CHAPTER 34

THE RETURN OF MYRA

I'm still in Highpoint when I have to say a reluctant farewell to Tracy, as she's being moved to East Sutton Park. We both vow to stay in touch.

The big news is that Myra Hindley will be moved back here, which causes a stir on the wing. This is a closed prison but is a Category C, which means there are fewer security measures in place, unlike Holloway or Durham. Myra is no longer a Cat A prisoner, which is why they've moved her here, I guess.

I'm unfazed. Myra and I have a kind of understanding by now. We tolerate each other, but I refuse to be overly friendly. There is a hardness to her that never seems to fade, and that indefinable feeling of darkness that seems to surround her like a black aura. I keep my distance and she keeps hers, or has done so far.

"Where are they goin' to put her?" I say to one of the screws, who is gossiping with the inmates in the breakfast queue. I'm back working in the kitchens, as a cleaner and server.

The kitchen is hot and steamy as I dish out porridge and chat to the girls as they pass my serving hatch.

"Dunno yet. They can't put her on the wing or she'll be lynched," the screw says.

"I don't want her 'ere. She's pure evil," a woman says in the queue.

I nod.

"I know each wing is locked, but all our cells are open and we can come and go as we please, so what'll they do with her?" I say as another inmate holds out her bowl.

The screw shrugs. "She'll 'ave to go somewhere. I don't envy the person makin' that decision."

It takes about a year before Myra Hindley, the most notorious female murderer in British history, arrives at Highpoint. The wing has been buzzing with the news for months.

"She's goin' in no man's land," says the same screw from last time, a tall, solidly built woman with brown hair and a sly expression named Margaret, who goes by the name of Marge. Yet again we're chatting while I dole out big spoonfuls of thick porridge at breakfast. No man's land refers to a couple of cells that sit between the punishment block and hospital wing. They're set away from the rest of the prison population for prisoners who can't be housed on the wing. It makes sense Myra will go there because the cell doors here aren't locked, only the wing doors, so anyone could go in and attack Myra in her cell.

"What d'ya think of that?" Marge says.

"What do I care where she goes?" I reply. "It's nothin' to do with me."

"You and Myra, eh?" the inmate with her outstretched bowl says and laughs. "You're friends aren't ya?"

I have to stop myself from shuddering.

"Yeah, you know her from Durham, don't ya?" the screw says. "That's what the guv'nor told me. Anyway, it'll 'ave to be you who keeps her company." I wonder if she's making me look like Myra's friend deliberately.

"Why's that then?" I respond. "There you go, darlin'. There's sugar and milk over there." I wink at the young woman who is in for arson. She wanders off carrying her bowl on her tray, seemingly satisfied with her meal.

"The guv'nor says you and Myra were friendly, so when she comes, you'll 'ave to look after her. Myra needs her to have her hair done and the guv'nor wants you to do it."

I turn to the officer, putting down my ladle, and narrow my eyes.

"I can tell you now that Myra and I were never friends, and I don't want to do her hair," I retort. "Didn't you know I slapped her in the face the first time I met her?"

"Good for you, Linda!" hollers one of the girls in the queue for breakfast.

Marge raises a single eyebrow. We're looking at each other now as if we're squaring up for a fight.

"Look, you're hopin' to go to open prison and she needs her hair done. Of course, you could always tell the guv'nor you won't do it..." she says eventually, knowing full well I can do no such thing. It doesn't go down well to disobey a request from the higher echelons of the prison. Everyone knows I'm desperate to go home and still fighting for my release, which of course is why they've picked me. They know I won't complain because I want a clean sheet so that they can't refuse my parole when I'm finally put in front of the board.

For a moment I have to fight the urge to tell this screw I absolutely won't do it, whatever the impact upon my case, but I know this would be a foolish move. I might even be put on report for refusing to do what I'm asked and this wouldn't help me at all.

"Oh, it's like that is it?" I say.

Marge just looks at me.

I nod, wishing I could wipe the smirk off the screw's face.

"If the guv'nor wants me to keep her company, that is what I will do," I say. Inside I'm fuming.

* * *

A couple of days later and I'm standing in Myra's area, which consists of two small rooms, one containing her bed and one for her work repairing prison library books. Myra had been sitting on a chair as I started to paint dark-red dye on her hair, but she suddenly shrieks and jumps up, almost spilling the contents of the bowl all over me.

"Linda! A spider!"

For a moment I think she must be joking. This is the hardest, most twisted murderess in Britain today, and she is terrified of spiders? Then I see it. The spider is huge. It's as big as my hand and has black furry legs. My nickname might be the Black Widow, named after a deadly arachnid, but I'm just as scared of them as Myra appears to be.

"Aaargghhhhh," I scream. "It's massive!"

I had been told in no uncertain terms that my job is now to keep Myra company twice a month, wash her hair for her. Once a month I'm also expected to come and dye her short thick hair as well. If this is some sort of sick joke at my expense, then I'm not laughing. I find every second in her company to be painful and abhorrent. She is evil. It radiates off her. I've fronted up and dealt with some of the toughest male criminals in the underworld over the years. Billy Blundell is a good friend of mine. The Krays, Ron Cook, countless crooks, blaggers and thieves, yet Myra is in a category of her own. Just being in her company sets my teeth on edge, and I have to keep reminding myself that I have to be here or it won't look good for me. Myra is chain-smoking cigarette after cigarette, so her cell is a fog of smoke. Her fingers are stained nicotine yellow, while her nails are painted bright pink. She is wearing a colourful kaftan and is now a middle-aged women.

"You kill it!" screeches Myra.

"I can't kill it!" I yell back. "I'm frightened as well!"

The irony. A child killer and the proclaimed Black Widow cowering and screaming over a large spider. I would laugh but I have to deal with Myra first.

Thankfully the beast scuttles into the space under Myra's bed, presumably fleeing by the same route it came in.

I crouch down on the grey linoleum floor and look underneath. The spider is nowhere to be seen but there is something unusual there. A battered-looking locked briefcase has been placed at the back of the bed next to the wall. Even though the cell is thick with smoke, I know what I'm seeing, and I also know that we're forbidden from having anything that we can hide things in, such as bags or cases.

Puzzled, I say: "What's that briefcase doin' there?"

Myra hesitates for a second, distracted from the threat of the spider reappearing.

"Oh, that's mine," she says cagily. "It's got my papers in..."

I blink. We're allowed to have papers in our cells, but we're definitely not allowed locked briefcases or anything like that.

"Your papers?"

Myra looks over at me. Her face is expressionless and I suddenly realise again who I'm talking to. My heart freezes. Something isn't right, but I'm damned if I want to make an enemy of Myra Hindley while I'm banged up with her.

When she doesn't answer, I return to her side and pick up the bowl of dye, feeling my hands tremble a bit. Why is there a case under her bed? Has she bribed a guard to keep incriminating documents in here? I realise she will never tell me and though I'm fascinated (and repelled), I decide to leave well alone.

That evening I ponder this in my cell. There might be something she has hidden from the police or justice system in there. I think of the deaths of those children on the moors, and shiver. What is she concealing inside that case? I realise I'll probably never know.

CHAPTER 35

FRACAS

The sky is grey through the visitors' room window. Rainclouds overhead look increasingly ominous and it's clear the heavens are about to open. I'm sitting, waiting for my son, daughter and grandchildren to come, and time is ticking past. I glance up at the clock. Already the visitors are 20 minutes late, a large chunk of our hour-long visit is already wasted.

"What's the hold up?" I say to one of the screws standing at the side of the room.

She shrugs.

"There's been a bit of a fracas at the gate," says the screw standing by the doorway that leads from reception where the visitors should be coming through.

"A fracas?" I echo, frowning.

Just then, the door opens and people start to drift in.

I look around eagerly but cannot see my family.

Where are they? I think, feeling a little annoyed. Visits are the high points of my days and I await each and every one eagerly. My grandchildren are growing up so fast; these times are incredibly precious.

After about five more minutes, Mel appears with Sammy, who is now 15 years old, and Emily, who was born in 1997. They skip over to me, beaming. Mel, who is carrying three-year-old Alana, on the other hand, looks pissed off, while Mia, who is now 11, is crying. Instantly, I realise something has gone wrong.

"Where's Neil?" I begin, but Mel stops me.

"They've bloody arrested him!"

"They've what?" I say.

"Yeah, him and another man. They're waitin' for the police now..."

Emily hands me a drawing she made me at school, so I break off to tell her how fabulous it looks and what a clever girl she is. When Emily is distracted by the chocolate bars I've brought for them, I turn back to Mel.

"What's goin' on?"

"It all kicked off when the prison gov'nor pushed over a couple of kids as he came in, including Mia. She fell over and hit her face against the wire as they were queuing up outside."

"Are you sure it was the guv'nor?" I say incredulously.

"Apparently so," Mel says. "He was pushin' people out of the way and Mia fell against the fence. Neil went mental. He started shoutin' at the man, as well as another guy whose child was knocked over as well. The guv'nor must've been late getting back from somethin'. Neil was shoutin': 'How'd you like it, mate. Bein' shoved? You can't push kids over!' Then Neil punched him, and then pushed him really hard..."

"He did what?"

Mel nods.

"He punched the guv'nor and pushed him. The governor grabbed a brolly and said: 'On guard!' like they were about to fight with swords or somethin'. It was bizarre... Then Neil was taken away by the police with another man who was involved."

For a moment I wonder if I'll laugh or cry with pure frustration.

"And now he's been arrested," she finishes.

All I can do is sigh. Why did it have to be Neil and Mia involved?

* * *

A few weeks later, I'm called to the wing office.

"Just to let you know, Linda, that your son has a lifetime ban on visits to this prison."

The screw doesn't even bother to look up as she speaks to me.

"Well, you'd better move me then, seein' as I'm servin' life!" I snap. "Perhaps I should ask my lawyers to check the security cameras that day and see what really happened..."

"The cameras weren't workin' that day," the screw replies, finally looking up at me, her gaze cold.

I don't reply. I don't trust myself not to shout and so I stalk out of the office, wondering what new punishment I'll receive for my attitude.

Days later, I'm called back.

"You're goin' to Styal prison," the screw says, smiling.

"Where on earth is that?" I say. I've not heard that name before.

"Oh, it's in Cheshire I think, up north." The screw looks at me, knowing that is exactly what I don't want to hear. "It's a closed prison up there. Pack your stuff. You'll be goin' as soon as there's room for you."

As I walk away I'm raging inside. So, this is my punishment, and it isn't even me being punished, it's my family. Knowing how much I hate my family having to travel long distances to see me, I'm being sent further away. They've got their own back in the worst way possible for me. To say I'm upset is an understatement. However, there is nothing I can do about it except pack my bits, my toiletries and slippers, my brush, radio and clothes, into a plastic bag and wait.

. . .

It is raining heavily when the sweat box pulls into Styal prison, somewhere in Wilmslow. It doesn't look too bad from the outside. It looks like a series of country houses pushed together, with a few trees dotted here and there. Inside, however, it's a madhouse.

There are women everywhere. The prison already feels overcrowded and I haven't made it to my house yet. It used to be an orphanage and so there are no wings, just houses surrounded by a fence with razor wire. The holding room is full of women awaiting a cell. I join them, keeping myself to myself, until I'm called up to the space I'll be housed in.

The place seems alive with chatter and shouting all night, bringing back memories of C1. In the morning there is a commotion when it is discovered that a woman has overdosed in her room overnight. Suddenly, there are paramedics and screws everywhere, and I wonder where the hell the prison service has sent me. There are no locks on the doors, and there is a maternity house with mums and babies being wheeled around.

At the same time, an actress from the hit show *EastEnders* has contacted me, writing to ask if she can visit me. I have no idea why she might want to come and see me, but I agree out of curiosity and a date is set for her visit.

It's the only time I ever get a closed visit, which means that we sit in a telephone box talking to each other through a phone and a glass screen. She introduces herself as Carol, and I realise she played a popular character, Louise Raymond, during her time on the soap. I recognise her immediately.

"Linda, it's so good to meet you," she says, her London accent still strong.

"It's my pleasure, Carol. I was so surprised and pleased to get your letter," I say. I realise I'm warming to this lady straight away, though I have no idea why she's contacted me and made the effort to meet me. She has blonde hair, a kind smile and the same accent as me.

"Where are you from in the East End?" I ask.

"West Ham, for my sins," Carol replies through the mouthpiece. We both giggle at that.

"So, I think there's a connection between us," she says.

"Go on," I reply, curious now to know how on earth I could be connected to a telly star.

"Well, my son's father is Jamie, Freddie Foreman's son. You're friends with Freddie, am I right?"

"I am." I smile. "Me and Freddie go a long way back. Tell him I said hello, won't you."

Freddie Foreman, otherwise known as Brown Bread Fred, has been a friend of mine for many years as we frequented the same circles back when we were crooks. I don't think anyone needs to guess what his nickname means in cockney rhyming slang! He was a gangster, a friend of Reggie and Ronnie when they ran the Firm together in the 1960s, and was known in the underworld for being able to dispose of bodies. How strange that our friends and families are so intimately connected.

"Is that why you got in touch, Carol?" I ask, still puzzled.

"Well, yes," she says, smiling. "That, and I've read about your case and your trial, and I felt there was more to it than they wrote about. I think I knew we might get on, does that sound strange?"

"No, it doesn't. I'm flattered," I say. Life throws up these surprises, and I've learned to flow with them and see where they go.

It seems strange to say it, but even though we're chatting in the most unlikely and brutal of places, a bleak booth in an overcrowded closed prison, it feels like we could be anywhere. The time passes so quickly, I almost forget to ask Carol why we've had to meet in one of these closed booths. Visits are always in the visiting rooms and this seems pretty harsh.

"Oh, Linda. It's so stupid. Last night I stayed in a hotel before coming 'ere to see you. I went for a meal somewhere, a pub nearby, and thought nothing of it. Well, I'm wearin' the same suit today as I was wearin' in that bar, and when I came through security, one of the drug dogs sat down in front of me. I was like, 'Search me!' I don't do drugs."

I burst out laughing.

"Oh my God, that's so funny! The one and only closed visit I've ever had and it's been with a famous actress!"

Carol starts laughing, too.

"The staff were really good about it. They said sorry and wanted to 'ave photos done with me!"

. . .

That night I smile as I settle down, knowing I've made a new friend, however unlikely and unusual the introduction was. I also realise I have unfinished business with the underworld, and by that I mean my ill-fated marriage to Danny Reece.

The next morning, I put in an app for a visit to where he is still imprisoned, at Whitemoor. My request is approved, and with a little trepidation I'm taken to Cambridgshire, to the Category A men's prison, to meet with Danny. I'm shunted through security, through metal doors that clang shut behind me, into a room where the visit will take place. Danny is already there. I smile. I've come to ask him for a divorce.

The visit is a success. Danny admits it's the worst thing we could've done, and made us look guilty of everything the court accused us of. He agrees to a quick divorce, and so I head back to Styal feeling relieved that one thing, at least, can't be held against me any more.

CHAPTER 36

SET-UP?

"You want what?" I say, thinking this is either a very bad joke, or I'm being set up. It seems obvious to me that it's the latter.

I was only in Styal prison for a few months and then I was sent back to Cookham Wood, and almost immediately then to East Sutton Park. I've hardly had time to process it all, but one thing I am now sure of – this is the beginning of the end of prison time. Open prison means they're sending me home. I don't know when. It's 2007 and I've been banged up since I was on remand in 1990. It's been a long, long wait, but my instincts tell me it's coming to a close. I don't dare hold out too much hope, but this has to be the final straight. Going home has become the focus of every hour of every day now. Not that it wasn't before, but the end feels like it's almost in sight; I can almost taste freedom. This is also why I can't help but hope I must've misheard the young screw who is sitting opposite me behind her desk. No one would ever ask what she is asking for of a prisoner about to go home.

"Can you arrange a murder for me?" The screw is a young woman with auburn hair. Her expression is pleading though her eyes are hard. "I want my boyfriend killed."

"Stand up," I say, slowly.

"Why?" she says.

"Stand up now," I say. My voice is low but she obeys. "Put your arms out."

I walk around the desk and rub her down, just as they've all done to us inmates for years.

"Where's your wire?" I say.

"What?" the screw looks genuinely dumbfounded.

"Your wire! Where's your wire? I'm assumin' you're settin' me up because you know it's only a matter of time before I get parole, and this is an attempt to stop me leavin' prison. Are you recordin' me?"

I look under the desk and behind the chair.

"There's no wire," she says. "Linda, I'm serious. This is no trick, I want my boyfriend murdered! Tell me who to contact and how much..."

"You're tryin' to set me up. You're tryin' to incriminate me so you can put me away for longer!" I'm starting to get angry now.

"No, really Linda. Please listen. I'm asking you a serious question. I'm in trouble and I need your help. My boyfriend hits me. He does bad things to me and I'm scared of going home. I need to get rid of him, but I don't know how. Can you do it?"

By now I'm staring at this screw in complete shock.

While I feel terrible that she has such an awful situation, I can't believe this is happening to me so close to release.

"I can't believe what you're sayin' to me. There's no way I'd ever, ever consider doing such a thing. I'm no killer."

There is silence between us now. The guard has the decency to blush and there are tears in her eyes.

"I'm waitin' for my parole and you're askin' me to arrange a murder. I find this really uncomfortable, sorry, I've got to go."

"Please don't repeat what I just said..."

Is a screw pleading with me? I don't hang around long enough to find out. With that, I leave her sitting there staring after me, and head straight to the governor's office. My heart is pounding and I feel sick. What do I do?

Before I get to the governor, I see my friends sitting at one of the tables and walk over. I must look shaken, because someone says: "What's wrong, Lin?"

Before I know what I'm saying, I blurt it all out.

The women look at me like I've gone mad.

"Bloody hell!" one says.

"Lin, they're fittin' you up, or if not she's a lunatic to do that. What you goin' to do?" says another inmate.

"I don't know," I reply, shaking my head. I can feel my body starting to calm down, but now the feelings of shock are being replaced by anger. How dare she do that to me so close to release?

"I'm really uncomfortable about this, I'm goin' to tell the gov'nor," I say, standing up again and marching as quickly as I can into his office.

"I need to see you, urgently," I say. "Someone in the prison asked me to commit a murder for them."

The governor looks up at me, his face already a picture of shock.

"I was asked if I could get a murder arranged..." I begin.

"My God, who is it? I'll get her shipped straight out..." he starts to reply. It takes me a second to realise he thinks it's a prisoner who asked me.

"Actually sir, it's not one of your prisoners. It's one of your staff!"

The governor leans back in his chair, and his expression changes instantly from shock to disbelief.

"One of my officers? I totally disbelieve that. None of them would've said that to you. That's not possible."

This gets my back up.

"Well, I'm tellin' you they did, this is serious. I want you to investigate. Actually, I want you to call the police."

"Linda, I don't believe this, and I won't be investigating my own staff. My officers are honest and I won't have them being investigated by the people they're looking after."

"Well, in that case, I'm goin' straight to my solicitor and he'll call the police," I say, robustly.

And, because I mean what I say, the police are called in.

Two officers from Maidstone police station question me about the incident. I tell them everything, including the domestic details, things I would never have known unless this screw had told me. They went off to interview her, and check everything out, but I didn't hear anything for a couple of days.

When the police officers return, they take me aside and say to me that they know I told the truth because of the circumstances I had described, and the things I would only have known if this screw actually did what I said she did.

"We can't charge her though," one of the Old Bill says to me.

"But why not?" I say.

"Because you're a convicted killer. No jury would ever believe you against the word of a prison officer. If we charge her with conspiracy to murder, it's her word against yours..."

"That's outrageous!" I say, feeling aggrieved but glad my side of the story has been believed at least.

"Sorry, Linda, there's nothing we can do."

The double standards in the justice system are glaring and unfair. Screws who ignore the women they've recently hired for sex. Screws who want to commit murder but will never be convicted. Screws sharing out stolen goods. Sometimes I wonder if the staff aren't as bad as the inmates, but at the same time I've met many kind, decent officers who are just doing their job.

The screw stays in her position and all I'm told is that no action will be taken because she has denied our conversation ever took place.

CHAPTER 37

PAROLE

My parole application is in with the board, and I have been waiting on tenterhooks for their answer since I arrived at East Sutton Park. I've been here six months now, so time has marched on and into 2008.

Meanwhile, I've been told I'm allowed out on day release. This is a huge step forward. My mum comes to pick me up for the first weekend I'm allowed out. Stepping into her modest car, winding the window down and feeling the early spring sunshine on my face as the car speeds off is heaven. She drives us to Maldon in Essex where the family is based, and I step inside my parents' home. Everything looks the same, except the television is bigger and they have a new sofa. Everything is just as it was and I feel almost giddy with the freedom of being able to walk around, without passing through security, or having gates locked and unlocked. I can move freely. I can make some toast whenever I'm hungry. I can sit with my grandchildren on my knee and laugh at silly things with them.

I could cry at my lengthy incarceration for a crime I didn't commit, but I find I don't want to waste a second of my new-found freedom with regret or sadness. Life is for living again, and that weekend is a shining, sun-filled rebirth. It is a full stop in some ways. The horror of Holloway, of C1, the indignities, the strip searches, the terrible food, the bullying and the overcrowding just vanish as I hug my daughter and son, and know how blessed and grateful I am to have a family like mine. When Mum drops me back to East Sutton Park, I wave her off gleefully, knowing in my heart it must be only a matter of time before I can step outside these gates. How much time, I can't say.

I'm given a volunteering job in a sustainability shop in Headcorn with another inmate as part of my reintegration programme. At the same time, Kate Kray invites me to come to her restaurant in Kent on the next Sunday I can leave the prison. Two of my girlfriends pick me up and we drive excitedly to the restaurant. It is here that I sit down next to a charming and rather portly man called George. The place is crowded and busy but we manage to start chatting. He asks me if I'm married and I tell him I'm widowed and divorced. He nods, and I see some sadness there as he explains he is divorced too, but I don't probe any further. At the end of the meal, George asks if he can take me out.

When I say I can only do Sundays, he seems surprised, until I tell him the truth.

"I'm only allowed out once a week."

George, who has a really kind face, looks puzzled.

"Why?" he says.

"Because I'm in prison," I reply.

George looks at me for a moment, before bursting into laughter.

"You're *that* Linda, Linda Calvey!"

"Yes I am," I say, and we both dissolve into giggles. "Does that mean you've changed your mind about takin' me out?"

"Absolutely not. I'd be honoured," George says, and I find myself blushing.

. . .

The following Sunday, I'm waiting at the prison for my date. George is late, and for a moment I think he won't come. I don't blame him. Ask anyone who Linda Calvey is and most normal men will run a mile!

Suddenly there is a commotion as girls line the windows along the front, poking their heads out and squealing.

"Linda. LINDA! There's a red roller turned up and it must be for you!"

I go to the window and, sure enough, George is standing by a red Rolls-Royce, waiting to pick me up. It's a strange sight, and I'd always wanted a red roller since seeing one driving along the grimy streets of East London as a child.

He takes me to a restaurant for lunch, then drops me back bang on the time I can stay out until, and that is that. Already I know we have a future, just by how easy it all is with him, and how unconcerned he seems to be by my criminal past. I've told him everything by this stage – about Mickey, about being an armed robber, about the world I was part of when Ron was murdered and I got the blame. I never expected someone to be so accepting of my past and so very quickly we have an understanding between us. On the third date a few weeks later, George asks me straight: "Did you kill Ron?"

When I reply: "No, I didn't," he nods, satisfied with my answer.

Then, one Wednesday afternoon I'm in the shop, making small talk with a customer, when George walks in.

"You're not supposed to be 'ere!" I hiss.

The other inmate who works here too is watching us and must have overheard.

"But I wanted to see you!" George replies. "And there's no harm in me buying some tomatoes, is there? Why can't I come in and buy some food?" He is holding a brown paper bag filled with the ripe fruit.

"You can't come 'ere, I'll get into trouble. You need to leave!"

I watch George go, a sinking feeling in my stomach. I turn around and the other inmate, a lifer like myself called Amanda, is staring at me.

Within a couple of hours of arriving back at the open prison, I'm called for over the Tannoy.

"TT0377, Calvey, to the office please!"

Oh God, what now? I think, knowing I must be in trouble.

"You're goin' back to Cookham for six months. You broke the rules. No engagement with your boyfriend or any acquaintance while working in the community," a particularly unfriendly screw says.

"But I didn't ask him to come, he just turned up!" I say, feeling this is very unfair. The inmate I was working with must have grassed me up.

"Doesn't matter. The rules got broken, so it's back to closed prison."

When I call George and tell him, he is beside himself.

"It don't matter," I say. "It's only for six months. I've dealt with worse."

George is inconsolable.

Back in Cookham Wood, George visits every chance he can. We're sitting in the visitors' room not long before I'm due to be moved back to East Sutton Park, when he fumbles in his jacket for something.

He draws a small velvet box out of his pocket.

Inside is a large teardrop diamond solitaire ring.

"Will you marry me?' is all he says.

I look up at him. My luck has always swung from very good to very bad, and back again. Finally, something wonderful is happening.

"I will," I say, and he slips the ring onto my finger.

I arrive back at East Sutton an engaged woman, to hear that I have my parole hearing in a few days' time.

George accompanies me, and we sit around a table with the probation officer and prison governor, all sitting and discussing my case for release. Halfway through, George suddenly starts to breathe strangely. He clutches his chest and I see he is sweating profusely.

"Oh my God, I think he's havin' a heart attack!" I say, grabbing his hand and calling for someone to ring for an ambulance. In the moments that follow, my hearing is abandoned as we rush to get help for my fiancé. When the paramedics arrive, they bundle him into the ambulance.

"Come on, Linda, we'll follow in my car," the governor says, and I find myself in the slightly bizarre situation of being driven by the prison governor to Maidstone Hospital.

A couple of hours later, the tests are back.

"Mrs Calvey, there's no need to worry. Your fiancé has had an angina attack. It isn't a heart attack, but still, though, he will need to take medication and this could be a warning."

"Thank you, doctor," I say, overwhelmed with relief.

I'm driven back to prison while George is kept overnight in hospital.

A couple of weeks later, my postponed hearing is held again.

"As you know, we've been concerned throughout your sentence that you'll return to your old life, mixing with criminals and gangsters," the governor says. "But now you've met George, we can see things are different. He is a decent man, with a fabulous home to go to, and we can't see any reason why you'll go back to a villainous life when you have so much to look forward to and can move on."

"Thank you," I say. "That's wonderful to hear." George squeezes my hand and smiles.

Just as we're leaving the room, one of the officers pulls George aside.

"Are you looking forward to getting married?"

George beams at me.

"Yes, of course I am," he says.

The officer clears his throat.

"I feel it's my duty to say this to you, but have you thought she may murder you?"

For a moment I think I've misheard him, even though I'm standing with George right next to this screw.

George shakes his head. He looks back at me as if to say: "Oh my God!"

"No, not for one moment," he says quietly.

The officer stares at him, then over at me.

"I think you should keep that in mind..."

"She says she didn't do it and I believe in her!" George says, and grabbing my arm he leads me out, both of us reeling.

CHAPTER 38

FREEDOM

It's summer and the grounds of East Sutton Park are bursting with flowers and home-grown vegetables and salad.

Every day, I await a message, breathlessly thinking: *Could this be the day?*

There's still been no word from the parole board, and I'm finding it hard to do my normal tasks and stay calm, I so desperately want to hear good news.

I'm sitting outside in the early evening, chatting with some friends. My friend Tracy is here as well, training to be a butcher, working with the pigs on the farm, and it almost feels like I'm an ordinary person, out enjoying the nice weather and having a laugh. Prison has been so different to – and so like – everything I've ever heard about it. Over the past years I've suffered all the usual indignities and lack of privacy and agency. I've seen horrendous self-harm from young girls who should be held in psychiatric hospitals and not in jails. I've witnessed bullying by both staff and inmates, and I've had my fair share of laughs and fun as well. Unexpectedly, I've found good friends while locked up, and even met the man I'm going to marry. Though I was angry at my conviction for many years, I've mellowed into it now. Perhaps because I'm so close to going home, I'm starting to value the brief moments of freedom, the camaraderie and the good parts, whereas before I was furious and grieving for the loss of my life and the terrible toll it was taking on my family.

My children have grown up and are now adults with kids of their own. They're all doing really well, and I'm grateful to have had a family that looked after them and supported us all through this travesty of British justice. I've always refused to say I'm guilty of the crime I was convicted of, and because of that I'm convinced my sentence has been harsher. If I'd done those courses on changing offending behaviour, I might have been home already. Who knows? What I do know is that I would do it all over again rather than admit to something I didn't do.

The next day I'm helping out in the kitchen when one of the lady governors comes in. She's quite an attractive lady in her forties, tall, buxom and well dressed.

"Can I have a word with Linda?" she says, smiling.

Well, everybody in that place puts their knives and ladles down because they all know I'm waiting for news of my hearing.

Everyone turns to look at her and she smiles back at them as well.

Can it be happening at last?

Instantly there are knots in my stomach as I turn to look at her.

"Linda, I've got your parole answer..."

I stare back at her. I can barely breathe.

"Linda, it's yes. You're going home."

"Say that again," I say, putting down the ladle I was about to serve lunch with.

"You got parole. You're going home in two weeks' time, on the first of August!"

"Oh my God, that's my daughter's birthday!" is all I can say. The governor walks over and gives me a hug.

The place erupts. People are all banging their tools on the metal surfaces of the stainless steel kitchen. Others are whooping. Several staff run in to find out what the commotion is and someone shouts: "Wonderful news! Linda's goin' home!"

Elation hits me. I'm smiling and crying, almost unable to believe this is really happening.

"I need to phone my daughter, and George, then they can ring Neil and Mum. Oh my God, I can't believe it!"

. . .

Guess what you're gettin' for your birthday present this year?" I say to Melanie on the phone minutes later.

"What, Mum?" she says.

"Me! I got parole at long last! They're releasin' me in two weeks!"

Immediately, Mel bursts into tears.

"Call Neil, won't you. Call Mum as well. They've let me 'ave two calls today and I need to use the other to call George," I say. "I love you. I'll be home soon."

The next two weeks whizz past in a blur. All I can think is that I'll be released. This time I give away my things – my toiletries and knick-knacks – knowing I won't ever return to claim them. No one wants my radio, saying it's too old-fashioned as I've owned it for so long in prison!

1 AUGUST 2008

The day dawns bright and sunny. I get up. I get washed and dressed. I hand out my remaining clothes and my spare shoes, and just as I'm dissolving into tears again, a screw puts her head around the dorm door.

"It's time, Linda."

Those might be the sweetest words I've ever heard.

I follow the screw down to the reception area, where I'm handed a clear plastic bag, inside which are the things I was wearing on the day

I arrived in Holloway 18 years ago: a pair of heels, my jewellery and my handbag. They seem like museum relics now, more like a piece of history than anything else. I take the bag and smile.

I'm wearing an outfit I had for visiting, a pretty blouse and skirt and modest heels, which I immediately take off and replace with the stilettoes. They still fit. I pull on the earrings I was made to take off, a bracelet and my watch too. The diamonds, though muted by dust and age, still sparkle.

"Linda, we'll miss you," the screw says. "And we don't ever want to see you back here!"

We laugh at that.

"Don't worry. I won't be, I can promise you that now," I say. I turn to the doorway. It's already open and it takes a moment to remember that I can now just walk through it, and I can keep walking, a free woman at last.

This time, the red roller pulls up on the gravel bang on time. Out of the window, girls are leaning out and waving. Some are blowing kisses, and I have to fight to stop tears from streaming down my face.

George opens the door for me on the passenger side. The gravel crunches underneath my heels. The summer sunshine feels hot on my skin. I turn my face up to the sun and I think, *It's over. It's finally over.* George coughs. He too looks overcome with emotion.

"Shall we?" he says, smiling and holding the door open for me.

I smile back.

"We shall," I say, savouring each second of this, my departure from prison.

I step inside the car. Inside is a huge bouquet of white roses, their scent already heady in the heat. George gets in beside me and starts the ignition.

The car purrs out of the driveway, away from the prison. I turn back and wave, and keep waving as we move off down the driveway and out on to the open road. *Am I dreaming?* I wonder as we pick up speed, and I find I'm laughing and crying at the same time. The window is open and I feel the breeze in my hair. It's like a blessing, a miracle that I am no longer a prisoner.

I'm finally free.

AUTHOR'S NOTE

Since leaving prison on 1 August 2008, I've turned my life around, though I had to serve another six months in a halfway house on probation before I could actually begin my life again.

I've stayed friends with only a few people I met along the way, who've all transformed from criminals to upstanding members of the wider community. Sue has left behind her life of crime to become a successful antiques dealer. Tracy has become a multi-millionaire, launching The Giggly Pig Company upon her release, and is one of the biggest prison success stories. Bobble is one of my closest friends and she runs a storge compay and lives a good life. I have seven grandchildren and five great-grandchildren, and I count my family as my biggest success through all of this. I became a widow again in 2015 when my beloved George passed away from cancer, two months after his diagnosis.

My life now is devoted to my work as an author and my family, and I hope this book serves as an inspiration to anyone who is banged up or facing imprisonment, who might think there is no life after prison. There is. I'm living proof.

My beautiful daughter, Melanie. She never ever stopped
visiting me all over the country.

My handsome son Neil and partner, the lovely Mandy.
They were also there for me and never ever let me down.

Me with my dearest special friend, more like family, the infamous Billy Blundell. He visited me all the way through my time. Much loved by me and my family, he is sadly no longer with us.

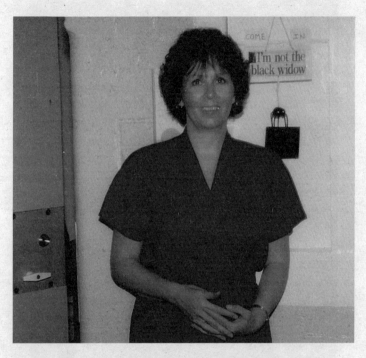

A rare photo taken on the wing of H Wing, Durham,
standing outside my cell door. One of the staff
made the sign *I'm not the black widow*.

I made this cup in the pottery in H Wing, Durham.
I made quite a lot of stuff but this is the only piece
remaining. My son Neil had kept it all these years.

The infamous inmate Charlie Bronson. He always called me
The Black Rose. He gave me this photo to be put in the book.

A drawing Charlie Bronson sent to be put in the book.

My dear, dear friend Sue. Her antics in Holloway used to
amaze me. She is now an honest, hardworking antiques
dealer. She is much loved by my family. This photo
was taken at my 75th birthday party.

This is a picture of my dear friend, the wonderful Tracy
MacKness, one of the prison system's true success stories.
She is the proud owner of The Giggly Pig Company. This photo
was also taken at my 75th birthday party.

I was a guest at the wonderful Julian Hardy's ladies night when he was master of his lodge. I can't sing his praises highly enough, a solicitor who always went above and beyond.

This photo was taken on my first day out from
East Sutton Park Prison. I was collected by my dear
friend Angie. Those six hours flew by.

Me and my dear husband George at my nephew
Ross's wedding. George always believed in me.
I miss him so very much.

Last but not least, a photo of Jason Moore, who is still in prison fighting to prove his innocence. I think his poem says it all.

ACKNOWLEDGEMENTS

There are so many people to thank. First and foremost, my agent Kerr MacRae, who has been brilliant and supported me through my career as an author. The wonderful Cathryn Kemp. The fantastic Oli, my editor who believed in this project and the whole fabulous team at Welbeck, including Wayne, James, Annabel, Nico, Rob, Tanisha, Isabelle, Kirsty and Rachel, who have all been incredible. As well as my family and friends, who have supported me through everything I've been through. I couldn't have done it without everyone here and I am very grateful to them all.